After migrating to Australia from Lebanon as an infant with his mother and three elder siblings, John Elias went on to lead one of the most colourful and controversial lives of any modern-day sportsman. John now lives in Sydney, where he hopes his story can serve as a warning to young footballers and men in general about the consequences of following in his footsteps.

SIN BIN

THE UNTOLD STORY OF A TRUE FOOTY BAD BOY

JOHN ELIAS
with JOSH MASSOUD

MACMILLAN
Pan Macmillan Australia

First published 2010 in Macmillan by Pan Macmillan Australia Pty Limited
1 Market Street, Sydney

Copyright © John Elias 2010

Reprinted 2010 (twice)

The moral right of the author has been asserted.

All rights reserved. No part of this book may be reproduced or transmitted by any person or entity (including Google, Amazon or similar organisations), in any form or by any means, electronic or mechanical, including photocopying, recording, scanning or by any information storage and retrieval system, without prior permission in writing from the publisher.

National Library of Australia
Cataloguing-in-Publication data:

Elias, John.
Sin Bin: the untold story of a true footy bad boy / John Elias

ISBN: 978 1 4050 4021 1 (pbk.)

Elias, John.
Rugby football players–Biography.
Rugby League football–Australia–Biography.
Lebanese Australians–Biography.
Cancer–Patients–Australia–Biography.
Criminals–Australia–Biography.

796.3338

Typeset in 12.5/16pt Janson Text by Post Pre-press Group, Brisbane
Printed by McPherson's Printing Group

Papers used by Pan Macmillan Australia Pty Ltd are natural, recyclable products made from wood grown in sustainable forests. The manufacturing processes conform to the environmental regulations of the country of origin.

The author and publisher have made every effort to contact copyright holders for material used in this book. Any person or organisation that may have been overlooked should contact the publisher.

To Rugby League: the game that probably saved my life

CONTENTS

Foreword by Alan Jones		ix
Prologue	The Quick and the Damned	1
1	The Seed is Sown	17
2	Getting Away with It	27
3	Rise before the Fall	39
4	Sitting in the Dock and the Bay	47
5	Big House to Big League	61
6	Dépêche Mode	77
7	Welcome to Wayne's World	91
8	A message from Wayne Bennett	107
9	Beautiful One Day, Dog Day the Next	117
10	Fibro Wonderland	131
11	Headless Chicken	147
12	Hot to Trot	157
13	Into the Eye of the Tiger	173
14	Keeping Up with the Jones Boy	191
15	Ticket to Roam	205
16	The Fix	221
17	The Fix-up	241
18	From Oberon to Lebanon	263
19	Don't Mention the C-Word	287
20	Coachjelias@hotmail.com	315
21	Ray	339
22	The Final Stretch	353
Postscript	You be the Judge	371
Author's Note		378
Index		379

FOREWORD

No matter the verbal or recitational skills available to any individual, the writing of a foreword to this autobiography is a very difficult task. The difficulty derives from the fact that I have known John Elias, until I read this I would have used the word 'intimately', for many years. I have always found him to be loyal, engaging, dedicated to whatever tasks I asked of him and with a redeeming love and fondness for his mother.

But then this manuscript arrived in front of me and it took me literally months to recover from the prologue alone which is compulsory reading for any prospective filmmaker. A slice of life unfamiliar to almost all of us. That John Elias, on the eve of joining me at Balmain, when I was to become the first-grade coach in 1991 and he was to become a star recruit – was out there as a debt collector, the nature of which is given emphatic presentation in the opening chapter of this book, is mindboggling.

With remarkable clarity and a chilling regard for detail, the scene is set of what, unknown to me, was obviously a dramatic double life. Here was an athlete at the height of his football career in 1990 being held at gunpoint over a debt, and the 'get square' was to kidnap a rival gang member and make him dig his own grave on the banks of the Georges River. Within weeks, I was coaching the same John Elias. But one can barely imagine what else must have been occupying his mind.

This is a story that has to be told. I say without any sense of gilding the lily that I have always found John Elias to be a thoroughly enjoyable, albeit roguish individual. I can well remember John entreating me to buy some suits out of the back of a car after training at Leichhardt Oval. It was an invitation that many players accepted. I politely declined, suggesting to him that if I put one on I might catch on fire. I'm sure John understood what I was hinting at, though few others did.

We read of John's life from when his father died three months before he was born, and a beautiful, caring and hardworking mother struggling in a new country to support four children alone. John Elias has never sought to excuse his errant behaviour on the basis that the beginning was, at best, awkward. However, without proper guidance at a young age, John was soon in trouble. Yet to be fair, while this is over 20 years ago, the same spider web of gangs and criminal youths is enticing the John Eliases of today and that is one of the central tragedies of this book. It is also one of the justifications for it being written. There have to be better ways of creating a more ordered society where there currently is disorder. There have to be better ways of making sure that the story of John Elias isn't wasted. While he

FOREWORD

stole his first car at age 14, the reality is today the incidence of such stealing is so rampant it is almost dismissed by law enforcement authorities. Report your car stolen today and the police merely give you a number and remind you that there were many thousands before you who made a similar report.

Then there's the issue of punishment. While this story demonstrates John's behaviour becoming more brazen, it also proves that the nature of juvenile detention is such that as with John Elias, so it is with many others, it is not a worthwhile deterrent. And just as teachers are increasingly under threat today in the classroom, this story demonstrates little progress has been made. John Elias was expelled from one school for masterminding a bomb threat. Today it is knives and guns.

What will we learn from this autobiography, which chronicles John Elias at 16 wrongly charged with stabbing a bus driver and spending 18 months in jail alongside some of the country's most dangerous and deranged criminals. If you want to learn something about life in prison, it's all here.

But so too in the book are the successes. The itinerant nature of a quite remarkable Rugby League career is revealed, and in particular a testing start with the super-coach Wayne Bennett which was to grow into a beneficial and influential friendship. Indeed, the ups and downs of a long and very distinguished Rugby League career are revealed here and they mirror in many ways the ups and downs of a life beyond the football field often lived with little regard to the law.

Chapter 17 is the chapter of special interest to me, because I was in charge of Rugby League at Souths in 1994 when what has now become an infamous game took place at the end of the season against Wests. I was so disturbed about suggestions that we had 'run dead' that I invited the then Police Commissioner Lauer to investigate the matter. To this day, I'm convinced of our innocence and a police inquiry found no evidence of such behaviour. Nonetheless John Elias reveals here that he was offered hundreds of thousands of dollars to arrange for his South Sydney teammates to 'run dead'. That he didn't accept the offer may well suggest an emerging morality which hopefully has blossomed in his later years.

Those years have been coloured to a very great extent by the crisis he faced with stomach cancer. But it wasn't all over, the flirtation with the law. A shooting incident over disputed winnings from a shared SP bookmaking syndicate led to John Elias being found guilty of shooting his betting partner. By this stage, law enforcement authorities, if not John, had had enough. The punishment was severe, four-and-a-half years and back to the dreaded Long Bay Jail from which our communications were regular and informative. On numerous occasions John indicated in writing to me that he'd learned the errors of his ways; that his new vocation would be to persuade other wayward young people not to turn down the long road upon which he had recklessly embarked so many years ago.

John Elias today faces the challenge of the straight and narrow. I am certain his most earnest wish would be that it would be a path that fewer young people would need to take because it only follows a long, harrowing and unrewarding march down a bent road. This book is about that march, but it's also about the turning in the road which hopefully remains straight and narrow forever.

FOREWORD

It's a measure of the John Elias I knew as a football coach that all the proceeds of this book will go to charity. It's a measure of our affection for John Elias that we hope, especially in relation to him, that the writing of it has not been in vain. Too many people close to John have been hurt by what you will read between the covers. I know it is his fervent wish that they not be hurt again. The fulfilment of that wish rests now with the man about whom all this has been written, the talented, colourful and enigmatic John Elias.

Alan Jones AO
Sydney 2010

PROLOGUE
THE QUICK AND THE DAMNED

'I'm going to die.'

That's my first thought. The gun is pressed against my head, shaking ever so slightly.

My next thought: regret. How the hell did I get into this situation? A gun to my head. It feels like a .44 Magnum without a silencer. There are five massive gangster blokes surrounding me. They're yelling threats in a foreign language. Maybe Greek. But I can't be 100 per cent sure. It's hard to think straight. I break into a cold sweat which is freezing my reflexes and melting my insides. I have to think straight, but instead I think back.

I'm going to die outside Belmore Oval, home of the Canterbury–Bankstown Bulldogs. There's a gun to my head on a warm afternoon in late 1990. It's just after 3 pm – kick-off time. My mind drifts back to days like these four years ago when I'd walk down the dim, cool tunnel beneath the main grandstand and into the roar of a 20,000-strong crowd. At my side were the true giants of rugby league – Steve Mortimer, Terry Lamb, David Gillespie, and Andrew Farrar. We would emerge into the sunshine, ready to defend our turf as the 3:05 pm service to Liverpool rattled past behind the northern goalposts.

The silver rush of a train brings me back to now – the reality of the gun's cold metal and its deadly intent. At this time on a Tuesday, the train would be filled with passengers. If just one of them happened to look left at that moment they would have seen a well-known first-grade footballer being marched towards a blue Kombi. Is the gun still there? Yes, it is. Oh shit. The side door slides open, revealing the dark and uncertain place I'm about to enter. I swallow only fear. My mouth is overcome by the same parched, breathless taste that last struck me as a 16-year-old on his way to Long Bay maximum security prison.

Everything in the back of the Kombi is crude steel: its corrugated floor and benches. Huge, hairy hands shove me down onto one of the seats. Then I see the gun. It's no longer at the side of my head but directly in my face. I was right. It was a .44 Magnum. The goon holding it was too big to stand upright. His steroid-inspired mass squatted before me and waited. The others clamoured like orcs before battle. They lunged and strained behind lowered baseball caps that masked their faces.

Then it began, first with boots and knees. I'm being kicked and punched from all directions. Under the blows, I feel my ribs and kidneys soften, like vegetables on a stovetop. I don't know how long the beating will continue or how it will end. But I was now certain of one thing: I'm not going to die. The gun has been put away, most likely nestled deep in the jacket of the man who stood back.

I'll call him Con. I hated him. He made a big mistake sparing me. I now lived for revenge.

In October 1990 I was many things. I was a top-grade rugby league player preparing for the upcoming season with the Balmain Tigers. The previous year had arguably been my best. A month earlier I had played my first NSWRL semi-final, against Manly. It was now the off-season, but I continued to train alone and kept in daily contact with my closest teammates from the Tigers – Steve Roach, Benny Elias and Tim Brasher. It was a rare and cherished month of the year when we could hit the bars of Kings Cross and Oxford Street at all hours without worrying about reporting for training on time the next morning.

In October 1990, I was also a convicted criminal who kept coming back for the buzz. Any chance I had of leading a straight, law-abiding life ended after spending 18 months among the state's worst felons at Long Bay jail when I was a teenager. It was unheard of to send a 16-year-old into maximum security, and still is today. I never recovered. I bashed people, robbed shops and then graduated to debt collection and stand-over work. I led a double life, which everyone suspected, but only a chosen few knew the whole truth.

One person who had my confidence was a businessman I knew from the Cross. He made an offer to me shortly after the 1990 season ended, when Canberra beat Penrith to claim their second straight premiership. My friend was not happy. He told me a Sydney-based criminal lawyer named Peter had been messing about with his trust account. There was $560,000 missing and the businessman wanted it back.

When the fulltime siren sounded, this became my line

of work. I visited people who owed money and used various means to get the debt repaid. Those who owed came from all walks of life, but were generally drug-dealers. Sometimes I hooked a big fish like a lawyer or an accountant. One time there was even a judge, who nearly had a heart attack when I turned up uninvited at his home. I'd normally be accompanied by a crew of guys I could trust – some of whom I had met in Long Bay almost a dozen years earlier. The key to collecting safely was to do your research and never use the same men twice in a row. There was only one exception to this rule: my good mate Georgie Boy. Georgie Boy covered my arse when we went on a job. He carried some pretty persuasive firepower, which could be revealed if the need arose with a simple flick of his jacket lapel.

I stood to earn $180,000 by getting Peter the lawyer to pay up. The next morning I rang his office in the city and made an appointment under a bogus name for that coming Friday. Because Peter made a living defending criminals, I was well aware of his background and reputation. He wasn't a dangerous man – just devious and untrustworthy. Or so I thought. It shaped up as a straightforward job. I assumed Peter didn't need a confrontation like this in his line of work. Being a lawyer, he was bound by a code of professional ethics. It wouldn't look good if the other legal eagles discovered he was being stood over by underworld figures for a six-figure sum he'd fleeced from a client.

As soon as I walked through the door with Georgie Boy, he recognised me. Most of them did, either because of my football career or my reputation on the streets. A few pleasantries were exchanged before we got down to the business of his debt. Peter responded in a strange way. While most of the people I confront offer excuses or ignorance, he acknowledged that he owed the money and immediately promised to return every last cent. We agreed on a date for repayment and shook hands. I place a large emphasis on judging a man's intentions by the way he shakes hands. A firm grip while looking you in the eye signals truth. Peter's grip was limp and clammy with his eyes directed towards the carpet. Still, I felt he had no choice. Georgie Boy and I left there confident things would run smoothly.

I felt even more assured when Peter phoned me the following Monday with some pleasant news. He told me a cheque was being organised and that he had arranged for a friend to hand it over.

His friend's name was Con.

I told Peter to have Con meet me in the park next to Belmore Oval the following afternoon, Tuesday. This was my favourite place to collect money because it was at the end of a cul-de-sac. There were certain advantages in having only one way in and one way out. It was also my home turf. I'd grown up in nearby Punchbowl after migrating to Australia from Lebanon as a baby in 1963. I knew the area intimately. We agreed that Con would meet me there at 3 pm.

The fact that Peter had set out to resolve matters so swiftly convinced me this would be an easy job. He clearly wanted this mess to disappear and then get on with his cushy life. And that's why I told Georgie Boy there was no need to shadow me at Belmore for this collect. It was a real break in convention, because Georgie Boy and I did every job together. Sometimes he would be by my side, at others he would be lurking out of sight. Either way, he was always there to cover my back in case someone decided to get tricky. Georgie Boy protested when I told him I'd be meeting Con alone. He wasn't worried about his cut, just whether or not I'd be OK. I dismissed his concerns out of the belief that Peter desperately wanted the matter resolved as soon as possible.

Tuesday morning was hot. I went down to Roselands swimming pool and did 20 laps before returning home to Punchbowl for more training in my backyard gym. I had 'borrowed' a rowing machine from the Tigers to do extras during the off-season. Balmain chief executive Keith Barnes – one of the best blokes I've met in rugby league – was none the wiser. But he would later be furious when I broke it and tried to smuggle the machine back into the weights room without his knowledge.

Mum prepared my usual lunch – salad with a can of tuna – which I ate before going to Belmore. Normally my mind is racing before a collect. But on this day I was calm and almost distant. Nothing could go wrong. I always liked to get there first. When I pulled up in my white 1985 Toyota Camry the cul-de-sac was empty. I parked, got out and waited on a nearby bench with my back to the grandstand that would shake with cheers and boos during the winter months. Today, however, it was soulless and still. No-one was around.

The sound of an engine made me look up. At the top of the street was a blue Kombi, driven hesitantly in my direction. As the van loomed up I made out the driver: Con. Our eyes met and we nodded in recognition. The passenger seat was empty.

I judged Con to be in his mid-30s. He was very Greek. As he stepped out of the car, I could see he was wearing a gold chain, exposed by his unbuttoned shirt. Con began shouting straightaway, 'We're not paying you a thing, you piece of shit!'

There were no pleasantries, no greetings. Just threats and abuse. I'd encountered this routine many times before and remained calm, although deep down I faced the difficult reality of being ambushed without Georgie Boy to back me up. I raised my hands in mock surrender and said: 'It's OK, mate, I'm just here on behalf of a friend. I know nothing about it. I've just been told to come here and collect something.' I wanted to let Con think he had intimidated me into backing down and disappearing. But what I really intended to do was get out of there, gather the boys and pay our lawyer friend a very serious visit that same afternoon. Peter had made an enormous error in hiring this goon to try and scare me off.

As I protested my innocence, Con moved in, close enough for me to see the self-congratulatory triumph flickering in his eyes. His look seemed to say: 'Now you know better than to mess with me, shitbag.'

I should have kept playing the game, pretending to be an unsuspecting middleman. To survive in the underworld you have to be a good actor, to know when to play charades. But on this particular afternoon my pride and bravado were too great to overcome. I couldn't let this flea I'd never set eyes on before stand over me like this.

I extended my hand towards Con. He grabbed it and shook. I returned his grip as hard as I possibly could and drew his chest into mine. I wanted to talk to him up close because there was always a chance he might be an undercover cop wearing a recording wire. If I was paranoid of anything in those days, it was plainclothes police. I'd heard the cops were keeping a close eye on my activities, which had featured some big rorts on the Friday night trots at Harold Park. The word was that these fixes had attracted the attention of the National Crime Authority.

I didn't utter a word until Con was close enough for me to almost taste his souvlaki breath. 'You've just made a big mistake, buddy,' I said. 'I eat guys like you for breakfast.' I even mouthed the words with a grin and a nod just in case there were hidden cameras.

Con was unmoved. His eyes were cold and steady. With my hand still locked around his, he turned and yelled out a single word: 'BOYS!'

I had time for one long and remorseful breath before the Kombi's side door whooshed open. Four hulking goons stormed out. It all happened in a split second, but my spirit plummeted like mercury in a thermometer. I'd been complacent and had paid the price. I'd dropped my guard and just invited a gun to be held to the side of my head.

The sunlight was harsh when I finally opened my eyes. It seemed like they'd been closed for hours, but no more than two minutes could have passed. I had shut them in self-defence as the kicks, knees and punches rained down in the back of the Kombi. The van was almost out of sight now, turning left at the top of the cul-de-sac towards Belmore Oval as I looked up. My ribs didn't feel right. Patches of red skin had been exposed by rips in my blood-splattered shirt. It was impossible to believe I had been sitting in my car five minutes earlier, so confident of an easy collect that I was almost counting my money. Stupid, stupid, stupid. I will never let my guard down like this again. Because I was collecting from a white-collar professional, I had relaxed. What threat could a lawyer like Peter pose? Plenty, it seemed. I couldn't afford to let something like this happen again. I had to finish Con. Show him who was boss.

There was one thing that consoled me – at least I knew Con wasn't a cop. All bets were off. I no longer had any fear of being caught, something that usually held me back. The fear of arrest made me tentative, which is not helpful in bloodthirsty moments like these. But now my mind was free to settle the score with impunity. Con and his lawyer mate were probably thinking I'd been scared off, but they hadn't done their homework. I was determined to make them pay.

As I drove to Georgie Boy's house my memory reached for any information it could retrieve about Con. I had to get some solid details on him. I knew nothing about the bloke – had never previously seen, met or heard of him. This was strange because I'd been working the Sydney underworld for almost a decade. It was hard to believe there was a stand-over man I didn't know about. I assumed Con had been paid by the lawyer to put the fear of God into me so I'd fade away.

Reputations and egos were at stake. Stand-over men are nothing without their reputations. And there's no better way of building one than taking down a rival collector. I assumed Con was a newcomer on the scene looking to bully his way up the food chain by getting one up on me. Everything I stood for – my very reputation – demanded that, in the most brutal way imaginable, he be prevented from doing so.

Whatever the reason behind Con's involvement, there was no doubting that he was the type of collector I despised. It might sound hypocritical coming from a person in the same line of work, but there are different breeds of stand-over men who can be classified according to the clients they work for. Although I have committed crimes and led a secret life away from my family and teammates, I lived by a crude code of honour. I never *collect* money on behalf of drug dealers and I never *protect* people who owe. I take pride in seeing the rich and powerful, like this corrupt lawyer friend of ours, return money to the less wealthy. I saw my job as a service for people who needed and deserved it – not those who used it as a means to avoid justice. And I didn't accept every job that was offered to me. I only took the ones I thought were right. Con was wrong because he was either trying to muscle in on my turf, or was being paid to protect a white-collar thief. Either way, he was a scumbag.

Georgie Boy didn't have to hear the story to know what had happened. Though we'd only met three years earlier, we'd quickly developed the understanding of lifelong friends. We met through football, where he worked in administration, and now we spent virtually every day in each other's pockets at training or games. Georgie Boy didn't want to give Con any more time to gloat. He demanded we gather the crew and pay Peter an unannounced visit in his office that afternoon. Every fibre of my body wanted the same thing, but somehow I remained calm. I told Georgie Boy that we'd wait until tomorrow.

Georgie Boy's girlfriend made the appointment this time. It was for 11 am the next day. But when the time arrived there was no petite brunette to be seen in the lawyer's office. Instead, a group of five thuggish-looking men burst through the door – myself, Georgie Boy and three of our Pacific Islander acquaintances.

There's not a shade of white that could do justice to the colour of Peter's face when he looked up from his computer. It was like a blizzard had descended on him. He began panting out excuses like: 'I thought you were going to have me killed' and 'I didn't mean for Con to beat you up, just scare you a little.'

When this drivel stopped, Georgie Boy opened his jacket to remind the lawyer how much shit he was in. We could have shot him dead on the spot. I could have strangled him. But instead I started asking questions. I was momentarily unconcerned about when the $560,000 would be repaid. I was only interested in finding Con and getting my revenge.

The lawyer didn't need any further convincing from Georgie Boy's jacket lining to give me the two things I had come for – Con's surname and address. Before we left I added: 'When we're finished with him, we'll be coming back for you.' It was a hollow threat, but Peter was so shaken that he had no choice but to believe it. I wanted to keep him terrified. If he was convinced that we might pounce at any moment, he was less likely to try something shifty again.

The crew split outside his office. Georgie Boy and I went back to Punchbowl, while the Islander boys drove straight to Con's home in Earlwood. He was to be brought to me. I didn't care how long it took. All I had to do was wait. And it didn't take long. At 5 pm the next day, a four-wheel drive purred past my house. Its windows were heavily tinted, rendering the occupants mere silhouettes. As soon as it pulled up, the front passenger door opened and one of the Islanders stepped out and said: 'John, we've got him.'

I didn't feel pleasure or elation, merely the satisfaction that comes with receiving what's due. I opened the back door and there was Con, fretting like a schoolboy who's just wet himself in front of the class. He knew something bad was coming, but the endless and brutal possibilities were what really terrified him. He was biting hard on a gag the boys had shoved in his mouth. I took my time to catch his eye and then turned away with the words: 'Boys, get the shovel.'

Although Con's kidnapping came well before I expected, plans were in place. I had thought of nothing else but this moment since staggering out of the blue Kombi two days earlier. I'd decided that Con was going on a drive to a secluded place I had visited many times as a wild 14-year-old. During those days, my friends and I would steal cars from Punchbowl shopping centre at night and take them for drives around town. When we felt like a change from the city or the Cross, we'd head to the National Park by the Georges River, in southern Sydney. Our favourite spot was down the road from Revesby train station. It was about a one-mile walk east from the car park through scrub. Although you could see the headlights from Henry Lawson Drive, no-one could see you. It was secluded and quiet. The perfect place for a grave.

The setting and the mention of a shovel sent Con into a panic when we arrived. Now it was Con's turn to face the Grim Reaper. As we disappeared into the bush, Con began pleading. We hadn't laid a finger on him, but his face was already creased with tears and sweat. He begged and name-dropped, but I wasn't interested. It was close to 6 pm when we stopped walking.

I tossed Con the shovel and ordered him to start digging. He looked at me like I was a lunatic. He didn't want to believe he was actually being asked to dig his own grave. It was simply too disturbing for even a morally-deprived shit-bag like him to contemplate.

A fresh round of pleas and name-dropping began, but it was no use. Con copped some physical persuasion and finally began to dig, moaning and whimpering with each strike of the shovel.

THE QUICK AND THE DAMNED

I didn't intend to kill Con. Sure I wanted to, but it was not my plan. I wanted to scare him beyond belief with a stunt so deranged he'd never come near me again. A gun to the head wasn't enough. It had to be something truly macabre and the prospect of being buried alive seemed to fit the bill. However, a sparkling performance was needed to instil genuine terror – for Con to believe I was deadly serious. A lot of my previous work in this business relies on bluff. You had to be a good actor and your associates also had to know when you are bluffing and when to play along. The boys put in an award-winning support role on this particular afternoon, goading Con about his impending death at regular intervals.

Con had not stopped name-dropping or promising to pay the money back with interest since he began digging. I was starting to enjoy myself, but I was also unsure of exactly how I'd let him go. The simplest idea was to accept his offer to pay the money back. Then he mentioned a name that got my attention: John Ibrahim. John was and still is a Kings Cross nightclub owner. We had been friends for many years and John is now arguably the most influential man of his kind in Sydney, a Lebanese immigrant like myself but with infinitely more connections. Con swore they were also friends and that if I contacted John favours could be arranged in return for his release.

I ordered him to stop digging and really turned on the theatre. I simultaneously threatened and cajoled. 'If you are lying to me, you'll be happy to be buried alive,' I said. Sensing a lifeline, Con furiously protested the truth. I nodded and told him to continue digging while I left to make a phone call. Few people had mobile phones in 1990, and I wasn't one of them. So I walked back to the cars and drove to a phone box. I rang John's home. As I waited I began to think about a new way to spare Con. I would tell him John had requested his release and that, being a good friend, I had reluctantly agreed.

John picked up, which was surprising because he was rarely home. When I finished telling him about the situation, he asked me to let Con go. He didn't know Con intimately, but he had been good mates with the Greek's late father. When the old man had died recently, John had promised to look after his son. They had a deathbed deal, the kind that could never be broken. I laid on a pained routine about wanting revenge against Con and so forth, but I always intended to agree. After a couple of minutes of mock negotiation, I promised John that Con would be alive tomorrow.

By the time I returned to the grave site, Con had finished digging his six-foot-deep hole. He sat cross-legged next to its edge looking sad and broken. There were no whimpers or pleas now. He knew his fate was in the hands of someone else and was resigned to it. It was the first time I'd ever seen the look of a man who is prepared to die.

That was enough for me. He would never threaten me again. 'You're a very, very lucky man,' I told him. 'Our friend wants to see you tonight. But if I ever see you again you'll spend the rest of your time in that hole.' Handed an unexpected stay of execution, Con nearly kissed my feet. He cried and gushed thanks as the night closed in. Then he did something that made me want to change my mind and kill him after all. He asked for a lift back to Kings Cross. We gave him the appropriate answer – with a few punches and knees thrown in for good measure – and left him alone. A man who has just cheated death should have no problems making his own way home.

I next saw Con about a week later, when he paid me a $20,000 'apology' fee that the nightclub owner had insisted on. The $560,000 owed by the lawyer had also been repaid to my client. At that meeting Con promised never to cross my path again, a promise he has kept because I've never seen or heard of him since. I left the meeting cashed-up and invincible. It was a good place to be in for the week ahead, which marked the start of pre-season training with the Balmain Tigers for 1991.

CHAPTER 1

THE SEED IS SOWN

All this trouble started three months before I was born. That's when Dad died.

My parents John and Susan raised our family in Hardine, a village among the mountains and cedar trees of northern Lebanon with a population of 200. My father died in his sleep from what doctors said was a heart attack. He had been rushed to hospital in Beirut for an operation but died before they could begin surgery. Mum later told me he had been sick for a long time, but medical knowledge in that part of the world was so hazy in those days she can't recall exactly what the problem was. Dad was in his 40s when he died.

Mum was left to support three kids on her own – my older brothers George and Joe, and sister Jennifer. When she gave birth to a fourth on 10 December 1962, he was named after his late dad. I was to be the last, but Mum had no means of feeding so many mouths. We were never rich, but just lived off the land like most rural Lebanese in the early 1960s. We weren't as poor as some families in Hardine, but our house was no mansion either. It was just one big room with curtains instead of walls to separate different areas of the house. All the kids slept together in one bed. On hot nights the bed became too crowded for comfort and we'd take turns sleeping on the threadbare floor.

Soon the strain of feeding all those hungry bellies got too much for my mother. She had to swallow her pride and ask for help from Dad's three brothers, who had moved to Australia a few years earlier. My mother was always the master of our house – a feisty and hard-working woman whose quiet handyman husband took a back seat in domestic arguments. They called her the pocket battleship. But the task of raising a family single-handedly in that culture was beyond her, despite her determination. So when I was old enough – about nine months – Mum packed our belongings for a three-month boat trip to Australia, in October 1963.

Our uncles paid for the fares and organised the paperwork from Sydney. I was too young to recall the voyage, but my eldest brother Joe later told me that the trip from Beirut to Port Said in Egypt was best forgotten because of the combination of a tiny boat and swells that induced widespread seasickness. He reckons the stopover in Egypt was great, solely because Mum bought all the kids hot chips. Who needs the pyramids? My brothers and sister also lapped up the three-month ride across the Indian Ocean on a much bigger liner named the *Galileo*. Joe, however, swears to this day that he spent the whole time worrying that I'd crawl overboard and be lost at sea.

I can't remember anything about life in Australia before we moved into our current family home in Punchbowl, in

THE SEED IS SOWN

Sydney's south-west, in 1966. That was the first and only home Mum ever bought. Dad's three brothers – George, Lou and Tony – had vowed to help Mum adjust when we arrived, but they had a strange way of showing it. We moved in with George, who had a terrible temper that saw him beat Mum and the older kids. When they weren't being hit, my brothers and sister would be locked in the chicken coop with the hens if George felt they had been naughty. The domestic violence against Mum got so bad that my older brothers even went up to the police station to report it.

The house was also overcrowded because George's wife and two kids lived there. Mum stuck it out for about six months, then she snapped and moved us in with Lou, who lived in Villawood, which is now the location of an immigration detention centre.

We weren't made to feel welcome by Lou and his wife. Within a week, we were back on the road, this time into the arms of a family friend in Bankstown, Joe Davis. Joe was much kinder and ended up keeping us for two years while Mum found a job in neighbouring Punchbowl. Joe would even drive her to and from work, while dropping my brothers and sister at school.

Although we now had a roof over our heads, Mum still faced the task of raising four kids alone. My uncles had promised financial help, but they never came through, leaving Mum to work tirelessly to pay for food, my older siblings' education and a deposit for a house. Sister Anne King from St Jerome's, the local Catholic primary school we all attended, helped Mum save a home deposit from her $25-a-week wages. Mum worked at a laundromat just down the road from our current house. She worked 14-hour days, folding sheets and ironing, for two years to make ends meet and save the deposit. I remember being left to play among the freshly-starched clothes when I was very young. Mum had to take me to work because she couldn't afford childcare. She worked at that same laundromat for 17 years. She couldn't even read or write Arabic, let alone speak English, when we left Lebanon.

Mum couldn't afford anything but the basics. Birthdays and Christmases meant nothing to us because there were never any presents. It was just, 'Happy birthday, John' or 'Merry Christmas, John.' Our clothes were donations from St Vincent de Paul or the Salvation Army. The Smith Family in Bankstown also gave Mum a $20 food voucher every week. I remember a handful of times when Mum simply had no money, and she'd have to beg the Smith Family to bring over boxes of food. We never had holidays and swimming lessons involved being thrown into Roselands pool by my brothers and told to fend for myself. We didn't get a TV until much later than everyone else – and when it arrived our favourite show was wrestling. My uncles used to come around drinking the old DA beer, convinced more and more that the bouts were real with each bottle they drank.

There was one brother left who hadn't burned us – Uncle Tony. When Mum had saved enough money for the deposit, she went to the bank only to be told their policy prevented single women from being approved for home loans. There was only one option open to Mum if she wanted the £3,000 to buy our own house – Uncle Tony. He was Dad's youngest brother, had not married and was in a position to put himself forward to guarantee the loan. He did, but on the condition that he and his mother – our Grandma Jennifer – live in the new house as well.

On one hand this was a good thing for Mum, because

THE SEED IS SOWN

she could leave us kids in the care of our grandmother when she was working five-and-a-half days a week. On the other it was bad, because Tony came with his own brand of tough discipline. Tony lived with us until he married – at least a couple of years. They weren't good years, particularly for Mum. Soon after they married, Tony and his wife discovered they were unable to have children and began to take an interest in their youngest nephew, John. Up until that point, Tony was probably the closest thing we had to a surrogate father – a dominant male figure who instilled some crude discipline. When my brothers and sister were cheeky, he'd put them over his knee. He used to get out the belt and issue some real floggings. That, believe it or not, was my introduction to violence.

But funnily enough, Tony would never hit me. He even helped me to learn to read, albeit from the yellow form guide in the paper. His gambling was almost as mad as his temper.

Eventually Tony asked Mum if they could adopt me. He wanted to take me because I was the youngest and he actually convinced Mum to give me up. I went and lived with Tony for about a week, but I was soon begging to go back to Mum. I was three or four years old, but it just didn't feel like home. I couldn't do it – I missed my family too much.

I often wonder what might have happened had I stayed with Tony. Looking back, I'm now certain that the root of all my troubles – the violence, the robberies, the stand-overs, the prison sentences – started with the fact that I never had a father figure. There was never any positive male role model. But perhaps more significantly, there was no male role model to advise against the stupid and illegal things I indulged in. No-one ever said *No* – and I never had the discipline or will-power to stop. When I was a kid, Mum was too busy and my older siblings too distracted to school me in the finer points of right and wrong. And when I got older, I was too consumed by the rush of crime to learn them for myself. As time went on, I strayed into more and more dangerous territory without bothering to find a moral compass that would have guided me out.

Apart from our poverty, my infancy was smooth enough. The biggest drama was the time Mum broke my right arm with a broomstick. I was about four years old and already an extremely cheeky kid. To be fair, cheeky is probably an understatement. Downright naughty would be more accurate. One of our neighbours was a rich family that owned a brand new BMW. They had a little boy about my age whom I took a liking to and on this particular afternoon I decided to teach him some dance moves – on top of his dad's new Beemer. Within about 15 minutes we had crushed the BMW's roof so that it looked like an inverted tent.

When our neighbour saw his beloved car crumpled beyond repair, he asked his son for an explanation. He was soon on our doorstep demanding Mum pay for the damage. Mum could barely afford a new roll of toilet paper let alone repairs to a BMW. So she refused in her uniquely defiant way, which consisted of hysterical hand-waving and finger-pointing. But that was hardly the end of the matter. I knew I was in big trouble when she came hunting with the broomstick, so I fled to the backyard. Mum chased me, waving the dreaded stick wildly, but I stepped like Freddy Fittler until . . . WHACK! . . . she struck my right forearm.

Mum toiled so hard in those days and was stressed a lot of the time, so her fury was understandable. The blow hurt like hell but I was too scared to say a word out of fear of another hiding. For two weeks I kept a silence better than any Trappist monk until the pain became too much. The doctor was amazed when I arrived at the hospital. My arm had been broken for the past fortnight. Even then I was a staunch bugger, but little did I know how well the ability to put up with pain would serve me later in life. Mum even made me tell the doctor that I had sustained the injury by falling over; because she was scared the police would come and take me away as a victim of child abuse.

Thanks to my broken right arm, I started school as a left-hander. The obvious and only choice was St Jerome's, but by the time I got there all of my siblings had left. George and Jennifer had gone up to St John's High School in Lakemba while Joe, the eldest, was forced to quit his studies at 14 to help support Mum. He worked long hours at a factory that injected mouldings, starting out at a miserly $6 a week, and I saw little of him for the rest of my childhood.

My time at St Jerome's was fantastic. It was an old-style Catholic school with a convent and strict nuns who took the classes. Like the area in which we lived, the pupils represented a diverse mix of ethnic backgrounds. There were a lot of Christian Lebanese kids – about half my class. My closest friends, however, were all Australian-born. My best mate was a kid called Peter Rix, who came from a big family that lived over our back fence. We remain as close today as we were when we started kindergarten.

I never really experienced any racism at school like so many other migrant kids did back then. My first taste would come many years later on the football fields of whiter suburbs. I can also thank St Jerome's for rugby league. It was pretty much the only sport the school played in winter – there was no soccer, or wogball, as it was called then. My introduction to the game came one afternoon in kindergarten when the teacher asked all the boys in the class if they were interested in playing. Although I had lived in Sydney virtually all my life, I had no idea about the sport. We didn't get a TV at home until after everyone else, so there was no opportunity to see it. I looked around the room that day and saw my two best friends – Peter Rix and Brad Hockey – with their hands straining above their heads. Well, if my mates were in it, so was I. This attitude would soon start to get me into a lot of trouble, but on this occasion it delivered something special.

We started in the Under-6s, the youngest possible team, and won the 1968 grand final. From the start I always played lock or second row, the two positions I would remain in until my final first-grade match 26 years later. All I knew at the start was that you had to carry the ball and put it over the other team's line. I didn't know anything about the first-grade competition. I had no idea about teams like the Bulldogs, Tigers and Rabbitohs, whose colours I would later wear. Back then I was like any other kid – I liked playing footy because it meant being with my friends. But on a deeper level, I loved the camaraderie of a team, the spirit of sacrificing your safety for your mates. I never missed a training session, never missed a game. And I loved tackling. Most other kids preferred to score tries or hog the ball, but I was happy for the other team to have it so I could line them up and smash them.

But the most valuable thing rugby league brought into my life was my second coach, Ron Miller. He lived up the road with his wife Carol and two children, Jamie and Andrew. Although most of the residents are now from the Middle East, Punchbowl was still very Anglo-Saxon back then. We were one of the first families from Lebanon to arrive there.

THE SEED IS SOWN

Ron had a family of his own, but took me under his wing. I'll never know why, but in no time he and Carol treated me like one of their own kids. Their door was always open to me after school and on the weekends. I'd go there for meals, even stay the odd night or two.

Now this might seem strange, but Mum didn't seem to mind because she was flat out working and maintaining the house. So was Joe. My eldest brother worked so hard in his teenage years and youth that his back is now gone, rendering him unemployable. By that stage George had begun to excel academically en route to being accepted into law school. George had also found a male role model of his own in the form of his godfather, who lived in Wollongong, and who came up every Friday night to pick up George and take him down the coast for the weekend.

So you could say I was a bit of a forgotten child. Not that I knew any better at the time. All that mattered was footy in the park with my mates and spending time at the Millers' house. We didn't have a car back then, so it was a big deal to be taken for a drive outside Punchbowl. One of the highlights was when Ron and Carol took me to Luna Park. They bought me show bags and paid for all the rides. Afterwards I was so tired that Ron carried me in from the car asleep. They also took me to the cinema for the first time, as well as on road trips beyond Sydney to try out for rep footy teams. So great did my bond with Ron become that he eventually sponsored me for my Confirmation.

Life was good with the Millers keeping an eye on me, but it was too good to last. When I was about nine, Ron and Carol split up. I never knew why or understood the reasons, but was quickly aware of the consequences when Ron suddenly moved away to Coffs Harbour.

That shattered me. I cried when he told me he had to leave. There would be no more weekends with him and Carol. No more drives. Ron was the father figure I'd been looking for, and he pretty much disappeared without an explanation that I could understand at such a young age. Looking back, it might have been a chance for a well-behaved life that went up in the cloud of dust that trailed Ron's car as it departed for the mid-north coast. But although it would be easier to convince myself that I'd have stayed out of trouble if Ron stuck around, there's no way of truly knowing. I really went off the rails after he left, and the only person responsible for that is me.

Around the same time as Ron's leaving I found an old black-and-white photo of our family that was taken in Lebanon when Dad was alive. It was hidden away among the stuff Mum had brought with her to Australia. For the first time, I found myself looking at my father. Mum and the other three kids were there, too, standing beside him in their Sunday best. The only person missing was me. I studied the photo for a long time, because it stirred something inside me. It seemed to enunciate what I'd been missing all my life – a father. My real dad had died before I even knew what one was; and when I thought I'd found a replacement in Ron, he'd gone away too. As if to remind myself of what I needed, I had the photo enlarged and framed. I then gave it to Mum to hang in the lounge room, where it is displayed to this day.

Up until Ron left I didn't get into any real trouble. Now he was gone, there was no stopping me.

CHAPTER 2

GETTING AWAY WITH IT

From Grade 3 I was among a small band of troublemakers who would talk in class, give a bit of cheek, neglect doing their homework, pinch the girls on the bum and steal lollies from the tuckshop. I recall that Peter Rix and I were first suspended in Grade 1 for something silly like not marching in line. I suppose it was a buzz having a reputation as a rebel who'd be summoned to the front of the class and whacked with a feather duster every day. I liked the mischievous part of being a ratbag and trying to get away with things. I paid no attention to the rules. When the other kids lined up for the school bus in the afternoon, I would just stride straight up to the front and get on. I was a little bit bigger than the others and that only encouraged me to throw my weight around.

There was no-one to pull me into line – and my behaviour was surprising because Joe, George and Jennifer were all angels when they went through the grades at St Jerome's before me. My misbehaviour earned a range of punishments like 20 Hail Marys and clean-up duty, but the feather duster was the worst. It hurt even more than the cane. The other kids – especially the girls – seemed to respect my tolerance of it. With the respect came popularity and immunity from being picked on. Everyone feared us – you could say we were the self-appointed school captains.

I started going downhill after Ron Miller left. I was lost for a couple of years. He was like my sponsor and, although we never spoke about it, he was the closest thing I had to a dad. Even footy lost its aura without him coaching. By age 10, I began to develop into a pretty handy player. The highlight of my childhood was when Ron told me I'd been selected in the Canterbury–Bankstown Under-10s rep side. The coach of that team wanted another player, but Ron pushed and pushed for me to be selected. That was a huge thrill, especially when I scored the winning try in our game against Souths. I held my own thanks to some handy footwork in attack and a huge work rate in defence.

Although there was nothing serious like fighting, my behaviour at school soon tested the nuns' patience. On one occasion I smashed a window while throwing a ball with Peter Rix in an out-of-bounds area of the playground. I was so bad that Sister Anne even visited Peter's parents, Ray and Margaret, to tell them not to let their son play with me. When I wasn't being whipped by the dreaded feather duster, I'd be detained after school, or made to clean up the playground. Ron's wife Carol tried to keep in touch – I remember she took me into the city for a couple of day trips – but it wasn't the same. I was going off the rails, losing respect for authority and adults, and would have been a real handful for her.

Eventually, St Jerome's had had enough. Mum was summoned by Sister Anne one afternoon and told that the school could no longer tolerate my behaviour. They wanted to transfer me to a boarding school because I was deemed uncontrollable. Mum was shocked and immediately began crying and begging for Sister Anne to reconsider.

Just as she would have no idea about my criminal activities in the years to come, Mum didn't know what I was getting up to at school. She was just too busy. There was always too much for her to worry about and I sort of fell through the cracks and was allowed to get away with whatever I pleased.

Mum was so busy that she never made it to a single game of footy to watch me play as a kid. In hindsight, the years I spent with Ron and Carol also placed a distance between me and my family – a gap that only got wider as I grew wilder. I gravitated towards Ron and Carol because there was a father in the house. With Mum, there was lots of love, but no time. You have to remember that she worked 14 hours a day, so I barely saw her.

Much to Mum's relief, Sister Anne extended me some mercy and I was allowed to finish primary school at St Jerome's. But it was only delaying the inevitable – a stay of execution. The freedom that would come the following year with taking the train to St John's High in Lakemba would soon land me on the wrong side of the tracks.

Although I was getting into trouble at school, life away from it was fairly mild. From age nine I began a newspaper round seven days a week for a bit of money. Sometimes I'd do both mornings and nights and quickly found I was a pretty good salesman. In fact, I wouldn't go back to the newsagent until all the papers were sold. If there were any left after my run, I'd just stand on the corner at the traffic lights and sell them to passing motorists.

My gift of 'the sell' came in handy as soon as I started at St John's at age 11. Students were roped into any number of walkathons and raffles to raise money for the school. For some reason I was really competitive about raising the most money, yet didn't give a damn about how my grades fared against other students. The kid that raised the most money would win a bike or something like that. People always wanted to help out a kid, even an over-sized troublemaker like myself. The key was to be polite yet confident in your approach to strangers – and you could safely say I had a bit of a brazen streak.

I'd go to Roselands shopping centre – in the early 1970s it was the biggest in Australia – and bug strangers to sponsor me for the 20 km walkathon. As for the raffles, I was so good at selling tickets that the teacher gave me permission to flog them up at Lakemba shops instead of going to classes. That lasted for a couple of months until the principal found out.

The teacher denied I had been granted permission, leaving me to cop 10 of the best. The fact he lied left me with a strange sense of disillusionment. I couldn't understand why he didn't tell the truth. How could an adult let an innocent kid take the rap? I believe from that day a bizarre sense of integrity was instilled in me. Although I've done all sorts of terrible things, I've always tried to be honest and transparent with my intentions.

The money I raised came in handy because St John's never charged Mum any school fees. The school knew she couldn't afford to pay for so many children. At that stage George, who is five years older than me, was still at St John's. The presence of a big brother certainly came in handy for a scallywag like me, who sometimes needed a hand with playground punch-ups. Once George stepped in, the older kids learned to leave me alone. Although I didn't really have too much interest in my studies (religion was my best subject, even though I didn't believe in God at that age), I never missed a day at St John's – even when things got pretty wild before my expulsion in Grade Nine.

We played touch footy on the oval before, between and after classes. One day after lunch Peter Rix and I decided we couldn't be bothered going back to class, so we just stayed in the playground getting into mischief. We found these megaphones, so what choice did I really have but to grab one and commentate a mock greyhound race at the top of my voice across the schoolyard while everyone else was in class? I copped the hardest six lashings ever for that stunt, and that's saying something. The frequency of beatings didn't change from St Jerome's to St John's. And neither did my attitude. I saw them as a badge of honour, limping away from the teacher's office with a red raw butt and a big grin to mask the pain.

The strangest thing about St John's was that one of my best mates was actually the bloke who would go on to be school captain after my expulsion. His name was Mark Cronk and we became good mates through the school footy team. I'd say he was the only person – aside from the teachers – who tried to get me to behave. He could see I was headed for expulsion and tried to step in before it was too late. Unfortunately, I didn't listen to Mark. I was having too much fun, although I did like him a lot despite the fact we were like chalk and cheese.

I can still remember the afternoon a couple of years later when Peter Rix told me Mark had died. He was killed in a car accident, aged 17. I was eating a sandwich at the time. When Peter gave me the news, I didn't know what to feel, what to think. So I kept chewing in silence.

By that time, I was pretty hardened. I was no longer the innocent-looking kid who could charm a couple of dollars worth of raffle tickets out of some kind-hearted shopper. I was something else altogether and the change happened at a place called Lucky Bills. Located across the road from Punchbowl station, Lucky Bills was a mixed business owned by a Lebanese family. It sold groceries and sweets, which were of no consequence to us. All we were interested in were the pinball machines. This was the place all the local kids gathered to hang out, and this apple barrel sure had a few rotten ones.

Lucky Bills became my second home after I discovered it catching the train to and from school every day. My brother George was the first person to take me there – he liked the pinnies too. But unlike me, the machines were all that he got involved with down there. I had the money from my paper round to spend, time aplenty, and limited supervision. It was a dangerous cocktail, ignited once and for all by the arrival to the area of a much older kid named Kenny.

Kenny was probably 17 when he came to Punchbowl – and the rest of us were barely teenagers. It's no surprise that we looked up to him and I was probably the most easily influenced. Within no time I was spending every spare moment at Lucky Bills. And yes, that included nights. The owners of the store lived in the same building, so they left it open for us to play the machines at all hours. Getting out of the house was no problem for me – I simply jumped out the front window after dinner when Mum thought I'd gone to bed. At the top of my street, I'd join a couple of mates and walk up to

Lucky Bills. We'd stay until all hours of the night – 5 and 6 am – sometimes so late that I would bump into Joe as he got ready to head to the factory that morning.

On some other nights I wouldn't even come home. Instead, I'd creep into the granny flat at the back of Peter Rix's house and sleep there. Although Peter's parents had been told to steer clear of me, Ray and Margaret were always kind-hearted and never asked any questions. As for my own family, they must have known something was up because the details of my whereabouts were pretty scarce, but no-one had the time to stop me.

And to tell you the truth, by that time I wouldn't have listened because Kenny was a much bigger influence. I can still vividly recall the night Kenny and I – a naive 14-year-old – sat in the front seat of a new EH Holden parked across the road from Lucky Bills. Every crim remembers the first car they stole, and this was my big break.

I'd been hanging out at Lucky Bills for a few months, and it quickly became apparent that the after-hours clientele had more on their minds than setting new pinball records. There was a gang of about 10 guys who hung out at night. It was a rag-tag bunch from all over the shop including a German, an Italian, a Greek, a couple of Lebos like myself and some Anglos. We were extremely tight and even developed our own language. For example, referring to someone as a 'Sal' meant they were a liar, while anyone we called a 'Warra' could be assured of being an imbecile. To alert one another to someone we thought was a copper, we'd touch our shoulder with our index finger.

Kenny was the ringleader because he was the oldest and had done the most stuff. So naturally it was he who taught me to steal cars. There was no great science to it – as long as you were a Holden-lover. We had a set of master keys that would fit any Holden door lock and ignition. If none of the keys worked on a particular car, the trusty old steel file would come out for some adjustments to the key's edges. We never failed to break in. Once behind the wheel, the trick was to jiggle the key up and down until you heard a click. That's when you'd turn her over and away you went.

Joyride time. No-one could count how many cars we flogged during those carefree, reckless nights. I even nicked Mum's car a couple of times. We probably stole about three or four cars a night, sometimes more. We'd start with the ones parked outside Punchbowl station – opposite Lucky Bills – and take them for a spin until we got bored, ran out of petrol or saw a better ride. We'd then drop the previous car and drive away with the next one. We never drag-raced or damaged the vehicles – we just drove them around in a convoy for a bit of fun.

My mate John was the exception. He became smitten with a white 1967 Holden station wagon. It was the first car he had stolen and he refused to let it go. He kept it in his driveway and washed it scrupulously for the entire world to see. Worried that his love affair with this car would spell the end of our fun, we ended up having to steal the car back from him. John was devastated, but we thought it was hilarious.

So that's how it really started in earnest for me – a life of crime conceived in the front seat of an EH Holden with bad-boy Kenny. He had no brothers and liked to have an influence over the younger kids. Without anyone else to look up to who took an interest in me, I was soon to become his pet student. I was an excited passenger the first couple of times Kenny and I stole cars together, but my moment behind the wheel didn't take too long to come. I was 14 and had no idea what it took to drive. I was still a couple of years off being eligible for my licence. The only inkling I had was from Kenny's joyrides, during which he showed me how to work the column shift gear stick most Holdens had back then. All I kept thinking was: 'How good is this?'

The first stolen car that I could truly take credit for was a green station wagon. It wasn't what you would call a smooth start. When I went to take off, the car was in reverse and we lurched backwards. Luckily there was nothing behind us, but maybe I should have seen it as an omen. Instead, I saw it as a green light. Within no time, stealing cars for our nightly joyrides became second nature.

Our favourite destination was Kings Cross. We'd cruise into town and along the strip clubs of Darlinghurst Road to perve on the hookers and check out the seedy characters. I'd never been to that part of town before I met the gang, so it was a real eye-opener. We were all too young to get into any of the establishments, so we'd just stay in the cars and keep driving around. It must have looked strange to see kids so young driving. But we never got pulled over. To tell you the truth, no-one was really that worried and that was probably half the problem.

Out of all the boys, Kenny was the best car thief. That's why everyone looked up to him. We didn't know any better. Apart from being very good at nicking cars, Kenny also had a knack for getting high. Luckily, I wasn't too interested in getting wasted. Most of the boys were into drugs, dope and the like. But Kenny and some of the others became addicted to heroin.

Like everything else, I would have been right up there with them had it not been for one thing: needles. I hate needles – they scare me to death. Back in those days I would sooner have done my homework than inject myself. Much later in life, when I was battling stomach cancer, the doctors told me I had to give myself a daily injection of white blood cells. I went to the doctor instead. That's how bad my needle phobia was.

But it was a godsend back then, because it probably saved me from becoming a junkie and following some of the boys to early graves. I steered clear of the 'softer' drugs as well, including cigarettes. The strongest ones I ever tried were Kools, but menthol must not have been my go because they turned me off smoking for life.

Rugby league was also a deterrent against drugs. Despite my spiralling life off the field, I began to take the game seriously again from about 13 after a couple of years break when Ron left town. St John's had banned me from playing on account of my behaviour, so I started playing for a local club side called Brothers. I remember St John's coach Brian McCullah saying, 'You'll never play rugby league,' when they kicked me out. His words made me even more determined.

I enjoyed the game, but didn't have any major ambitions to make it a career. I didn't idolise any of the big players, and wasn't obsessed with making the Canterbury Harold Matthews or SG Ball rep sides. In fact, I couldn't have cared less about the NSWRL premiership. I casually supported Souths because my brother George was a Rabbitohs fan, and took me to my first game at Redfern Oval. But apart from that one outing I had no interest in following rugby league live or on TV/radio, despite the buzz I got from playing.

A bit of a turning point came when I was 14 and George asked me to accompany him down the coast to watch his side, Bankstown Collegians, take on Port Kembla. At the last moment he made me pack my boots, which was strange because I was four years too young to play in George's grade. He told me I was going to be the ball boy. But when we got to the ground, George revealed his true intentions: I was needed to play because his team was short.

I was terrified. I thought there was no way I could set foot on that field because all the other players were 19-year-old men and I was this little 14-year-old boy. I was frozen with fear, but George wouldn't take no for an answer. So I started and actually played OK. I handled myself, made the tackles, wasn't scared of anyone and pretty much belonged. The older boys were impressed. That gave me a lot of confidence about my ability as a rugby league player. As we drove back up Mt Ousley towards Sydney, I was a different person. I thought there might be something in this game for me.

But before I could get too carried away, my activities off the field came home to roost. My first and inevitable brush with the law was waiting back in Sydney.

CHAPTER 3
RISE BEFORE THE FALL

Apart from Lucky Bills, in 1977 the other place we liked to hang out was a petrol station on Canterbury Road owned by a guy called James. It had pinball machines. One night there was an unregistered Holden waiting for repairs at the garage and, fast becoming the life of the party, I decided that it needed to be taken for a joyride.

Now the funny thing about this stolen car was that I actually filled it with petrol and returned it! No damage done.

Or so I thought. The following day I walked past the service station and James told me there were a couple of coppers who wanted to have a word with me. Naively thinking I had done nothing wrong, I spilled the beans and told the police everything. They responded with my first criminal conviction for illegal use of a car, which resulted in a two-year good behaviour bond. I was filthy with James, who it later emerged was a well-known police informant. That experience left me with a huge mistrust of strangers and the cops, but no will whatsoever to change my ways.

Only a few months later, it came home to roost. It was an ordinary night at Lucky Bills, meaning that we had just finished a few games of pinball and it was time to go joyriding. I was in the process of breaking into a Holden when a passing security guard yelled out. I tried to run but he caught me and held me to the ground until the cops arrived to arrest me, for the first time. Riding in the back of the paddy wagon, I was terrified.

I can still remember smelling the fingerprint ink; a 14-year-old not knowing where it would all end. I called home and Joe came down but the police refused to release me because of the prior conviction at James's servo. Instead, they held me on a second charge of illegal use of a car, which spelt four weeks detention at a juvenile justice centre known as Minda Boys' Home in Lidcombe, until my sentencing date at the children's court.

Mum was absolutely shattered and I had no idea what to expect. The centre had kids much older than me – up to 18. But none of my fears were realised. It was just a big dormitory with beds – sort of like an army camp for children. There were chores and lessons, but also recreation time outside. Within a few days I had made friends and it wasn't so bad. In fact, I remember it as being fun and I probably behaved better there than anywhere else in my youth. Whatever Minda was, it wasn't a deterrent. Nor was the good behaviour bond the magistrate handed me four weeks later.

As soon as I was back in Punchbowl, I was back at Lucky Bills. By then we'd formed a proper gang, calling ourselves the Punchbowl Bulldogs. We needed a name because a lot of the other areas around Sydney had gangs of their own. The closest one was in Revesby, the riverside suburb where I would toy with burying Con all those years later. There were also gangs from Rockdale in the St George district, the city, and Eastwood, way over the other side of town in the north-west.

Inevitably, the gangs came to blows but there were never any weapons used. The brawls, however, could get willing. And it was rarely a case of man-on-man. If one gang successfully ambushed another's territory, they would often have their entire group belting a couple of helpless guys. The fights would generally start with one gang cruising into another's turf in cars, honking the horns and yelling abuse. Most of the time they'd get away, but sometimes they didn't and it was then the action started. The other way was to sneak up on individuals on foot and ambush them. The same would happen to us on our turf. It was give and take, cut and thrust. Although there were some scary times and we became regulars in the emergency departments of Canterbury and Bankstown hospitals, no real damage was done.

My brawling at night stirred an invincible and aggressive attitude. I'd take on kids much older than me without thinking twice. This came in handy for Peter Rix, whom I bailed out of strife on a couple of occasions. Peter used to sell ice creams and meat pies at the footy. One day in the late 1970s he took me along to North Sydney Oval. Midway through the match he stepped into the toilets, where two mean-looking 17-year-olds were waiting to rob him of his takings. They took his bag and Peter came out screaming for me to help. I rushed straight in and belted the both of them. I didn't care how big they were. My brain just snapped because I saw my mate being hassled.

On another afternoon when I was about 14, Peter's 12-year-old sister Lyn was being hassled by some hoods outside Punchbowl station. Lyn was terrified and had locked herself in a phone booth. She was surrounded by this leering group of low-lifes when I spotted them. Again, there were no thoughts of sorting it any other way than with my knuckles. And that's what happened. On most occasions you only had to identify the ringleader and give him a flogging. The rest of his mates, although they had the numbers, would always be too pissweak to stand up for him.

The most feared rival gang member was an older Lebo named Ray Khoury, who was from Eastwood. Ray was raging mad, especially when it came to drug dealers. He was angry because his brother was hooked on heroin. Ray eventually joined us, meaning he would ride along for our nightly cruise through the Cross. It was a place full of junkies and dealers, perfect for a man of Ray's tendencies. He always told me that if I was going to steal from anyone, I should steal from a dealer. They always had drugs that could be on-sold, as well as money. I remember one night he knocked a dealer out cold for selling drugs to his younger brother. It was pretty chilling, even for a kid like me, who was growing up all too fast.

It didn't take Einstein to figure out that theft was the next stop for all of us. But my first lot of robberies were motivated by revenge, not easy money. That came later.

On the corner opposite Lucky Bills was a gambling and drug den owned by the local big-shot, a Lebanese guy called Eddie. Eddie was all fast cars, flash clothes and jewellery. He not only owned the gambling place, but five other businesses in Punchbowl – the supermarket, smokes shop, gift shop, laundromat and fish shop. His prized establishment accommodated all sorts of shady characters – from SP bookies, to drug addicts, to hardened criminals, and, yes, local coppers. Everyone knew Eddie entertained members of the constabulary with topless girls, booze and card games to keep them onside and prevent his operation being closed down.

I had just turned 15 the first time Eddie spoke to me. Peering out the window, he yelled across the road in Arabic for me to bring him up some drinks from Lucky Bills. Because of Eddie's reputation, this was a big deal for me – to be invited into his joint. I paid for a couple of Cokes and took them to him. This became a nightly event, me taking him bottles of Coke and paying for them myself. Eddie only really trusted me and the other Lebanese kids in the gang. He felt he couldn't trust the other kids from different backgrounds, even the Aussies.

I must admit that – away from football at least – my work ethic was not (and never has been) great. The super-coach himself, Wayne Bennett, could never work it out when I played for him in Brisbane in 1985, saying one day: 'John, I don't get it – you don't dare take any short cuts on the field, but off it you are always looking for one.'

Some of the guys from the gang and I tried a bit of manual work at Punchbowl Pipe and Bricks, but there was much easier money to be made illegally. My first payment came thanks to Eddie's supermarket. After six months of never getting paid back for buying his drinks, we'd had enough. So we decided the best way to get our money back was to rob his businesses.

The planning was pretty thorough, and my time with other young criminals in Minda came in handy. While I was there the inmates had taught me all the tricks of the burglary trade. It was pretty basic stuff, like knowing which coloured wire to cut to disconnect an alarm and knowing to walk on the beams of a roof because otherwise you'd fall through. The other good one was how to wedge a screwdriver between a window and the frame to gradually break it from the bottom and gain access.

All these tips were put to the test on a rainy night when we decided to hit Eddie's supermarket for what would be my first robbery. The alarm for that building was actually on a telegraph pole out of reach and we'd spent the previous nights throwing rocks to damage it. Our plan worked, because the alarm only sounded softly when we broke in. Eddie and his mates across the road couldn't hear a thing. Once inside, we grabbed the only items of value: cigarettes, and made a quick $4,000 selling them to a service station owner in Lakemba. That was huge money back then, even when it was divided among the gang.

As with the proceeds of my future earnings, I splurged on clothes, food and my first girlfriend, Lee Flood. Lee was a blonde stunner who went to Wiley Park girls' school, which was just up the road. I used to sit up on the seat opposite the station and watch her walk down the steps in her lovely green uniform every afternoon. Our relationship was nothing serious, but a lot of fun. I was always on the lookout for ways to impress her with the latest fashions.

All the boys had a crush on some girl or another from Wiley Park. Then one night, we hit on a perfect way to impress them all at once. There were about 15 of us joyriding at this stage, so we decided to take all the cars from Punchbowl one night and park them outside the girls' school. By the morning there were 40 stolen cars filling up the car park. Then, to complete the stunt, we slapped 'For

Sale' signs on all of them with ridiculously cheap prices. Not only was there a huge rush of potential customers, but one of the cars we stole also belonged to her school principal.

I loved pulling stunts like that, but my next one was a bit more sinister by today's standards. In 1979 – Grade 10 for me – I'd been expelled from St John's and transferred to Punchbowl High. This was a huge difference – one was a good Catholic school, the other a public school full of every undesirable kid in the area. You could say it was a match made in heaven, but I wasn't interested in going to Punchbowl High. While I never missed a day at St John's, I would have been lucky to go once a week to Punchbowl in the three months I lasted there before my first jail term. Instead of going to school, a few mates and I would go to the races – Canterbury, Rosehill, or Randwick – where I'd get older punters to lay bets for me with my paper-round money. We'd bring a change of clothes to get in, but I can't remember too many wins in those days.

The trots at Harold Park, Fairfield and Bankstown were popular outings at night. Peter's dad was heavily into the trotting scene and used to take us out there. So the gambling bug bit me from a young age. But even then I realised there was no money to be made by punters, because the odds were stacked in the bookmakers' favour. I would later try my hand at this (albeit illegally) in earnest, but my first foray came at a very young age at St John's, when Peter and I used to frame a market on 'Wacky Races', a kids' cartoon that screened on TV every afternoon. Each episode was a car race between the same characters, one of whom was a hack driver called Dick Dastardly. Dick never won a race, but we still had this one kid – John Conway – who would place 20 cents or a dollar on him every day. He wrote his own ticket – 500-1 sometimes – because we knew Dick would never win. One day, however, he crossed the line first. Peter and I started fretting about the payout until there was a protest that was upheld later in the episode. We should have trusted the scriptwriters a little more.

Without school friends and the endless games of footy, things got pretty boring during the day. So one morning, a mate named Steve and I decided to hit Punchbowl High with a bomb scare. Not surprisingly, it was left to me to call the principal, Mr Cox, and tell him, in what I thought was a very threatening and mature voice, that a number of bombs had been planted around the school and were set to go off repeatedly. Then I hung up and started giggling. That was one of the few days we actually went to school – just to see what happened. Lo and behold, during morning maths class an announcement was made that the school had to be evacuated because of a bomb threat. Everyone was told to gather on the oval and there was panic everywhere.

Unfortunately, it overwhelmed Steve, who thought I was so convincing on the phone that he actually believed the bombs were real. He couldn't hold out and went straight to Mr Cox and spilled the beans. Of course, I denied it. There was no proof and no way of tracing the phone call back then. So, even though the police were called, I escaped criminal charges. But it wasn't too late for expulsion. Two terms short of my Year 10 School Certificate exams, I was given my marching orders from the second school in three months.

Little did I know it would not matter at all. I was soon answering roll call at a much bigger institution – Long Bay jail.

CHAPTER 4

SITTING IN THE DOCK AND THE BAY

Eddie never said anything about the robberies, but something told me he knew it was us knocking him off. Soon after the first hit on his supermarket, he came up to me with a sly look on his face and simply said, 'How are you John? Very well, I hear.'

He never said anything specific, and at the time I was convinced he didn't really care because his insurance covered all the losses. And even if he was bent on revenge, it wouldn't have bothered me. By that time I was completely off the rails. I was without school, without routine, without supervision – and without a care in the world.

We continued to hit Eddie's businesses in Punchbowl until we'd robbed all five of them, always targeting cigarettes because they were the only thing of real sale value. But just because we were crims, don't think we didn't have a sense of irony. When we robbed his laundromat, we scored some expensive suits. Thinking of delicious revenge rather than profit, I removed the tags and sold them back to Eddie. I thought I was so clever. On another occasion, we hit the gift shop and donated the stolen items to St Vinnie's and the Salvos. I figured it was one way of paying St Vinnie's back for helping Mum for all those years when we were kids.

There were other robberies aside from Eddie's joints. A friend of a friend worked in a nearby factory, and claimed to know the whereabouts of the safe. So we went there in a stolen car, but not just any stolen car. Fate would have it that the car we used that night was the same green Holden station wagon I had stolen for the first time two years earlier. We broke in through the back door and discovered the safe but no keys. There was no time, so we stole the entire safe. Luckily for us, we knew a bloke with an oxyacetylene torch who was able to blow it open. And what did we find inside? More than $8,000 – meaning we pocketed a very, very cool two grand each.

It was easily my biggest haul and it served to entrench the vicious cycle I was getting caught up in. Easy money spelt expensive tastes and a healthy gambling habit. Both were taking hold over me, meaning I'd spend the money quickly and soon need another earn. Because the money didn't come from work, I thought nothing of blowing it on friends or taking Lee to the Harold Park trots on a Friday night. Whatever the price, we always shouted. It felt great. But everyone knows the good times don't last. And when they are this good, they are bound to end more quickly and savagely.

The bell tolled for me in the middle of one night towards the end of 1979. The doorbell, that is. Standing on the front porch of our house at 1 am were two detectives. They had arrived to arrest me on three charges of assault relating to the punch-ups we got in with other gangs from around Sydney. But there was something worse. Much worse. They were also charging me with attempted murder for the stabbing of a Roselands bus driver some weeks earlier.

When I sat down to write this book, I knew I had to do so with an open and transparent conscience. If my experiences are to teach today's youth a lesson, I have to be truthful about everything – no matter how embarrassing or damaging to my pride and reputation. So when I say I never stabbed that bus driver, I'm telling the truth. The simple truth is that I never caught a bus. Why would I need to with all those stolen cars at my disposal? Sure, we were bad kids. But nothing we did came anywhere near stabbing someone. As I said before, we never used weapons – just bare knuckles and street smarts against the rival gangs.

My mind boggled when I was told about the bus driver. It simply wasn't true. I couldn't comprehend why the police wanted to charge me with such a crime. I was arrested and kept overnight at Albion Street detention centre in Surry Hills, thinking one word over and over and over: How?

The next day I appeared in court and the prosecution demanded I be refused bail and await the hearing in a maximum security jail – an adults' jail full of the worst criminals in New South Wales: murderers, rapists and drug dealers. It was mid-1979, and I was only 16. I was scared shitless. The prosecutor argued that the chances of me re-offending while on bail were too high to justify release. The magistrate agreed, despite the valiant protestations of innocence from my legal aid solicitor, Andrew Young. The magistrate's hammer came down – no bail and an indefinite booking at Long Bay.

So there I was, handcuffed in the back of a prison van with nine other inmates – all much older and more fearsome-looking than me – headed for Long Bay. Everything was spinning, but I tried to keep concentrating on how I had come to be here. No-one said a word, but my head was screaming with questions. Why did the police want me to go down for this? Why me? Why? I was too young to work it out back then, so I just thought they wanted to pin something big on me to make up for all the other crimes – the stolen cars, bomb threat and robberies – that they were unable to prove.

These days, however, I've begun to think a little more clearly about the reasons for my charge. One of the detectives who had me charged was none other than Neville Scullion, who later left the police force under a corruption cloud. And one of the detectives used to frequent Lucky Bill's. I have no proof, but their relationship weighs on my mind, given Eddie would have been looking for a square-up for all his businesses that we robbed.

But none of that mattered as we were led through the huge sandstone gates of Long Bay. I was taken for a briefing that all new prisoners have to undergo when they arrive. I can still recall the shock of one prison officer when I told him my year of birth. 'You mean 1960, don't you?' he said. 'No, it's 1962 – I'm still only 16.' I could see that he couldn't believe they'd send a kid so young to a place like this. The next thing they asked me was whether I was suicidal.

It was a shocking turn of events for me. An extended stretch at Long Bay among hardened criminals was the last influence I needed at that stage, when there was still hope for me to change my ways. At Long Bay there was no shortage of male role models to aspire to – and none bigger than multiple murderer, rapist and heroin dealer Arthur Stanley 'Neddy' Smith, whom I would soon befriend.

But on that first night I knew no-one and said nothing. I spent the night in a single cell with a scabby pillow, foam mattress and stainless steel toilet. They fed me roast beef and veggies, followed by sponge cake and custard for dessert. Having not eaten since my arrest nearly two days earlier, it might as well have been lobster and prawns. I was transferred to my new home the following morning – Ward 11.

I had no idea how long I'd be inside. I would know more when the Supreme Court reconvened for my hearing, but that could be years away. Having accepted that – and it took me several weeks to do so – there was nothing else to do but survive in the meantime. Survival meant keeping my mouth shut and not drawing any attention to myself. We were all kept in single cells for most of the day, so it wasn't a big problem to begin with. We were woken at 6 am every day and escorted to collect our breakfast.

To be honest, the food was pretty good back then – a lot better than the pre-prepared junk I was given in stretches I did later. It was all cooked hot and fresh on the premises. Breakfast was cereal, toast and even eggs. For lunch there was usually sandwiches. Dinner, which was served at 7 pm, were hot meals like you'd get at a cheap RSL buffet. We were always served in the kitchen, but had to take our meals back to our cells to eat. I suppose that's because the guards didn't want us using the knives and forks as weapons in the mess hall. After breakfast, we'd be allowed outside into a semi-concrete yard, before heading back in for lunch. We'd take showers between 3 and 4 pm, then we'd be locked up for the night apart from the trip to collect our evening meal at 7 pm.

The three-and-a-half-hour morning yard time was obviously the best chance for socialising. But with prisoners mixing in such a small space came trouble. I witnessed no shortage of brawls and violent assaults. Long Bay was full of weapons – and most inmates carried something sharp to protect themselves with. But the funny thing was the so-called activities that everyone on the outside believes happen in the prison showers. Like everyone else, I had heard rumours about inmates who forced others to have sex with them. But never once did I witness anything or encounter a threat myself.

My first few weeks were spent wandering around the yard alone. I'd sit in solitude, trying not to attract attention to myself. Everyone seemed older, meaner and better connected. There were groups and cliques I couldn't see any way into. Prison isn't like primary school – the others don't approach the new kid and ask him to join in their games. He has to earn their respect and mateship.

The most obvious fit for a kid like me was a group of young prisoners. Again, football was my saviour. Along with basketball, games of touch were popular in the yard. With a bit of talent and plenty of experience, I impressed on my first couple of runs and soon became mates with the group, most of whom were at Long Bay for a string of armed robberies in the Maroubra area. Their names were Danny Williams, Wayne Finlayson, Mark Merriman, Jim Koutonos, Steve Rhind and a couple of brothers named Roy and Ray Carrion.

Steve ended up being murdered five months after I met him – stabbed to death with a shiv in the yard. It was a tragic end to a dispute over drugs, a common disagreement in every prison. No-one was charged, but the bloke who was suspected of killing Steve copped a savage beating in Parramatta jail soon afterwards.

Our crew was pretty tight and we formed an unbeatable footy team for the big games on the grass oval every Thursday morning. The slower, older prisoners had no answers to our youth and speed. The daily games – plus regular sessions in the prison gym and on the boxing bag – fuelled my desire to have a red-hot crack at rugby league if I beat the charges and got out. I vowed to myself early on in Long Bay that I would give football everything I had and go straight in doing so, if I ever had the fortune to get out of Ward 11 and return home.

The chance came much earlier than expected. After six months hard time – and with no indication when my court hearing would take place – our gang hatched an escape plan. Now, I've pulled some foolish stunts in my time, but this would have to win the gold, silver and bronze medals. A stupid bunch of kids, our grand plan was to jump the two screws on duty at night, steal their clothes and simply walk to freedom. I had no excuse for believing that such a breathtakingly naive scheme would work because I'd never seen any prison escape movies. It was so unbelievable not even Hollywood would have had a bar of us.

The night of our planned escape was in early 1980, but fate intervened and saved me from playing a role in such a harebrained scheme. As we were being taken back to our cells that afternoon, a screw I disliked intensely was on duty. I spotted him and gave him a cheeky grin, because I also knew he was rostered on that same night and I was savouring the thought of the boys giving him a few for his trouble as they stole his uniform en route to freedom. The daydream was so overwhelming that I kept smiling, so he asked me what was so funny. Feeling cocky, I replied, 'Don't you worry, because we'll be seeing you real soon.' And that's all this screw needed as an excuse to place me in indefinite lock-up.

That meant I could take no part in the escape. The other boys, however, were determined to push on. They got word to my cell that they would come and release me after they had jumped the screws, using stolen keys. So I waited, and at 8 pm they came rushing up to the cell, unlocked the door and let me out. It had begun. They had really gone through with it, belting two of the guards, stealing their uniforms and tying them up.

But before we could start planning our new life outside, we were brought back to earth by blaring sirens and a voice over the loudspeaker telling us to 'freeze'. It was immediately apparent we were no chance of escaping, more so when an entire riot squad came tearing through the ward moments later with batons and shields. We had no option but to give ourselves up. We were scared stiff. However they merely handcuffed us and threw us all into isolation.

Isolation is another story. No windows, no light, no time outside. After 72 hours, we were all taken to Maroubra police station for interviewing. Luckily for me, there was no evidence of my involvement in beating up the screws – aside from the fact I was outside my cell when the riot squad arrived. Had one of the boys said I was in on the plan, I'd have been in big trouble. But all five remained staunch. I'll never forget their solidarity. While the rest were all transferred to Parramatta jail and slapped with another three years, I was returned to Long Bay with a severe warning.

The value of not snitching was impressed on me from that moment. So when I witnessed something a couple of months later that could have legitimately delivered my freedom, I kept my mouth shut. One day after footy on the oval, I was coming out of the toilet when one of the most savage attacks I've ever seen behind bars occurred in broad daylight. One prisoner began stabbing another wildly with a crudely-made shiv. The assailant was crazed, the victim helpless. I had made it away by the time the screws arrived. Somehow, the victim survived. Under questioning, he told the cops that I had witnessed the whole thing.

That same night, there was a bang on my door and I was taken to the detectives for an interview. They were suddenly very kind. 'Elias,' one of them began, 'if you just tell us what happened we'll release you straightaway and make the charges regarding the bus driver disappear. All you have to tell us is who did it. You'll be out of here tonight.'

The coppers were desperate to nail this bloke, because they didn't want to release him. I later found out his name was Dave, an extremely dangerous and violent man. Many, many years later he would walk back into my life and change it forever.

Their offer was as unexpected as it was tempting. But I couldn't accept the offer because it meant snitching. And there was something else, too. Because I hadn't stabbed the bus driver, I wanted to be found innocent in court. I didn't want to get off it this way. So I denied everything. I denied being there. I denied any knowledge of the stabbing on the oval. I lied and told the cops the bloke who was stabbed must have been delusional. I was not yet 18, but my beliefs were entrenched. They hammered me with questions for three straight hours, but I refused to budge.

I returned to my cell no closer to release. But things changed from that night. In the coming weeks I noticed that I was treated better by my fellow prisoners, especially the ones at the top of the Long Bay hierarchy. The most notorious were Neddy Smith and corrupt detective Murray Riley. They pretty much ran the yard, and enjoyed unimaginable privileges like alcohol, seafood and civilian clothes.

One day, Neddy approached and congratulated me for not snitching. It was the first time he had spoken to me. I was aware of his reputation and, as a kid, I knew better than to provoke him by saying anything unnecessary. Neddy's reputation on the outside filtered through the walls of Long Bay. He was a man not to be messed with. Standing at well over six foot (1.8 m) tall and weighing more than 100 kg, Neddy was a fearsome customer. He was at his physical prime in 1979 – aged 35 – and already serving his third prison term after convictions for drug dealing, rape and murder. Nothing seemed to faze or move the man.

But it seemed that Neddy was impressed with my sacrifice. He began to take me under his wing, ensuring the inmates on kitchen duty gave me bigger servings or the screws gave me a couple of extra minutes with visitors. He even arranged for a top lawyer to organise my release.

Neddy said all the lawyer needed was $5,000 to pay the cops, and all the charges would be dropped. He even offered to pay. Again I refused. I had my heart set on beating the charges fair and square, because I knew I was innocent. And $5,000, back in 1980, was a lot of money. And finally, part of me didn't want to be indebted to a heavy like Neddy Smith.

Like it or not, however, I was now one of his boys. He worked as a floor sweeper in the library – probably the sweetest gig an inmate could have. Others helped in the kitchen, or cleaned or whatever. But there was none of that for me once Neddy took an interest. He got me a job in the gym – distributing and collecting footballs, basketballs and weights for the prisoners during their yard time. I also cleaned the gym. I was paid $11 a week, money that could be used to buy supplies from outside like soap and toothbrushes. The screws handed out order forms every week and you'd fill out what items you wanted, hand over the money and it would be delivered to your cell in a brown paper bag.

Cigarettes weren't on the order form because they were actually supplied free of charge by the prison back then. White Ox was the brand everyone smoked.

Unless you had some pull with the screws it was impossible to get other items like porn magazines or weapons into Long Bay. But Neddy had plenty of pull. One just had to visit his cell to realise that. Long before anyone got a TV, he had his own – and a Beta video player to boot! His cell was at least four times larger than average, even equipped with an en suite. I remember he invited me inside for Christmas in 1980 (his cell door was mysteriously never closed), where we ate prawns and even drank a couple of beers in T-shirts Neddy demanded we put on instead of our green overalls. Neddy never wore the prison clothes – he had a whole wardrobe of his own and even a range of jewellery.

He always had bits of advice, but the one thing I really recall him saying is never to leave yourself 'weak' if you intend to embark on a life of crime. When I asked him what he meant by 'weak', Neddy replied: 'Don't get married or have kids – they can leave you open to be exploited.' Whether by choice or not, it's a piece of advice I've followed until this day. Even in this book, I'm not prepared to mention the names of extended family like nephews and nieces.

Thanks to Neddy's generosity, I found a daily rhythm that made prison life bearable. But that didn't mean my freedom was any less anticipated. During the time I spent in Long Bay on remand, Andrew Young approached the Supreme Court four separate times to try and secure bail. It was never any good. I would have to wait until my hearing, which didn't arrive until January 1981.

By the time I finally faced the jury I was 18, and far different from the naive kid who first stepped into Long Bay 18 months earlier. It was 9.30 am and I was sitting in court feeling extremely uncertain. I knew I was innocent, but had no idea how Andrew could convince the jury when the prosecution was saying otherwise.

The key was a witness the prosecution produced to testify that I had stabbed the bus driver. Apparently, this fellow was on the bus and had seen me commit the bloody crime. But under cross-examination from Andrew, he came unstuck. Andrew was brilliant that day. He was inexperienced and from legal aid, but he expertly wore the witness down under questioning to admit that the police had instructed him what to say. With that, the judge immediately dismissed the case. It was over in a couple of hours – I was innocent.

I felt on top of the world as I sat in the car that afternoon, headed back to Long Bay to collect my belongings. But something was still weighing on my mind. I still had three assault charges to beat to be totally in the clear. Andrew had earlier told me that if I didn't beat those, I could be facing another two years at the Bay on top of the 18 months I'd already served, because I was now deemed an adult in the eyes of the law.

It was an agonising eight-week wait until that hearing, which took place on 5 March 1981. The judge was Justice Cameron Smith, who boasted a particularly strong reputation for handing down severe punishments. I was not optimistic. But my attitude changed when a familiar old face stepped into the courtroom. It was Sister Anne King, the principal from my old primary school, St Jerome's. Although I had consistently tested her patience until the point that she wanted to send me to boarding school, she was now volunteering to be a character witness in my favour.

As Justice Smith was preparing to hand down his sentence (I pleaded guilty to the charges, which related to our brawls with the other Sydney gangs), he looked over at Sister Anne, who was saying the rosary. I was later told that Justice Smith was a devout Christian, despite his ruthless streak, and this must have played a big part in his decision to place me on probation. I couldn't believe I'd avoided a trip back to Long Bay. And I never forgot Sister Anne's help that day. I visited her regularly until her death in a nursing home a few years later.

Everything finally worked out. Not only was I a free man, but it was also early autumn. There was still just enough time to find a side for the upcoming rugby league season and I had my sights set on the top.

CHAPTER 5
BIG HOUSE TO BIG LEAGUE

Long before my release, I had promised myself not to fall back in with the same crowd at Punchbowl when I got out. I was determined to give rugby league my best shot and mixing with the wrong elements would not have done my endeavours to get fit in jail any justice.

Staying out of trouble wasn't easy. Temptation beckoned me every day upon my return to Mum's place. The boys were still hanging out at Lucky Bills, and they had progressed to even more brazen crimes like armed robbery. Their drug habits had also escalated to the extent that two of the group – a German bloke named Greg and a Lebanese called Sam – died from heroin overdoses. The money they were making from crime was breathtaking – about $2,000 a job.

But having spent 18 months inside, I knew the cops had their eyes on me. One more stuff-up and I was gone. So, despite emerging from prison a bitter and distrusting teen, I stuck to my guns. There would be no more nights at Lucky Bills, no more joyrides in stolen cars. Rugby league was the only thing I wanted to do.

I was released just in time for the Under-19s trials for my old local side, Brothers. My old mate and former school captain of St John's, Mark Cronk, was still playing and he encouraged me even more. I didn't have a licence, so he'd come from his house in Clempton Park (about a 15-minute drive) and take me to and from training. Although I had previously ignored his pious advice, I now listened to him about staying out of trouble and giving footy a go. When he died in a car accident the following year, I was devastated. From that day, I vowed that if I ever had a son I'd name him Marcus after one of the most pure-hearted, generous guys I've ever met. It's true what they say – the good really do die young.

Before the trial I also saw Peter Rix for the first time in ages. I remember grabbing him and walking a lap of Clempton Park – which takes about 15 minutes – and just repeating over and over and over again: 'I'm never going back there.'

I was pumped for a big game and played like I never had before, snapping the opposition – St George Dragons – left, right and centre. All their players knew I had just come out of jail and I think there was a lot of intimidation in that. My training behind bars had made me lean, strong and hungrier than the other kids. I felt I had an edge over them, given I had been imprisoned with some of the most dangerous men in New South Wales and lived to tell the tale. Nothing scared me any more. I breezed through the trials and played the first half of 1981 with Brothers, training three nights a week and working during the day as a labourer.

The pay was lousy, particularly compared to the easy

money I could have made by returning to Lucky Bills. For a kid who had never really known the value of a hard day's work, it was a crash course. Without a driver's licence, I'd wake at 5:30 am every weekday to get a train to wherever the building site was located. The hours were 7 am to 3 pm. Throw in three nights training and footy on the weekend, plus the extra fitness work I was doing, and I was simply too tired for anything else after hours. This was a blessing, because I was now 18 – old enough to start frequenting the bars and nightclubs of Kings Cross that had seemed so alluring before my first jail stint.

During my free time, I finally began to take an interest in following rugby league. It was more of a job for me – I still didn't get any great buzz out of watching other people play, but at the same time I knew an education in the broader aspects of the game would help me pass through the grades more quickly. I watched NSWRL first-grade matches regularly on television, and read about the stars and scallywags in the newspaper every day.

With that knowledge, it was a big moment when a fellow called Leo called my home on a chilly night in late June. Leo was a selector for the Newtown Jets, one of the top teams in 1981. I knew the Jets were coached by one of the sharpest minds in the competition, Warren Ryan, and captained by one of its toughest players, Tommy Raudonikis. They proved an awesome combination that would eventually propel Newtown to a shock grand final appearance later that season.

Leo's call came thanks to Peter Rix's dad Ray, who played golf with the Newtown official at Marrickville. Ray tipped his friend off about my performances for Brothers when Leo asked if there were any players he could recommend.

Leo asked Peter if I was any relation to Benny Elias, who was the gun hooker for Holy Cross Ryde in the schoolboys' competition – the Commonwealth Bank Cup – back then. I told Peter, 'Yes, of course I am,' even though I didn't know Benny from a bar of soap. I needed to get a start and was willing to bend the truth to get one.

There were about five matches remaining in the regular season when Leo invited me down to Henson Park to train with the third-grade squad. Back in those days, there were simply three grades with no age restrictions. That meant that if I got a start I would be playing against men with many years worth of experience.

Newtown was a tight-knit club, where all the players regardless of their grade trained at the same time. I recall my first day walking past a room where the first-grade team was assembled. Along with Raudonikis there were other big names like Ken Wilson, Bruce Bowden and Phil Sigsworth. The other bloke with a bit of presence was Phil Gould, who went on to become one of the game's most successful coaches and more recently commentators. Although Gould is widely respected, we would end up locking horns about a decade down the track. But more of that later . . .

And of course there was coach Ryan, whom I had little to do with in 1981 but would later play under at Canterbury and Balmain. On my first day at Newtown, I recall seeing him scribbling Xs on a whiteboard in the weights room, barking all these theoretical instructions to the players. I was intrigued. What did all this technical stuff have to do with football? Compared to where I had come from with Brothers, it was like another world. I could see Ryan had a presence that was infinitely more switched-on than any other coach I'd encountered. But I wasn't intimidated or nervous. When you spend 18 months at Long Bay jail as a teenager, it takes a lot to make you gun-shy. Such was my confidence that not even an intimidating character like Ryan had it over me.

In the penultimate game of the season, one of our starting back-rowers Grant Ellis rang the third-grade coach Johnny Rea to say he couldn't make it. Ironically, Grant is still a dear and loyal friend to this day – and the man who I will always remember for giving me this break. We had travelled to North Sydney Oval to take on the Bears and, at best, I was just hoping for some time off the bench. All of a sudden Johnny came across and told me I would be starting in place of Ellis. It was a big shock, but also the chance I'd worked so hard for over the past six months. I was hell-bent on making it count.

Luckily for me, my old teammate from Brothers, David Puckridge, was playing halfback. We had a bit of a combination from park footy, and this no doubt helped me to see a bit more of the ball. But my strength was my ability to stand and off-load, which created a few tries for David that day. The coach was so impressed that he kept me in the starting side for our final game of 1981 against St George at Kogarah. We finished on a high by winning, with another good performance earning me a meeting with Newtown officials about a playing contract for the following two seasons. My mum and family were too busy to watch either game and I had to rely on good old Peter Rix to drive me south to Kogarah that day.

With the contract negotiations, the time had come for me to do something that came very naturally – selling myself. All those raffle tickets and walkathon sponsorships didn't just sell themselves, and now was my chance to begin making some real money doing what I loved. I remember asking my brother George – who by this time had begun a law degree – to pretend to be my manager. So we fronted the Newtown board and before they could say anything, George slyly mentioned that the Bulldogs had already tendered an offer. There was no offer, of course. George was just trying to pump up my price, because he knew Newtown were keen.

Knowing very little about me, the board then asked again if I was related to Benny Elias, the promising Balmain hooker who would later go on to captain New South Wales and represent Australia. Without thinking I said 'Yes', even though Benny and I had never met. And it's still a question I get virtually every day all these years later. The truth hasn't changed – Benny and I aren't related. Elias is just a very common Lebanese surname.

George and I succeeded in nabbing a contract with a base salary of $1,000 plus $1,000 for every five matches I played.

Heading into the summer, I was on cloud nine along with the rest of the club. Newtown had just made the grand final – losing narrowly to Parramatta – and were primed to go one better in 1982. By the time we returned to training in late November, I had my driver's licence and had saved enough money from my labouring job to buy a red Austin off my uncle. Like most people's first car, it was a bomb. But at least it wasn't stolen.

Now that I could get myself around, the chances of falling back in with the wrong crowd at Punchbowl increased. The boys were still hanging around, their reputation growing worse and worse by the week. In fact, the whole suburb seemed to be sinking into a morass of crime and drugs. My old mates would contact me fairly regularly, but the promise I made myself in Long Bay remained intact.

When I first arrived at Newtown in 1981, I didn't tell a soul that I had just suffered a broken collarbone. It happened a fortnight before they brought me on board and I was nowhere near fit when I made my third-grade debut against Norths. Fortunately, the stoicism I learned in prison – and from Mum's broomstick that broke my arm all those years ago – came in handy.

Now, however, I was as fit and strong as could be. I was 19 and ready to let rip. Even though the off-season resembled an army camp, I soldiered through with the best of them. In those days, teams did conditioning without the ball during the summer months. The idea was simple – get these bastards as fit as possible. The methods, looking back, were crude. We did ridiculous road and stair runs through Coogee. It was like doing a mini marathon three times a week and some players simply gave up. They just walked and vomited their way through it.

But I was running on all cylinders when our first trial rolled around in February 1982. The third-grade side was drawn to play Easts at the old Sydney Showground. I had never been so pumped for a game. I was counting on breaking into first grade at some time during the year, and this was where it all began . . . and ended.

Just before halftime, I was hit hard in a tackle and heard a massive snap around my right ankle. The pain was incredible. They stopped the game and the Easts medico – Dr Neil Halpin (who now works with the Sydney Swans) – treated me. I can remember him screaming at me not to look at my ankle as they carried me off. I was later told my foot was at right angles to my lower leg, hanging off the stretcher. When I arrived at Auburn Hospital for treatment, the doctor said he had never seen such a severe compound fracture.

I was operated on that night and immediately my season was declared over. I was condemned to two months in plaster and 10 weeks on crutches.

The trip to hospital was also my first encounter with the high a lot of my drug addict mates had become hooked on. The nurses gave me Pethidine and within no time I felt on top of the world. After I emerged from surgery, one of the nurses told me how I tried to chat her up under the effects of the painkiller. I've always fancied myself as a ladies' man and never backed away from having a go at a girl I fancied. You only live once, after all.

But the bliss induced by the drugs and attractive nurses soon wore off, leaving me with a terrible boredom that persisted as I recovered alone at Mum's house. Back in those days there were no therapists or counsellors to help players deal with the feelings of isolation and worthlessness that come with a serious injury. I couldn't work or train. I was totally cut off from the rest of the world. It was shattering.

I'd been true to my word, kept out of trouble and worked hard, only to be rewarded like this. Within no time, the doubts began creeping in. Mentally, I started to become weak and vulnerable. Punchbowl was calling. Even on one leg, I would still belong up at Lucky Bills. I was part of the furniture, despite a three-year absence. The boys were phoning . . .

It was just so easy compared to the excruciating road that lay ahead by returning to football. The blinkers were on. I couldn't see or think of anything else but getting that hit of adrenalin, having a bit of fun. Footy had been a decent surrogate, but now it was gone. To be honest, I was filthy on the game. Back then, I couldn't understand how someone could train so hard for such an unfair result. It just pushed my resentment of hard work to another level.

When I finally showed up at Lucky Bills one night, I felt no guilt. I felt justified going back, given the fate that had befallen me. It didn't take long for me to settle back into the old routine. I was even flogging cars while on crutches. I figured the act of hitting the accelerator actually helped to strengthen my right ankle.

Eddie was still hanging around at his joint across the road. Strangely enough, he seemed happier than ever to see me. He invited me upstairs to eat and play cards and I didn't think anything of it. But now, looking back, I can't help but think that his smiles were a show of satisfaction that I had been thrown into Long Bay at such a young age. He later died a brutal death – the word around town was that he informed on one too many.

We never robbed any more of Eddie's businesses, but instead began to expand into other suburbs. Jewellery shops were our new favourite. Soon I was making big bucks stealing cigarettes and necklaces, more than I could ever dream of earning in league at such a young age. I thought, 'Screw rugby league, screw Newtown.' The saddest thing was that the third-grade side were having an excellent season in 1982 and were bound for the semi-finals.

It was around this time I met Danny Karam. During my time on the dark side, I met no shortage of mean characters. But none came close to Danny. He was one of the most dangerous individuals I have ever come across, purely because he just didn't care about consequences. Danny wasn't afraid of death and that made him as good as invincible.

Danny was also Lebanese, but that's about where our similarities ended. He was short, stocky and completely mad. The genesis of his lunacy came thanks to the Lebanese SAS, of which he was a member before emigrating to

Australia and getting involved in crime around the Belmore district. He would eventually be slain by his own crew in a sensational ambush, getting shot 16 times in Surry Hills, in 1998. That was a huge story that made the front pages of all the papers and sparked tensions between rival Lebanese gangs and families for years to come.

I met Danny through trips to nightclubs in the Cross that we'd take in stolen late-model Holdens. There was no need to drive the red Austin any more. Danny was in his mid-20s and had graduated well beyond the activities I was involved in. Danny was a debt collector. A ruthless, uncompromising, intimidating debt collector. His favourite targets were drug dealers who owed friends or clients money. He worked in tandem with another dangerous Lebanese bloke called Alex Shalala. I think they got on so well because Alex was also mentally unhinged.

Later in my career while I was playing for Balmain, a big Islander in the crowd was bagging out my good mate Steve 'Blocker' Roach. Knowing Blocker and I were close, Alex – who was in the crowd – simply stepped over and clocked the guy; knocked him out cold in front of thousands at Leichhardt Oval. These blokes just didn't care. That incident was typical of Alex, who is a good friend and always supported my football career.

Hanging around them, I quickly developed the same mindset. I was always looking for older male role models and consistently picked out the wrong ones. Looking back, my sense of daring attracted me to the likes of Danny and Alex over more wholesome types. Every decision was my own and it's disappointing to think back and see that there were times when I went straight and enjoyed myself. A clean lifestyle was within my reach, but also a lot harder to maintain than simply falling back into a life of crime and easy money. And the money was irresistible. Falling in with Danny and his mates made me take after them. I began to not give a stuff about the rules governing society. I became an outlaw.

I'd park cars anywhere I pleased – across driveways, or in disabled spots. I'd barge my way into concerts and football games with a group of tough-looking mates. It was pure fun. I was even enjoying dressing as a gangster, preferring long trench coats and a jockey's cap that Arthur Beetson also liked wearing during his coaching days at the Roosters. When I was feeling particularly bold, I'd stop the car at traffic lights, get out and fetch a long stick from the boot. I'd then aim it at the car next to me like a shotgun and they'd scramble quick fast. It was all a big laugh for me, not caring what the consequences were any more because of my injury.

Danny and co. took a liking to me because of my size and Lebanese background. Danny could see I was young and strong and would make a good 'accessory' to take along to his collections. My task was simply to stand in the background and look big. I didn't have to say a word or do a thing.

By the time I'd dipped a toe into Danny's collection business, my ankle had begun to recover. I was feeling a lot better and from nowhere began toying with a return to football in late 1982 as the third-grade side challenged for the premiership. I started going back to training once a week and also began a bar job at the Newtown Leagues Club.

It was this ray of hope that opened the door for me to get out of crime again. Amazingly, Danny made it easy. He understood that playing football at the highest level was an unfulfilled dream of mine, and actually encouraged me to return. That was the thing with Danny – he was the most loyal friend one could hope for. But heaven help you if you got on his bad side. He told me that if the coach didn't put me in first grade, then he would shoot him.

The club doctor, however, put an end to my belated attempt to come back in 1982. The risk was deemed too great, and because I was so young they felt it better that I be saved for a full-on tilt in 1983.

One of the last jobs I did with Danny before starting pre-season training was a collection from this bloke who paid us in leather jackets. They were good items, easily worth $100 a piece retail. Danny needed the cash quickly, so I took the leather jackets in a van to training at Henson Park one afternoon to sell them to the boys. Well, they went quicker than John 'Chicka' Ferguson on our left wing.

The funny thing was that Newtown legend Brian 'Chicka' Moore had taken over the head coaching role that season. Chicka Moore, believe it or not, was a copper, so it said something about my skills as a salesman that I was able to offload dubiously obtained jackets from the back of my van without raising his suspicions. In fact, he was my best customer – snapping up six jackets at the bargain basement price of $35 each. Everyone in the team bought one, meaning that although we weren't the best performed side of 1983, we were definitely the best dressed.

Another good spot to sell the gear was outside Harold Park trots after a Friday night meet. Being a terrible punter in those early days – I sometimes lost more than $10,000 on a single card – it was often a necessity for me. I'd walk out of the course penniless and open the back of the van to the punters as they left the course. I'd make about $1,500 a night, recouping a small part of my losses. Melbourne Cup-winning jockey Malcolm Johnston was an excellent customer.

BIG HOUSE TO BIG LEAGUE

Determined as I was 12 months beforehand, the 1983 pre-season went well. So well, in fact, that Chicka Moore selected me for the first-grade trial against North Sydney in February. Although nothing intimidated me after prison, the size of the Bears pack which included the giant copper Don McKinnon was cause for slight alarm. I hadn't played a game for a year and was not entirely confident after the injury. The ankle felt OK and steadied me well enough to make 45 tackles on that steamy late summer afternoon.

But first-grade was quicker than I had anticipated, and I must not have quite played the part because Chicka dropped me straight back to thirds. I can't lie, I was filthy. I didn't understand why Chicka had teased me like that. I would much rather have worked my way up from third-grade as the season went on. Chicka, however, told me that he just wanted to see how I handled it. He was moderately satisfied, but still needed more convincing to give me another shot.

I had a solid year in 1983 and stayed out of trouble off the field, working at the leagues club and training hard. Despite the first-grade team's poor showing, the spirit among the players was good. We enjoyed meals together at the club or Henson Park Hotel after training. I went about my business honestly. Despite a chequered past of theft and robbery, I didn't steal a single 20-cent coin when I emptied the poker machines at the club. Towards the end of the season I stepped up to reserve grade and was eventually summoned to the first-grade bench over the closing month. That season was a poor one for Newtown. The first-grade side won only a handful of games and finished with the wooden spoon – a huge letdown from the heyday of 1981.

When a hot St George side came to Henson Park for the second-last game, we had nothing to play for. After going around in reserve grade, I was sitting on the bench during the second half twiddling my thumbs. The thought of actually running on didn't even enter my mind until Chicka started yelling my name with 20 minutes left. 'Elias! You're on!' he shouted. I didn't need to be asked twice. I felt my contribution on debut against a Dragons pack that included the likes of Pat Jarvis and Craig Young was solid. And to make things even better, we held on for a rare win – probably our best of the season.

I was back to reserve grade the following week for our final match against Canberra. That game was played at Campbelltown, where the Jets planned to relocate the following season because of declining crowds in the inner city. Another driving force was the fact that the club's benefactor, advertising guru John Singleton, lived on a property near Campbelltown. It was tipped to be one of the big growth areas for Sydney and Singo insisted it made sense for a league team to be based there because of all the juniors who would soon crop up.

After the season finished, Singo asked me to come to his farm to talk about a deal for 1984. He was willing to give me a big pay rise – up to about $5,000 a season.

But we didn't get around to signing anything. No player did. Unknown to all of us, Newtown was on the brink of insolvency. The first I heard about it was reading a story in the paper that declared the oldest rugby league club in Australia would not field a team in 1984. It was incredible – not one official told me a thing. I was none the wiser, and I truly believe that all the players who ran onto Campbelltown Oval for that fateful game against the Raiders had no idea it would be the Jets' last outing in the top-flight competition. Tight-lipped officials finally called a meeting on the day the story broke. We gathered at Henson Park and they confirmed the truth. There was no money left and it was uncertain whether we would ever see what was owed. Back then, we got paid twice a year and I was still waiting for my money from the second half of the season. It eventually came when the creditors sorted out the mess several years later.

But money was the least of my worries, because my football career had hit an unexpected wall. Instead of savouring my break into first-grade at age 20, I was faced with retirement. No other Sydney club was interested – they all had their rosters finalised for 1984 – and the future again looked grim.

CHAPTER 6
DÉPÊCHE MODE

With the death of Newtown, my football career had lapsed into a coma for the second time in two seasons. Well aware of what had happened last time, I was determined to do something to avoid falling back in with Danny Karam and his crew. Danny and I were still in touch, but I hadn't done a thing wrong since the 1983 season began. Even though I was only young, I was smart enough to realise that without footy my life would eventually descend into the familiar cycle of crime, easy money and gambling. By that age, I was beginning to really enjoy a punt and spent a lot of time at the races and trots. Back then it was merely a hobby, something I managed without damage to my bank balance. The bigger stuff would come later.

One of the few things I had in my favour was a passport. I started thinking about travelling and the possibility of playing footy overseas. My mind went back to a newspaper article I had read earlier in the season about the Parramatta front-rower Paul Mares, who had returned from a season in France. Mares reported that the experience had made him a better player, as well as waxing lyrical about the European lifestyle.

Since there were no options in Sydney, a season overseas began to make sense. Although I had debuted in first-grade, I was, for all intents and purposes, still a lower grader. I was also keen to see a bit of the world outside Punchbowl and Long Bay jail. But perhaps the biggest motivation was the chance Europe offered to get away from Sydney and the bad influences I knew would eventually overcome me.

It so happened that an Italian-raised Bulldogs player by the name of Tas Baitieri was holding seminars at the NSWRL headquarters on Phillip Street in the city for those interested in going to France. Tas had plenty of connections in Europe, something that has led to him now holding a post high in the ARL as International Development Officer. He gathered about 50 players together in October 1983 to discuss the opportunities to play in France that season.

The French season had just started (they played in northern hemisphere winters back then) and there wasn't any time to waste. Tas basically conducted a draft, matching different clubs with the type of players they were after. Because I was light on experience, I was left towards the end and sent to a club called Avignon. Tas told me I was lucky, because Avignon was a strong club interested in back-rowers like me. Within a week I was at Sydney airport with all the other guys ready for the big flight to Paris. I had never been on a plane, so even though I maintained that nothing scared me then, I was feeling a few butterflies.

The flight went well, but I gave little thought to the cultural challenges that waited at the other end. I couldn't

DÉPÊCHE MODE

speak a word of French – aside from 'croissant' – and knew nothing about day-to-day life in the south of the country. When we landed at Charles de Gaulle airport, Tas paired everyone with their club officials. Virtually every CEO in the comp was at the airport that day waiting for these Aussies to come through customs.

Waiting for me was an Avignon director named Michel, who could speak a bit of English. He drove me the four hours from Paris to Avignon and we struggled for conversation. I didn't mind, however, because there was plenty of scenery to take in. I was completely awestruck by the history of the place. I thought, 'Geez, how good is this. It sure beats Long Bay!'

Avignon was a pretty big town with a population of about 400,000. But I didn't know a soul. I stayed the first couple of nights with Michel and his family before the club moved me to an apartment that would be my home for the rest of the season. They covered all the rent, gave me a car and paid me around A$300 a week, which was pretty good back then. The only thing I had to pay for was food, and most meals were provided at training anyway.

Our coach, Jean-Paul, had played for the famous French team that defeated Australia in 1974. I'm guessing that was his only claim to fame, because the bloke was definitely no coach. Compared to Warren Ryan, he was a dunce in terms of the technical aspects of rugby league. For example, he insisted every player eat a piece of steak an hour before every match under the mistaken belief that protein was needed for maximum endurance. They also drank a glass of red wine with a dissolved sugar cube for energy. Thinking this was crazy, I stuck to the carbs – potatoes and bread. My teammates thought I was crazy, but it never seemed to dawn on them why I had so much energy at the end of a game when they were tiring badly.

The only thing Jean-Paul was big on was motivation. He made all these stirring speeches that I couldn't understand. Even training was pretty lax – it typified the ad-lib approach to the game the French loved. We didn't practise moves or anything like that; it was just a case of playing what was in front of you. I found the style refreshing, but at the same time it also encouraged me to step up as a leader of the team. Big things were expected of every Australian who arrived at a French club and I was no exception.

The people at the club were very generous, inviting me to dinner and on outings with their friends. Better still, Avignon was also home to an international university, which meant there was no shortage of pretty girls. We used to head down to – wait for it – an Aussie-themed joint called the Koala Bar every Friday and Saturday night.

Rugby league was big in France in those days, bigger than soccer in that part of the country. We got 5,000 to every home game, which was a buzz for a third-grader like me who was accustomed to playing in front of friends and loved ones at midday. When we went out, we were treated like minor celebrities.

Thanks to the language barrier, I matured as a player. Because I couldn't communicate with my teammates all that well, my actions had to speak louder than my words. This made a big difference, because I was constantly setting an example. And then there were times when being lost in translation was a bonus. Australian players delighted in calling the referees every name under the sun in English. The funniest times were when you'd call the ref something like a 'fucking cheat' and he would smile back sweetly and say 'Merci'.

DÉPÊCHE MODE

The Aussies were very tight over there, despite being scattered across different parts of France. Later in the season, Tas put together an invitational side called the Koalas to take on the French national team. The standard of French rugby league had dropped dramatically since that famous win over Australia a decade earlier and we won easily.

In a buoyant mood that night, I stole the team bus and drove the players to the tiny alpine country of Andorra – locked in the Pyrenees Mountains along the Spanish border. It was about a three-and-a-half-hour drive. I remember the other boys being pretty keen on the idea, but Tas wasn't involved because he was purer than the driven snow. We came back the same night and although they knew the bus had been nicked, no-one could prove who the mastermind was. I'm sure they all suspected me.

The standard of footy was nowhere near first-grade in Sydney – closer to third-grade, in fact. But on the score of thuggery, nothing else I've ever experienced came close. Every game would degenerate into an all-in brawl at some point. When this happened, the Aussie players would generally retreat for a rest and a chat while those crazy Frogs belted one another's lights out. However, there was no escaping the eye gouges, bites and kicks to the head that would regularly sully each tackle.

Although I led a dubious life away from the field, I never resorted to dirty tactics or cheap shots on it. But there was one time I didn't have a choice. We were playing the Pia Donkeys – the same club I would end up coaching almost two decades later – when this lunatic front-rower booted me in the head after I'd been tackled. Blood gushed from my nose. I was livid and gained my revenge by upending the bloke in a lifting tackle that would be considered very dangerous today. In France, however, it was by-the-by. Anything went in that competition – fingers ripping your nostrils, being spat at. The only thing I didn't encounter was a squirrel grip.

I played well and began to feel like the king of the town. Here I was, having just turned 21, a strong player in the prime of his youth running free in a foreign country. Life didn't get much better. I was so comfortable; I didn't even bother to learn French. Most of the locals spoke enough English and were kind enough to humour me through everyday situations. Over time, I began to rediscover my cheeky streak. I committed nothing illegal in France, just a few of the practical jokes I loved back in high school. On one bus trip to an away game, I tied the shoelaces of all the officials to the seat bases. It made for a hilarious scene when we arrived and they all tripped over as they tried to get off.

The opportunity to see the rest of Europe during our free time was also snapped up. Along with a few other Aussie players, I made several trips into Spain and Italy. We returned to Andorra to go skiing a few times. But the most memorable getaway was a weekend in Monte Carlo. That was my first visit to a real casino, and as a budding card-lover it was a real buzz. I recall taking 4,000 francs and betting on black on the roulette table. My timing, however, stank. I jumped onto an incredible run of reds and within no time was left with just 500 francs. I decided to bet it all on black, knowing that another loss would have left me without any money to get back to Avignon. Fortunately my colour came up – and then some more – for me to break even and return home with my shirt on.

In January 1984, midway through the French season, a Sydney-based player manager, George Coorey, got in touch to say South Sydney were interested in signing me for the upcoming season. Although my contract with Avignon prevented me from returning to Australia until May, they were still keen to sign me up for the rest of the year for $2,000 plus bonuses, under coach Ron Willey. It was a decent contract and I agreed almost immediately. My old Newtown buddy Paul Ackery also signed with the Rabbitohs on the same day. The money was very good, but my main reason for coming back was the desire to prove myself in Sydney. I wanted to test what I had learned in France in the toughest rugby league competition of all.

Avignon finished the 1983–84 season in fourth spot, earning a place in the semi-finals. We were knocked out in the first week, meaning that my farewell party was held sooner than desired at the local clubhouse. The club threw a really nice party with gifts and balloons – I was genuinely moved by their gesture and pleas to come back the following year. It tugged at my heartstrings a little, but then reality set in. I still had much to prove in Australia.

When I touched down at Sydney airport in May 1984, I also landed on my feet. I was headed straight for Redfern, where one of the most promising teams in the country was being assembled. At Souths, I would join the likes of Phil Blake, Mario Fenech, Craig Coleman, Les Davidson, Ian Roberts, Neil Baker, David Boyle, Bronco D'Jura and Tony Rampling. Few team rosters boasted so much young talent, many of whom would go on to represent their state and country.

I immediately felt like I belonged at Souths. The big thing was its multiculturalism. There were Greeks, Italians, Maltese, the lot. It was like Punchbowl in a football club. I felt very comfortable and was accepted straightaway. Although

Souths had won more premierships than any other club, they were the perennial battlers of the league because of their roots in down-and-out Redfern. Given I was raised by a single mother and went to prison at 16, this suited me fine. I was also taken by the sense of history at Souths. As a player, you could feel you had joined a club steeped in pride and tradition. Although Newtown was established first, I found that Souths placed a greater emphasis on celebrating the past.

I could also detect that there was no shortage of like-minded characters at Souths. I can't really explain how it works, but scallywags just have a knack of seeking one another out. In a very short time, I became tight with Craig 'Tugger' Coleman, Bronco D'Jura and the reserve-grade hooker Rick Montgomery. Out of the three, Rick was a real wild card. He is currently serving time after being fingered in a huge drug bust with the late Mick Hurley and Les Mara in the infamous baggage handler scam at Sydney airport.

The training at Souths under Ron Willey was no different to Newtown. We had a run three nights a week and played on Saturday or Sunday afternoon. I was drafted straight into the third-grade side, which was coached by club legend Paul Sait.

I returned from France confident in my ability to make it to the top by the end of 1984. Third-grade was no problem and I was soon promoted to reserve grade under Wally Watsford. By the end of the season I managed three or four first-grade games off the bench, but didn't get a run for either semi-final match the Rabbitohs played at the SCG. We had a very exciting team that season and could have gone all the way. But after producing a memorable come-back from 14–0 down to beat Manly in the first week, they were narrowly downed by St George in another epic seven days later.

Knowing all too well the trouble that lurked in Punchbowl (I was back living with Mum), I asked Souths CEO Terry Parker to get me a job. He came up with something perfect – selling advertising space in the 1985 team calendar. Revelling in the chance to relive my days flogging raffle tickets and walkathon sponsorships, I sold out in two weeks. I could have bludged and taken the rest of the year, but I didn't know any better. I was like a bull at a gate with everything. It was all or nothing. Looking back, I reckon I was hyperactive back then. I simply couldn't stay still. I always needed someone to talk to, something to stimulate me.

So within a fortnight I was back to the dreaded idleness that had so easily brought me undone in the past. I had money and time – an awful combination for me and these days for other young footballers, who seem to get into trouble every time they go out for what should be a regulation night on the town. Trying to cement a place in first-grade just wasn't enough any more. I missed the thrill of the collects, the robberies and the punt. It was like a wicked siren calling, her voice now so close to where I slept every night.

Inevitably, I made contact with Danny Karam again. He was happy to hear from me and immediately got me work on a couple of collects from drug dealers or blokes who owed. The jobs had become bigger and more lucrative. On one occasion we went as far as Brisbane for a collect. We drove up there non-stop with a couple of Islanders. The drug dealer got a bit smart, but we eventually got our money. We'd usually drive to the location in a stolen car, then just leave it there and catch a plane back.

Wherever we went, Danny was always armed. He carried

a weapon on every job. This wasn't spoken about, just secretly acknowledged. Even though Danny had several screws loose, I never thought he'd actually pull the gun or use it. But all that changed when we turned up for a collect on behalf of the Lebo bloke who owned a restaurant in Surry Hills. This was a very old debt and because Danny loved his compatriots, my friend was extremely determined to settle the ledger that evening.

However, there was a problem. The guy who owed the money was a real heavy from the Cross. A big stand-over man. The meeting shaped as a real clash of Sydney's underworld titans. Danny left nothing in the locker room. He stormed into the room, where this heavy and his mean crew were waiting, and immediately whipped out his gun. He pointed it straight at the heavy and calmly said: 'I'm going to count to three and on the third count I'm going to shoot you.'

Standing behind Danny, I was shocked. There was no warning as we made our way to the job that this was going to happen. The rest of the people in the room were also stunned. No-one knew anyone would be armed. For the first time since going to prison, I shat myself.

Danny began to count. 'One . . . Two . . . ' his finger now poised to squeeze the trigger, when the bloke yelled out, 'OK, OK all debts are settled.' He knew Danny would have shot him. Would have killed him then and there. There was no point just shooting that bloke, because of all the witnesses. Had he not spoken up, I shudder to think how many people Danny would have killed that night. But he didn't care about body counts or prison terms, because he was happy to die himself. There is no more dangerous enemy than a man who doesn't value his own life.

That incident shook me up and I soon reverted to footy.

But in those couple of months with Danny in late 1984, I learned the basics of stand-over work and debt collection.

Danny was always big on researching his target. He did plenty of groundwork before the collect to learn what type of person they were – aggressive, sneaky, well-spoken, or a snivelling coward. His approach on the day would then depend on how he thought they would respond from his research. Generally speaking, the more violent and aggressive the target, the more violent and aggressive Danny would be in his approach. His decision to produce the gun first and ask questions later that night in Surry Hills was a perfect example. As for arranging meetings, that would also depend on the subject. If they knew us, we'd make contact and arrange a place. If not, we'd pay them an unexpected visit.

At the time, I was certain there was no other player in the competition who led the double life that I did. It was crazy. I had the blinkers on by that stage and would stay out till 4 am doing collects and playing cards before training or playing the next day. I really don't know how I did it.

But it would be a naive person who believed all the other players were cleanskins. Players used recreational drugs back then, particularly marijuana. At Souths, this culture would take six more years to come to the surface, when a bunch of players tested positive in 1990. Dope was usually smoked on the weekend, but it definitely wasn't the drug of choice. Alcohol won that prize hands down. There was a big culture of train hard, drink hard at Souths and most other clubs those days.

I was never a big drinker. I've never liked the taste of beer and if I do have a drink it might be a bit of red wine or a cocktail. I could count on one hand the number of times I've been drunk in Sydney. To be honest, more than my distaste for alcohol it was the fear that I could drop my guard and get clocked by an enemy while out on the piss that stopped me from drinking to excess. I'd made quite a few enemies over the years.

Away from Danny, I knocked about with Tugger, Rick and Bronco. We were all cut from the same cloth, although I'm sure they didn't get up to anything near as bad as what I was doing on a weekly basis. However, we all shared a love of the punt. Tugger, especially, was mad keen. He used to spend entire days at Souths Leagues playing the pokies before strolling across Chalmers Street for training at Redfern Oval. One day, Tugger got a big tip from the trainer Johnny Lee on a horse racing out at Hawkesbury. So he, Rick and I skipped training and headed to the north-western outskirts of Sydney for a big lash. I think we all had $2,000 on the nag, which was backed in from 8/1 to 2/1. We got on early and absolutely cleaned up. But our celebrations were soon dampened when Terry Parker called me into his office the next day to explain myself. He gave us all an absolute tongue-lashing before giving me this cheeky look and adding: 'But what I'm really angry about is the fact you didn't let me in on it. Make sure you don't make the same mistake again.'

Terry was a streetwise official and had some inkling of my activities. I didn't help my cause by fencing stolen clothes and leather jackets at training, which was a surefire way of converting them to cold, hard cash. I was actually very keen to stay with Souths beyond 1984. With the likes of Davidson and Roberts rising fast, the future looked very promising at Redfern. Willey also had the players' respect. He was a quiet coach, but beneath his soft demeanour raged a burning passion for his team and players. During one game late in the season against Canterbury, the referee was giving us such a raw deal that Willey actually relayed a message for us to abandon the match. But we stayed on; such was the never-say-die attitude of Fenech and co. They taught me the value of endurance and competing through pain.

Terry, however, baulked at coming to the party for 1985. He kept saying there would be a new offer, but when we asked about details he went silent. Time was running out for me and with nothing in Sydney for the following season I began to think about going to France again. In essence, I had not progressed from 12 months ago. I was again without a club after playing a handful of first-grade games the previous year. And I really needed to leave Sydney and its temptations.

When Terry signed a couple of back-rowers from Norths, I knew my days at Redfern were numbered. I got on the phone to my old mate Tas Baitieri to enquire whether there were still any opportunities in France. Tas then contacted Hubbie Abbott, a Brisbane-based contact who also had links to France. The offer Hubbie came back with wasn't what I'd imagined. Little did I know it would open the door to the best year of my life.

CHAPTER 7

WELCOME TO WAYNE'S WORLD

I'd never heard of Wayne Bennett. Twenty-five years ago I didn't have a clue who he was. Apparently, he was a pretty decent fullback from Queensland who played for Brothers in the Brisbane comp and also represented Australia in 1971. This was all a mystery to me when his name was first mentioned at the end of 1984. For all I knew, Wayne Bennett was just another retired footballer trying to survive the treacherous crossover into coaching. At the time, Bennett was coaching a club side in the Brisbane competition called Brisbane Souths. They had made the grand final the previous season, but were comprehensively flogged 46–8 by an almighty Wynnum–Manly team that boasted the likes of Wally Lewis, Greg Dowling, Colin Scott, Gary Coyne and Gene Miles.

Back then, the Brisbane comp was very strong. It wasn't quite the same standard as Sydney, but not far off, with big crowds and television coverage. On top of that, Queensland rugby league was enjoying a renaissance thanks to the State of Origin concept that had been conceived four years earlier. All of a sudden, it seemed that a lot of the best players in Australia were being produced north of the Tweed River and many of them resisted Sydney's lure of big bucks and stardom to stay in Brisbane and play in their own competition.

I knew little of all this when Hubbie Abbott got back to Tas Baitieri and mentioned that Brisbane Souths were keen to take me on board for 1985. In fact, I knew very little about Brisbane itself. My fleeting visit for that collect with Danny Karam was my only trip to the Queensland capital and we weren't exactly there to go sightseeing. Apparently word of my solid season in France had reached the scouts at Brisbane Souths. They were also keen for a hard-hitting back-rower in 1985 as the club sought to somehow exact vengeance on the glamour boys from Wynnum for their grand final humiliation.

I agreed to go there. The money was decent – about $8,000 – and well above what Souths had paid me the previous season. But once again the need to get out of Sydney was a bigger motivator. Anywhere but Punchbowl, I kept thinking. If I stayed in that environment for too long, I would eventually be dragged back in.

Despite taking a break from Danny, I was still treading the precipice. My favourite extracurricular pastime before leaving Sydney was hosting illegal card nights. They were full-on affairs with tens of thousands in cash changing hands. Manilla was our poison. Some sessions lasted for 18 hours at a time and interfered dangerously with my preparation for matches. But the money, as always, was just cause. In return for organising and hosting the nights (and accepting the criminal responsibility if the cops raided us),

WELCOME TO WAYNE'S WORLD

I got a cut from every hand. Each session would net me at least $2,000 for doing little else but making sure there were cockatoos out the front looking for cops.

In short, all the well-intentioned promises to stay clean upon my release from Long Bay had been broken. My recklessness and addiction to living life on the edge had rendered every single one of them futile.

Brisbane Souths put me up in a fully furnished one-bedroom flat in West End and I lived by myself. Having tasted independence in France, I enjoyed being away from home again. Although Mum loved and would do anything for us, the house at Punchbowl was just too hectic. By that stage my older brothers Joe and George were building families of their own and I needed space to give football a real shot.

But I wasn't able to get away from them that easily. By coincidence, George had become smitten with a Lebanese girl in Brisbane and decided to marry her. The wedding coincided with my trip north, so 10 cars carrying our entire family and friends wound their way up the old Pacific Highway for the ceremony in November 1984. After a couple of days everyone returned home – except me.

Although it meant I had to cook for myself, I revelled in the solitude. It was lonely at first, because I didn't know a soul in Brisbane. During our first training session at Davis Park, I felt like an alien. It was completely different from South Sydney, which was a genuine melting pot of cultures. Brisbane Souths was less eclectic. While West End was home to a large proportion of Brisbane's Mediterranean community, the 'wog' population was tiny compared to Punchbowl's. Aside from some Aborigines and a few Papuans, Souths was a predominantly white club in those days.

Now this wasn't a problem per se. Over the course of

that season, everyone in the club was fantastic to me. It was just something that I couldn't ignore. Having grown up in such a multicultural area, I suddenly felt very exposed without any Lebanese, Italians or Greeks beside me. Again, it's hard to explain why, because I'm a proud Australian. Many of my best friends are Anglos as well. But it was a feeling I couldn't dismiss. And I'm sure many immigrants and second-generation ethnics can relate to what I'm saying. No matter how Australian you are, no matter how well you speak English, no matter how fair dinkum your accent, there's still a weird attraction between wogs. During those first weeks, it was something that really struck me.

I fronted training just shy of my 22nd birthday with an Afro and a wild look in my eyes. By that stage I'd discovered that Bennett was a copper. What a match made in heaven. To make matters worse, most of the players were hand-picked from the ranks of the constabulary. In fact the whole place was swarming with them – even the statistician Jim Banaghan (who is now a player manager) was a boy in blue. Peter Jackson and Mal Meninga, both of whom would go on to star for Australia, were also in the force, as was the forward Ash Lumby. I felt like a round peg in a square hole from the get-go.

The weather, as well, was like nothing I'd encountered before. Summers in Sydney can be hot and uncomfortable, but they don't have the same oppressive sting of humidity you get in Brisbane. Pre-season training during those sweltering days was nothing short of hellish.

The weather might have been hot, but the reception from Bennett was decidedly cool. He was never rude, but never warm and welcoming either. I remember turning up in green clothing at that first training session, which in combination with my wild hair must have got him thinking about the Libyan revolutionary Gaddafi. So that was my nickname – Gaddafi. It stuck to me all year like my sweaty training shirts during the summer.

Aside from condemning me to this strange moniker, the only thing Wayne said was: 'Hello, John, welcome to the club – I'll talk to you later.' I didn't realise how much later it would be until we really spoke face-to-face.

When I wasn't training I was completing torturous days on construction sites as a brickie's labourer. Every day I would be up at 6 am for work, home at 2 pm for lunch, then train until nightfall. Within weeks I was knackered. Hard work and me simply don't mix, a sad hallmark of the easy money I made while cutting corners out of the rulebook as a youth. I was so averse to hard yakka that I was the only labourer who wore gloves on the building site. My boss and the rest of the boys found that hilarious. I was working with a young prop called Scott Tronc, who represented Queensland later in his career. Souths had a pretty handy side that year, with a young fellow named Gary Belcher also slotting in at fullback. Meninga, however, was not due back until May because he was committed to finishing the English season with St Helens.

The hard days of labouring and general loneliness had pushed me close to breaking point by the time our first trial against Valleys arrived in February 1985. I was also missing the rush of crime. My life seemed to have flat-lined and I was getting itchy feet in Brisbane. At that age I was on the horns of a terrible dilemma. I loved the highs of the illegitimate lifestyle but also felt a huge guilt that I wasn't doing my football career justice. Then, when I went the other way and worked hard, I'd become bored and agitated. There was no in-between with me. As my career wore on I tried to have it both ways, to juggle stand-over work and race-fixing with playing first-grade. More often than not, my life degenerated into a dangerous, frantic mess.

The return of football should have brought relief, but it was to be short-lived. After playing first-grade against Valleys, Bennett dropped me back to reserves for the start of the season. I was livid. I hadn't left Sydney, trained and worked like a dog, to play reserve grade for some Brisbane side. Feeling let down, I rang Bennett and asked him for a release to go home. He didn't flat-out refuse, but did end up convincing me to stay. 'It's a long season, John,' he said. 'This bloke or that bloke might get injured, might lose form and you'll get a start.' He didn't, however, make any guarantees. That's something I respected him for.

As hard as I tried in reserves, I couldn't break into the top side immediately. One game I made 50 tackles and couldn't believe it when my name was still absent from the first-grade team list. Again, I fronted Bennett. 'Wayne, I made 50 tackles last weekend and I'm still in reserve grade,' I said testily. 'Just what the hell do I have to do?'

He looked at me and gave me some advice I'll never forget. 'Gaddafi, I know you can tackle,' he said. 'But what about when we've got the ball? What are you doing for the team then? Defence is only half the game. I know what you can do without the ball, but you haven't shown me what you can do with it.' It was true. I saw myself purely as a defensive player and felt that making heaps of tackles justified my position in any team.

Such an approach gained less favour from a coach like Bennett. There was plenty of emphasis on attack and flair in his pre-season training program, more than any coach I had ever played under. The skills he taught us were much more advanced than I had learned under either Warren Ryan or Ron Willey.

Even though I was almost ashamed to produce it, I did have a decent left-foot step. After talking to Wayne, I vowed to make the effort to try it on in matches. But the first step was forming combinations with the other players at the club. Everyone at the club was amazingly friendly, particularly CEO Jim McClelland. By that stage I had forged a bit of a social network with members of the Greek community that lived in West End. Card nights had bobbed up at my apartment – although nothing rivalling what I used to organise in Sydney – and eventually the other Souths players started coming around. Meninga and Banaghan – both coppers – were the most ardent players from the Souths side.

I struck up a good friendship with Peter Jackson. Like Craig 'Tugger' Coleman at Souths, Jacko was a bit of a knockabout. I didn't know what he got up to off the field in 1985, but it's now well documented that he ran into some major personal problems after retiring. Sadly, Jacko died in 1998 from a drug overdose. By that stage he was struggling with bipolar disorder, but there was no sign of any of that at Brisbane Souths. He simply came across as a bit of a rascal. That attraction transcended the state border and we got on well, despite the fact no-one at the club knew anything about my past.

Back then my first jail term was not common knowledge in football circles, so I doubt Bennett knew about my dark secret. But he soon learned that I was aggressive and hotheaded. As for the rest of my life, I was never certain how much he knew. But I had a feeling he was aware of my past and the activities I liked to engage in. He was, after all, a senior police officer. It wouldn't have been too hard to get the good oil from his New South Wales colleagues. Bennett, however, didn't say a word to me about anything aside from football.

Our stand-off was finally broken during a team dinner when we sat next to one another. We used to eat at a ribs and pizza joint in West End every Thursday after training, but this was the first time Bennett and I had ever dined alongside one another.

Until that point in time the most personal interest he had taken in me was at a pre-season bonding camp on the Gold Coast. The entire squad was gathered around a bonfire as Bennett peppered us with motivational lectures and quotes from his favourite figures. Then, without warning, he turned to me and said: 'So John, what do you have to say that can motivate us?' I couldn't believe he put me on the spot in front of my peers without warning. I felt the embarrassment of not being able to think of anything until I recalled an old book I'd read in prison. It had a Roman saying to the effect of: 'They who believe shall conquer.' So that's what I repeated. Bennett looked suitably impressed, but nothing really happened between us after that.

It all changed over the course of that fateful dinner. Bennett wasn't as advanced on the science of the game as Ryan, but he made up for it by ensuring there was an unbreakable bond between his players. The dinners were a big part of that. As we sat together he began to ask me about my past. He asked what my father's name was and I told him it was John. 'But wait a minute, your name is John – how can that be?' Bennett shot back. 'Because my father died before I was born and Mum decided to name me after him,' I replied.

That revelation seemed to spark a bit of a thaw between

WELCOME TO WAYNE'S WORLD

us. From that moment he became the first positive father figure I'd had since Ron Miller left Punchbowl in the early 1970s. I wasn't the first player to feel that way and I sure won't be the last. He continued to ask questions about my background, how our family migrated from Lebanon and what not. But he didn't stray into the other stuff, so I kept quiet.

That night was also a chance for me to find out a little more about him. I knew he had a disabled son, Justin, who used to come and watch training. Justin was about eight at the time and sometimes he'd have a fit or get into a bit of trouble and Bennett would have to rush off and sort it out. Seeing your coach in that situation stirs certain feelings. I don't know if 'inspiring' is the right word, but as a player it certainly made you look beyond the bloke holding the clipboard and into his soul. Having shunned a lot of responsibility all my life, I can't comprehend how he has managed to juggle such sensitive demands while building a one-man coaching dynasty. I have to hand it to the man.

After that night Bennett and his wife, Trish, would continually invite me to dinner at their house in Mt Ominy. I kept politely turning them down and after about six attempts the invitations dried up. Privately, I didn't want to create any more work for the Bennetts given the challenges they had with Justin.

We did, however, start speaking outside training. I didn't have a telephone in my apartment, so I'd walk down to a public phone on the corner and dial Bennett's number whenever the urge took hold. He and my mother were the only two people I phoned while in Brisbane. My time up there was a true seclusion and one that I began to savour once I made the first-grade side mid-season.

I took Bennett's advice and, in doing so, perhaps taught the old dog a new trick. One day at training he pulled me aside and said: 'You know, Gaddafi, I used to only look out for blokes with flair at training, but you're different. I've come to realise that the blokes who put in that extra one per cent make a much bigger difference.'

For some reason, Bennett knew how to reach me. He communicated in a language I responded to, despite not saying a whole lot. But what he said – and more importantly did – hit the mark more often than not. One example was a training session I ran late for on account of a big Friday night card game. As they awaited my arrival, Bennett gathered all the players together and barked: 'When Gaddafi arrives, don't say a word to him.' So I copped the silent treatment. I pleaded some cock-and-bull story about saving a man with a heart attack on the way to training, but Bennett was too cluey to have a bar of such baloney. Those silent hours really reminded me how much I'd let the team down. It played on my mind that I'd lost the trust of those who meant most to me. I'd put myself above the team and when I'd been sprung I still didn't have the guts to tell the truth. That was very selfish of me and Bennett's unique way of dealing with it made me determined to make it up the only way I could: by playing out of my skin.

The return of Meninga and Chris Phelan from England really got us on a roll. Although Wynnum beat us both times that season, we still managed to finish first. By the end of the season, I was a starting member of the first-grade side. And what's more, I felt like I truly belonged at the club. I was so happy, playing my best football under the best coach I'd ever had. The temptations of Sydney faded away. I didn't think about Punchbowl or Danny and his quick earns. Between the

WELCOME TO WAYNE'S WORLD

Greeks at West End and guys like Phelan and Jacko, I was surrounded by new friends. I thought, 'I could get used to this.'

Wynnum, however, stood in my way of achieving total bliss. That side contained the best player I ever faced – King Wally. He had a quality no other player I'd ever seen had – he was able to play the game at his pace. He played a different game to the other 25 blokes on the field. On a different level altogether. But they could only manage to finish fourth, while we earned a week off for being minor premiers. We beat Brothers to progress straight to the big one, while Wynnum had to win three straight to force a grand final replay. They did just that.

Grand final week in Brisbane back then was exactly like you get in the NRL these days. The whole place succumbed to grand final fever. It was an amazing week. The media attention was also incredible. Before arriving in Brisbane I had only done a single interview – with *Rugby League Week* to explain my decision to move north. If only the journos knew the rest I would have made a pretty decent story. But no-one ever asked, so I kept a low profile. But once Brisbane Souths started going well, I was being featured in the *Courier-Mail* almost every second day. The big story about me was whether I'd hang around the following year. I remember the veteran Brisbane journo Steve Ricketts asking that question several times. I always told him the truth – I didn't know.

The night before the grand final six of my family and friends from Sydney arrived to watch the game live. My eldest brother Joe was among them. They all piled into my one-bedroom apartment for the night, which hinted at a less-than-ideal preparation for the biggest game of my life. Then, to make matters worse, Joe insisted we go to the

Albion Park trots. 'Are you joking?' I asked. 'I've got a grand final on tomorrow and you want me to spend the night on the punt?' Joe, however, was adamant. He wanted to see Prix Chevalier, a trotter he considered to be Australia's best, go around that night. Because he was my older brother, I agreed and we went. Funnily enough, Joe lost all his money before the super-horse raced.

I wasted no time getting out of there but couldn't stay home. There was just too much distraction with all these noisy relatives crowding the joint. It was like my idyll had been destroyed at the worst possible moment.

Desperate to get some rest, I called up a family friend, Ben Andary, to ask if I could sleep at his place. He agreed and I went straight over thinking about nothing else but a decent night's sleep. Those hopes, however, were shattered when Ben led me to the spare bedroom and introduced me to the resident waterbed. I had never slept on one and found the floating sensation very disturbing. Soon enough I was tossing and turning, wondering how I would ever get to sleep. And to tell you the truth, I was a bit nervous about falling asleep on the damned thing. It just felt weird.

I didn't get a wink of sleep. But when I got up at dawn on grand final day I felt strangely refreshed. My head was clear and my mind ready. Ben took me to breakfast at a café, then it was off to Lang Park for the most important 80 minutes I'd ever spend on a football field.

The cauldron was packed to its 32,000 capacity that afternoon. The mood was decidedly pro-Wynnum given they'd thrashed us 12 months earlier and now fielded an even stronger side. We were 2/1 outsiders with the bookies, while Wynnum were near unbackable at 3/1 on.

Unknown to most, a lot of our players had invested. This,

WELCOME TO WAYNE'S WORLD

of course, was at my urging. About six weeks out from the grand final our chances were posted at 11/2. The weekend before we had beaten a desperate Redcliffe side in one of the toughest matches I'd ever played. Their tough pack – which included internationals Wally Fullerton-Smith, Greg Conescu, and Bryan Niebling – threw everything at us that day but we emerged 12–8 winners. From that afternoon I was certain we'd win the comp, despite what the experts were saying about Wynnum. So I took a few of the boys down to the bookies' ring at the Gabba and loaded up at a healthy price. We stood to win over $10,000 each by beating Wynnum that day.

In my eyes, a player puts more pressure on himself by backing his own team to win. There's just enormous pressure not to make a single mistake, to make every pass stick. That's the way I felt that afternoon, but Bennett expertly defused the tension.

In the week leading up to the game he didn't change a thing. Our routine had worked all year, so why deviate? Although Bennett never said it openly, everyone's season culminated at this point: Wynnum on grand final day. We didn't have to be better than them – just better on that particular day. There's a big difference. They outranked us on paper, but a freak 80 minutes could put paid to reputations. Like a stayer trained to perfection for the Melbourne Cup, we were prepared especially for that afternoon at Lang Park.

In the dressing room Bennett made a speech that was unlike any other he'd done all year. 'You've done everything for your family and friends,' he said. 'Now do it for the bloke standing next to you.' I was already crying in the corner before he started to talk and now my emotions really started to overflow. I thought that's what players did before a big match like this. There was less than 10 minutes before kick-off. Bennett immediately broke the mood and quipped, 'Gaddafi, you are supposed to cry after the game, not before it.'

That made the tears stop, but before long my nervousness prompted a flow of a different kind. Early in the game as Wynnum lined up a shot at goal, I was struck by an irresistible desire to relieve myself. There was no time to rush back to the sheds and holding on was so uncomfortable that it would have compromised my performance. So I had no other choice but to head over to the goalposts, turn my back to the crowd and pee in the northern in-goal area. Talk about marking territory. Lang Park must have had a strange urinary effect on players because a couple of years later big Don McKinnon was sprung on TV doing exactly the same thing while playing for Manly against the Broncos.

We started well but could not translate our dominance to the scoreboard. After 30 minutes the scores were locked at 2–all. Then came the highlight of my career. From deep within our own territory, Jackson and Belcher combined to produce a big break. The Wynnum defence was all over the shop and from the next tackle the ball was shifted wide to me. I had support on the outside but elected to use my trademark left-foot step and head back against the grain. Taking the line on, I evaded two tackles before straightening, drawing the fullback and sending our halfback Norm Carr on his way. He crashed over with Lewis on his back for the first try and we led 8–2 at halftime.

The second half saw Wynnum lift. After we edged ahead 10–2, they finally scored a try to make it a two-point nail-biter with about 12 minutes left. It seemed like they were camped on our line the entire time. They attacked and attacked with all the big names – Miles, Lewis and Dowling – going for glory. But our defence was resolute. I was certain we'd hold out and we did. Lewis later said it was the best defensive effort he'd ever encountered, State of Origin included. Final score: Souths 10, Wynnum 8.

The siren was a blur – screaming fans, exultant players, shattered Wynnum opponents. I went over and shook all their hands and then did a lap of honour with my team-mates. Can life get any sweeter? I don't think so. With the exception of being told I had beaten cancer later in life, that lap of honour was the greatest single moment for me. I was so far from Lucky Bills, so far from Long Bay, so far from the deadbeat, good-for-nothing lifestyle. And it felt so good. In fact, it felt like home.

I've got a tape of the game which I watch from time to time. Bennett, however, refuses to live in the past. Speaking to him from jail during my last stint in 2007, he told me that Justin was watching that very grand final on TV in the background. It was the first time he'd seen it since 22 September 1985.

The celebrations were standard stuff – a glorious bus ride back to Davis Park to party with the fans, followed by a three-day bender and pub crawl. If I remember correctly, Norm Carr was the best stayer. True to form, I drank little in the aftermath. I just didn't need the alcohol to have a good time.

After the game the media began speculating about who should be awarded man of the match for the grand final. Back in those days, the officials had a quirk of not handing out the award until the gala QRL dinner a week later. Most of the experts in the papers, however, had nominated me. I felt confident because I had set up the first try and made a heap of tackles as Wynnum pressed for victory late in the game. When my name was announced at the dinner, it was an extremely proud moment. Standing there being photographed with the $500 cheque was surreal, given that 12 months before I had been standing in a Surry Hills drug den waiting for Danny Karam to blow some guy's brains out.

I finally felt settled. I knew where I wanted to be. It's just a shame certain people in Sydney felt differently.

CHAPTER 8

A MESSAGE FROM WAYNE BENNETT

Had I known John Elias spent time in prison before coming to Brisbane Souths, he would never have played for us. But what I didn't know turned out to be the ultimate blessing in disguise. Because if John Elias didn't play in the 1985 grand final, I'm prepared to say we wouldn't have beaten Wynnum that afternoon. That season, there was life before John and life after him. They were two very different phases. John's character was completely different to all the other players at the club. I had never encountered anyone quite like him before. He just turned up at training one day during the pre-season. Someone on the board had obviously recruited him, but I had no idea about it.

John soon let us all know what he was all about – himself. He wasted no time trying to stamp what was a very strong and at times overbearing personality on training sessions and team activities. He was the hotshot gangster from the big city who'd come to teach us Brisbane yokels a few tricks. As anyone from Queensland will attest, that Sydney routine wins neither respect nor friends north of the Tweed. It was divisive. His strident individuality bred uneasiness between John and his new teammates. No-one quite knew how to react to his comments or behaviour. And I'm not too proud to include myself as one of them. My philosophy as a coach has always been to stand back and observe the players at first, to get an idea of what kind of person they are. I did plenty of observing with John, and he continually challenged and surprised me.

The real flashpoint came after I'd omitted John from the first-grade side following a trial match in February. He rang me at home and really tried to stand over me about his non-selection. He tried to intimidate me. John said he'd made 50 tackles and thought that pure defensive effort should automatically warrant selection. He talked quickly and upped the tempo. 'You can stick the bloody club up your arse,' he yelled. 'I didn't come all the way up here from Sydney to play reserve grade. I want a release now.'

Given no player had ever confronted or spoken to me like this before, I was slightly taken aback. But I stayed calm and agreed to let him go if that's what he really wanted. I also told him a few home truths about his attack. John thought that he could get by on tackling alone. Not on my watch, he couldn't. In fact, John's attitude during that phone call was a reflection of the way in which he believed people should treat him. He thought that just because he could play football, then they should have to tolerate everything else.

A MESSAGE FROM WAYNE BENNETT

Standing up to John and flatly refusing to be bullied by his tough talk was the turning point. I think John had a lot more respect for me as a coach and for our entire club after that conversation. He had to win my confidence, not the other way around. I brought him into first-grade about three or four weeks into the season and neither of us looked back from there.

Still, John had requirements that differed from the other players. Everything about John is individual. I didn't encounter another player with such self-belief until Wendell Sailor came along almost a decade later. His lifestyle of late-night card games and frequent visits to the racetrack was difficult for the other players – who enjoyed nothing more than a drink together – to comprehend. On and off the field, it was difficult for them to accept John, regardless of how well he was playing. It wasn't an issue for me. I'm not concerned about your past, your skin colour or whatever else. I learned to handle his differences. But for many of the older players, who'd been at the club for a while and guarded watch over its culture, John could be very difficult to deal with.

The turning point in his acceptance came when Chris Phelan returned from England midway through the season. John and Chris struck it off real well, and I believe Chris's acceptance of him was a signal for the rest of the team to do so as well. John also played his best football alongside Chris. I'll always remember that game late in the season against a desperate Redcliffe side at Davis Park. They threw everything at John that afternoon and he kept coming back for more.

We also gave John a nickname – Gaddafi. Now he might like to think it had something to do with him wearing a green T-shirt, but that's not how I remember it. In those days, Gaddafi was a big deal as he set about revolutionising Libya in a violent and abrupt manner. His motives might have been admirable, but the means were questionable. He reminded me a lot of John – honest and explosive. One minute John could be planting a letterbox bomb, and the next day, after your mail was splattered to smithereens, he'd be on your doorstep apologising and wanting to be mates. So Gaddafi it was and John didn't mind one bit. One of the most impressive things about John was that he could laugh at himself.

John was right about the Redcliffe game. That toughest of wins convinced us we could win the premiership. But true to form, John had to do things the hard way. He turned up late for our final training session on the morning before the big one against Wynnum. When it became apparent that John was a no-show I gathered all the players for an urgent meeting. Under normal circumstances, I'd have axed him from the side – no arguments. But this was a grand final. Dropping a starting second-rower on the eve of the biggest game of the season would have caused far too much disruption.

Nevertheless, John had to be taught a lesson. Even if I wasn't going to sack him, it wouldn't hurt if he thought that was a possibility. I ordered no-one in the club – no-one – to utter a single word to him when he arrived. They were to treat John as if he were invisible.

He turned up 40 minutes later. Even if I hadn't

vowed to ignore him, I was too disappointed for words. Realising that the whole team was intent on giving him the cold shoulder, John finally managed to collar me one-on-one near the dressing rooms. And what he said only made things worse. 'Wayne, you've got to believe me – a man near my house had a heart attack and I had to help him,' he said. 'I called an ambulance – you would have heard it go by the oval.' I looked at him with disgust. If John had simply put up his hand and said 'Sorry, I stuffed up,' I would have been prepared to move on then and there. But that wasn't his caper. There was always a tall story, a colourful excuse. And this one took the cake. 'John, there was no friggin' ambulance because there was no heart attack,' I replied. He could see he was in trouble and started to backpedal. I couldn't let it go on forever. There was a fine line. While I wanted John to suffer for being late, I didn't want the punishment to impact on his preparation for the game. I sent word to the boys to start talking to him again.

But John's pre–grand final high jinks weren't done there. Moments before kick-off he did something I've never witnessed from any of the hundreds of players I've coached. He cried before the game. I've been to a few grand finals with the Broncos since that day, but never once seen a player break down into tears before we started. He was sitting in the corner of the home side dressing room at Lang Park, bawling. I went over and said: 'John, what are you doing?' He replied: 'I'm crying, I thought this is what players are supposed to do before a grand final.' I couldn't believe what I was hearing. 'John,' I said, 'you are supposed to cry after the game when we win, not before.' And that's exactly what he did.

The flipside to John's personality was how easily he can be led. I suspect this was the main reason he got into trouble in Sydney. But it was a double-edged sword. On the positive side, it made him a wonderful and loyal friend who'd never knock back a request. He just has a unique way of doing you a favour. As with the many clubs John played at during his career, there were mysterious gatherings around his car boot after training at Brisbane Souths. Being a police sergeant at the time, I had my suspicions. But I never wanted anything to do with it, so I kept well clear when John took the players to the car park.

But there was one time when I had to intervene. Two police officers came to training midway through the season and I suspected that they wanted to speak with John. I didn't know any specifics about what he was getting into off the field, but I knew plenty about his lifestyle – the racetracks, the card nights and car boot sales. He seemed like the obvious player they would want to speak to.

Before the police reached the sheds, we were able to get word to John about their arrival. We quickly hid him behind a couple of dirt mounds the crowd used to sit on to watch the game. Convinced he was safely concealed, we returned to greet the police. As luck would have it, they wanted to speak with an entirely different player. But that's a different story, for a different book.

I only asked John for a favour once. That was enough to learn never to do it again. The problem wasn't John's willingness to help. It was his bull-at-a-gate approach.

A MESSAGE FROM WAYNE BENNETT

When he was too willing, he went too far. I was coaching Queensland for a State of Origin game in Sydney a couple of years back, when John rang to ask if he could be of any assistance. He always rings to offer his services. Nothing specific came to mind, but I was curious whether New South Wales would take the field with the same starting 13 they'd announced a week earlier.

'Well, John, if you like, you could go down to New South Wales training and see what you can tell me,' I asked. John couldn't agree quickly enough and I thought nothing else of it until he rang again the following night. 'Wayne, my mate has a panel van with a peephole in the side that we can video the whole session through,' he said. 'I'll give you the tape and you'll be able to see everything yourself.'

John thought he was doing me a big favour by going the extra mile – he genuinely did – and in a strange way I appreciated his thought and effort. But what he was proposing was insane. If New South Wales sprung them filming from the van, it would have been World War III. The news would have been on the front page for days. And that sums John up. He doesn't have the instincts to know when to stop, when enough is enough. Simple tasks were never enough. John had to make them into something more thrilling and illegitimate to satisfy his hunger for a buzz. He was a gambler. He loved raising the stakes.

It's no secret John bet on the outcome of matches involving teams he played for. For the record, I haven't got a problem with that. And John definitely wasn't the only player to back himself before the NRL outlawed the practice. In my view, it does no harm. It only adds extra motivation, which can only be a positive. The problems start when they go the other way.

I wasn't happy when John decided to return to Sydney – for him or Brisbane Souths. It didn't take Einstein to figure out that trouble awaited him there. Had he stayed, I'm convinced his considerable potential would have been more fully realised because there weren't so many distractions. But John said he had to go. And so he went . . . and never came back.

His departure hasn't stopped us from talking, though. Even when he was in prison, I'd still get calls from an operator asking me if I wanted to accept a conversation with John Elias. The answer was and always will be the same – yes. John is a great friend who never forgets what's important to his mates. That's why he calls my house every Christmas to say g'day and pass on season's greetings to my wife and kids. His family is also forthcoming with invites for dinner. It was only earlier this year that I enjoyed a wonderful Lebanese lunch – cooked by none other than his mum Suzie – in Punchbowl. I look at that woman and can't help but admire her toil to support the family single-handedly when they arrived in Australia.

My wish is that John learns a lesson from her about the value of hard work. While he never cut corners on the training paddock or football field, he wasn't one to do the hard yakka on a building site or behind a cashier's counter. If he can bring himself to accept hard work, then I'm sure a lot of the hard work in his attempts to re-assimilate into society will be taken away.

I started by saying that I could never have played

A MESSAGE FROM WAYNE BENNETT

John at Brisbane Souths had I known he spent time in prison. He is not asking to play anymore, but unfortunately nothing has changed. As much as I'd love to help John's coaching career by offering him a start at my new club St George Illawarra, it's just not possible. He called to ask for help and it wasn't easy to knock him back, because I know he'd do anything to help me.

I feel torn and a little helpless about John's situation. On one hand we say prisoners have done their time and should be treated equally upon release. But it's never the case. We are hypocrites when we say that. I'd love to help John. If I worked in a warehouse or a shop, I'd offer him a job tomorrow. But it's not like that in the NRL, where you have responsibilities to so many other stakeholders. Someone would be bound to complain – and unfortunately that's all it would take for me to have to tell him to walk away. In my view, that would be more hurtful than giving him a straight answer to begin with.

In life, you have to foresee consequences. I hope John can understand that when rugby league refuses to give him another chance. But I also hope he keeps trying, because there's nothing more inspirational than a man who refuses to give in.

CHAPTER 9

BEAUTIFUL ONE DAY, DOG DAY THE NEXT

'Bring my boy home!'

Those were the very words that sent me back to Sydney against my will. And the person who roared them was none other than legendary Canterbury supremo Peter 'Bullfrog' Moore. A genius administrator who built the Bulldogs' four-premiership dynasty during the 1980s, Moore was without peer when it came to street smarts. As I celebrated our grand final win, Bullfrog was on the phone to his good mate Bob McCarthy, the great Rabbitohs international who was based in Brisbane at the time.

'Who was the best player in the grand final up there?' Moore asked McCarthy. His friend replied, 'It was John Elias.' It didn't take Moore long to realise I was a Punchbowl boy and therefore a local product of the Canterbury district. So when he contacted my brother George soon after, he demanded I come 'home' to Canterbury. If it hadn't been written in black and white, Moore's offer would have been unbelievable. He was willing to pay $28,000 a season for 1986 and 1987, plus $5,000 for every 10 first-grade matches I played. This was more than three times what Brisbane Souths could afford to keep me.

Nevertheless, I was adamant when George called to relay the rich Canterbury offer. I told my brother to forget it. I was finally settled in Brisbane and had formed an unbreakable bond with Bennett and the players. My dream for 1986 was to make the Combined Brisbane side that competed against the Sydney teams in the midweek Panasonic Cup. As unlikely as it seemed, this was my home now. The last thing I needed was to go back to Sydney and fall back into the same old cycle of gambling and crime that always seemed to hook me.

But being a business-minded man, my solicitor brother would not give up. The money was huge. It would set me up, he said. Buy me houses. Knowing that fiscal responsibility wasn't my forte, he offered to sign the contract in his name and then pass me on a weekly wage. The rest would be invested into property and shares. I could not compare such an arrangement with the contract being offered in Brisbane. Then, there was the chance to play with what was then the best rugby league side on the planet. Canterbury had just won the past two NSWRL premierships and were coached by the best in the business, my old mentor at Newtown, Warren Ryan. Their roster was a mix of fearsome forwards and skilful backs – Mortimer, Folkes, Lamb, Tunks, Dunn, Bugden, Kelly, Gillespie, Hagan. Looking back, it was a ridiculously good team.

The more I thought about it, the more George's argument made sense. My brain started to rule my heart and I imagined being part of this world-renowned pack from

Belmore. It was a privilege to be invited to play for Canterbury in that era and what's more I was being offered more than some of their international forwards were earning.

But it wasn't the money or the opportunity. As much as I resented it, the urge to get back into the funny business had never left me. It just lay dormant until an opportunity arose to release it once more. Being offered to play for Canterbury was like being handed the key to Pandora's box. I could still choose not to open it, but temptation always seemed to get the better of me.

Brisbane Souths were disappointed when I told them a month after grand final day. But Bennett respected my decision and wished me all the best. I was really torn as I packed my bags. Although I only lived in Brisbane for a year, I truly felt I belonged at that club. At their centenary dinner in 2008, I was named Best Import, an honour I will always cherish.

So, with $25,000 cash stuffed down my underpants, I embarked on the long drive south. The money was a combination of my contract, winnings from the card games and, of course, my big collect from the Brisbane bookies on our grand final win. I remember returning with a kid my own age named Ray Dib, who played juniors for Canterbury. Ray had come to Brisbane to get a friend, Kenny Isaac, a start. Ray is now a director on the Bulldogs board.

Warren Ryan already had the players back at training for 1986 by the time I arrived. No matter what anyone says about Canterbury, there is something special about that place. There certainly was in those days, when it was renowned as the 'family club'. This was an institution that didn't admit outsiders lightly. Thanks to Moore, the place was founded on familial bonds that saw the Mortimer and

Hughes brothers dominate the successful teams of the early 1980s. There was an aura of confidence and pride at Canterbury I had never experienced. As someone who did not come from Moore's inner sanctum, it indeed felt like a privilege to be part of such a club.

Ryan hadn't changed a lot from his Newtown days. He was technically brilliant and would furiously shout down anyone who dared to suggest there was no science in rugby league. He was also fiercely loyal to his starting side and would only drop a player in extraordinary circumstances. But he wasn't Wayne Bennett. I felt with Ryan that it was impossible to form a bond away from football. If you followed his game plan you would win any game on the field, but off it you were on your own. I liked Ryan, but there was nothing else happening between him and the other players from the moment the fulltime siren sounded. He was more like a schoolteacher than a father figure. He commanded plenty of respect, but no love.

Without Bennett, I began to feel homesick after only a couple of weeks. How ridiculous. Here I was training under the world's best coach just a stone's throw from my family home and I'm feeling homesick. I couldn't help it – my head and my desires were still in that little one-bedroom flat in West End. I enjoyed my independence, something I missed upon returning to Mum's house. By that stage the place was overrun with relatives night and day because George and his wife had moved in. There never seemed to be a chance to think clearly like I could in Brisbane.

So, before the start of the 1986 season I went and told Bullfrog I wanted to go back to Brisbane. I was still secretly speaking with Bennett on the phone, as well as Brisbane Souths CEO Jim McClelland. Both were willing to have me back in a heartbeat. But the Bullfrog was just too good, too convincing. He persuaded me to stay put, arguing that my pining would disappear once the season began.

Then a strange quirk of fate occurred to justify me not going to Brisbane. Thanks to red tape in the QRL, Bennett was made to step down from coaching Brisbane Souths because he had taken on the Queensland State of Origin job for 1986. The QRL had a rule preventing club coaches from taking the state reins, to prevent the perception of bias. Bennett didn't want to quit Souths, but was forced to. So even if I did get my way, I wouldn't be playing under him. His absence lessened the attraction of returning, but I still wanted to be there rather than at Belmore.

I even went to the extent of flying up to Brisbane one weekend early in the season when Canterbury had a bye to touch base with my old teammates. The defending premiers were struggling a little, having lost the nucleus of their 1985 team. Both Mal Meninga and Gary Belcher had followed me out the door – the two of them were poached by Canberra in what would become one of the great recruitment coups for a NSWRL club.

I was despondent after falling in line with Peter Moore's stance. One of my fatal flaws – and there are quite a few of them – is that I just can't say no. This obviously got me into trouble from a very young age, being easily persuaded into a criminal lifestyle as a teenager. But there's another side to it as well. A big part of me just wants to please people, no matter who they are. I hate letting people down, the guilt that comes from seeing them disappointed. In truth, my will was no match for a master of the mouth like Peter Moore.

You had to earn respect at Canterbury and it was harder work than anywhere else. The players were a very tight-knit group and they tested newcomers mercilessly. Just before the season started we were scheduled to play a trial match in Newcastle. The senior players must have decided that the three-hour bus ride would double as my initiation. I remember they hassled me the whole way – saying stuff about my hairy legs, my surname, whatever it took for me to crack. My short fuse burned out by the time we passed Hornsby, but somehow I maintained control. After about an hour I was really ready to snap and they were all clapping and laughing at my expense.

The worst was Paul Langmack, whom I've never had much time for. I found him to be a big-mouth who only looked out for number one. We ended up having a run-in a few years down the track when I was selling suits to players at Wests, the club he switched to in the 1990s. I got the feeling Langmack was envious that he wasn't in on the deal, because he told his teammates to stop buying them. I found his attitude entirely hypocritical because Langmack had bought clothes from me previously. He was dirty that there was no money in it for him this time around – pure and simple.

Noticing how well I was doing to stay composed on the bus, Ryan turned to me and said, 'Don't give them anything, son. Keep it up, you're doing well.' His advice inspired me to make it to Newcastle without jumping out the window and from then on I was accepted. Peter Tunks approached me when the bus stopped and said: 'John, you've done well, you've passed the test.'

Although my heart was still with Bennett in Brisbane, I reproduced my 1985 form and played five of the opening eight rounds in first-grade. Incredibly, I did not make my top-grade Sydney run-on debut until that season. All my previous appearances had been off the bench.

My chance came against Easts in round two, when Steve Folkes was ruled out with injury. Ryan came up on game day and told me not to bother with reserve grade, because I was to be one of his starting second-rowers. I recall all the players coming up to me in the sheds with advice, wishing me all the best. That made Ryan mad. He snapped: 'Leave the bloody kid alone, I wouldn't have picked him if he wasn't ready.' I ended up getting man of the match that day, but couldn't hold my spot when Folkes overcame his injury.

If there was any friction among that brilliant side it was probably between Ryan and the captain Steve Mortimer. I witnessed nothing outward, just a cool vibe that ran between them. In my opinion, Ryan probably thought Mortimer was a bit past his best by then. I respected Mortimer a hell of a lot. Despite being an asthmatic, he did his best at training and would never cut a corner. The one player who held everyone's respect was Terry Lamb. I remember the Bullfrog used to buy him a bottle of spirits every week.

Canterbury was a wonderful club, but my heart just wasn't in it. I went there for the wrong reasons and inevitably got caught up in the wrong scene again. Danny Karam was still hanging around, but by now had progressed to robbing jewellery stores. He was also in league with a certain inner-city nightclub owner. Given my lack of passion at Canterbury, I was ripe for the picking. I begged the manager Garry Hughes to find me a job on the council to keep me occupied, but I was left to my own devices.

By the start of 1986, I was involved in a couple of inside jobs on jewellery stores around Sydney. The trick was to always make it seem real. So, after opening the safe with the combination, we'd have an explosives guy there to blow it up. After a few jobs with Danny's crew, I realised how much I had missed the buzz of living on the edge.

It was a crazy double life. By day I'd be training alongside the best footballers in the country, living a lie as someone who dreamed only of being an elite athlete. At night, however, my true dark desires would be fulfilled through robberies and illegitimate debt collection. I'd get home at 4 am every night, wake up at 11 am and go straight to training. It didn't make sense, but I kept getting away with it. I couldn't wait until training finished to get on with the next job, the next payday. The funny thing was that I didn't need the money. I had plenty. Adrenalin, however, was something I could never get enough of.

The worst time I burned the candle at both ends was a trip up to Newcastle for a collect on a Saturday night about a month into the season. The job went well as always – the scumbags always paid without too many problems when Danny was involved – but I didn't get home until 3.30 am. I was due to play reserve grade against Manly 10 hours later, so things were already pretty tight.

It felt like I'd hardly slept a wink when the phone started ringing. It was just past 9 am. Warren was on the other end with some interesting news. He told me that Folkes had succumbed to injury again and that I would be playing first-grade that day. Our opponents, Manly, had a star-studded pack that included Noel Cleal, Ron Gibbs and Paul Vautin. It was a huge game and a capacity crowd was expected to pack into Belmore Oval.

Considering my unique preparation, I went well and set up a try for Lamb. But I can only wonder how much better I might have done had I given myself every chance. Not just in that game, but for my entire career. I suppose the answer lies in that perfect season at Brisbane Souths.

No-one at Canterbury ever said anything about my activities off the field, so I've got no reason to believe they knew. But, as with Wayne Bennett, I'm convinced they suspected something. The Bullfrog wasn't stupid and club president, Barry Nelson, was a senior copper.

Nelson had already banned me from the leagues club for two years because of a violent altercation earlier in the season. My old mate Peter Rix and I were there one Friday night when a couple of big Islanders started hassling him over a dropped drink. Peter is tiny and can't hold up his hands, so as per usual I came rushing over to step in on his behalf. I dropped the Islander right there on the dance floor. It was a complete overreaction, but I just can't stand by and see my loyal mate get stood over. And I hate blokes that pick on easy targets.

The bouncers rushed in and broke us up. We were escorted down to the bistro, where Nelson came and met us. He said that if we shook hands it would be forgotten. I went to approach the Islander with an outstretched hand and then . . . KABAMM! I threw a couple of haymakers instead. I didn't trust the shaking hands routine and wanted to make sure I got in first. Nelson was speechless. After throwing us out, he told me I was banned for two years.

Looking back, my reaction on that night was way over the top. There's simply no excuse for carrying on like that – then or now. In those days I was still a wild kid who could never stay still. I was permanently on edge, looking over my shoulder. I was that pumped up that I genuinely believed the Islander would have decked me had I not lashed out first. It's scary to think back to how insane I could get.

Little did I know how soon I'd be gone from the

Canterbury team altogether. My exit was sparked by a friendly-natured wrestle with Peter Moore in his office one night after training. Bullfrog and I got on quite well, actually. As we were wrestling, his wallet fell to the floor and a credit card dropped out. He didn't notice, so I pocketed the credit card and decided to play a little trick. I gathered three other players – all first-graders – and took them on a little outing at the club's expense. We were headed for the local brothel on Canterbury Road, where I intended to pay for the services rendered with Bullfrog's card. At the time I thought it was a hilarious stunt. I was too narrow-minded to think Bullfrog wouldn't see the funny side of it.

As for the choice of venue, well, brothels are an old favourite of mine in which to splash a bit of cash. I'm not too ashamed to admit I've shouted mates to a good time after a big collect on the races. I've never slept with a prostitute myself, however. I understand that sounds strange and even impossible to believe, given the number of these establishments I've frequented. But for me, the attraction of brothels was the scallywags who hung out there. I enjoyed joking with the madams and prostitutes, who never took themselves too seriously. At least with those girls, you knew their agenda: money. But in those days sex didn't have to be paid for when you were a first-grade footballer, and although many still did, it wasn't my go.

The four of us entered the brothel, where we were met by a pretty receptionist. She organised girls for the three other players and I handed over Bullfrog's credit card. Payment was always received before the services were rendered. A moment later, the manager out the back let out a big yelp. He must have been a big Bulldogs fan and immediately recognised the name on the credit card, which I must stress had never been used at an establishment of this ilk before. The manager rushed out the front and began asking for Peter Moore. I gathered he wanted to give Peter some complimentary extras.

Upon discovering that Bullfrog was not there, the manager cottoned on. He refused to hand back the credit card and kicked us out. I still thought nothing of it – we were all laughing, in fact. The smile, however, was wiped from my face when Bullfrog rang the next day. His voice was stern. I was to see him immediately. The brothel manager had dobbed me in. For some reason, I was the only player he recognised. I will never reveal who the others were, but let's just say I was flabbergasted that he recognised me over them.

Bullfrog was furious. He demanded to know who the others were. I said nothing. In these situations, my lips are always sealed. I learned the value of not ratting in Long Bay and stubbornly adhered to that lesson that day as Bullfrog hammered me for information. He was furious at my refusal to tell him who the others were and began bringing up other stuff. Among them was the case of a stolen cigarette truck. Bullfrog believed a club official had helped cover up the case to help me avoid police suspicion. I again denied any knowledge.

Bullfrog's anger was obvious, but beneath it there was something else that drove him to sack me there and then. He had been embarrassed. The man was a revered icon of the club and here was some 23-year-old punk flogging his credit card and trying to use it at a brothel. It was a direct strike on his standing at Belmore – an unprecedented insult.

He had every right to show me the door. Bullfrog had bent over backwards to bring me home and this is how I repaid his faith? By flogging his credit card and trying to use it to shout players at the local brothel? Now it sounds too stupid to be true, but unfortunately that's exactly the type of stunt I thought was cool in those days.

Being too big for my boots at the time, however, I didn't really care. My heart was still inclined towards returning to Brisbane. But Bullfrog was too smart. He said I would not be released to play in Queensland. He would only pay me out for 1986 on the condition that I play for either Cronulla or Wests. To this day, I still don't know why he insisted on either of those two clubs. But his reason for preventing me from going back to Brisbane was obvious. He was denying me what I truly wanted, as punishment for the humiliation I had brought upon him and his beloved Bulldogs.

I don't recount this story with any sense of pride. Peter Moore was one of the most respected men in rugby league and he always treated me with respect. Many years later I visited him on his deathbed at St Vincent's private hospital to make final peace. He was succumbing to cancer, a disease I had just recovered from before my visit. I apologised for embarrassing him and he accepted. He was pleased that I had gone out of my way to do that.

But he couldn't help taking a parting shot at the man who replaced Warren Ryan as Bulldogs coach in 1988 – my old Newtown teammate Phil Gould. Although Gould delivered the Dogs a premiership in his first season, Bullfrog was not a fan of the bloke they called Gus. He talked long about how Gould had tried to destroy everything he had built at Canterbury. I listened silently, nodding my head. Bullfrog was preaching to the converted, because I'd had a few moments with Gus that we'll get to very shortly.

The media were told that my split from Canterbury was

'amicable'. So where to now? Cronulla or Wests? Standing outside Belmore Oval on the day of my sacking were Magpies CEO Rick Wade and coach Steve Ghosn. They desperately wanted me. On the other hand, Cronulla's coach at the time – the late, great Jack Gibson – was nowhere to be seen.

So the decision was made for me then and there. I'd come from a family of battlers and now I was about to realise my true calling. I was about to become a Fibro.

CHAPTER 10
FIBRO WONDERLAND

My first training session at Wests' home ground – Lidcombe Oval – was not one to remember. As soon as I walked onto the ground I could feel an icy blast coming from the direction of my new teammates. Only four of them made an effort to welcome me – the bald yet bearded prop Ian Freeman, John Bilbiga, Brett Gale and Allan Fallah, a fellow Lebanese. The rest of the boys stood back and emitted silent rays of jealousy and resentment. It was a Tuesday afternoon and, although I had yet to complete a single training session for the Magpies, my name was in the starting side for that weekend's match against Canberra.

In hindsight, Steve Ghosn should have started me in reserve grade. Every club's culture always carries a heavy emphasis upon earning your stripes. I might have been on the same big bucks as I was at Canterbury (Wests had signed me for 1987 as well), but my reputation counted for naught among these blokes. I hadn't proved that I was willing to sacrifice for them, to bleed for the black and white. Their hostility was understandable.

Unfortunately, it got beneath my skin. Heading into my first game for Wests, my mind was a mess. I was at a new club, had the players hating me and was still getting up to all sorts of stuff away from football. It all seemed to be catching up and on a chilly afternoon at Seiffert Oval in Canberra I was collared.

My first game for Wests will go down as the worst I've ever played. I dropped balls and missed tackles. I was an embarrassment to myself and the team. I felt sick. To make matters worse, we were flogged by 40 points. And to make matters even worse, my former Brisbane Souths team-mates, Gary Belcher and Mal Meninga, had a front-row seat to the most humiliating 80 minutes of my life. Both of them starred for the Raiders that day and I could hardly bring myself to look them in the eye as we shook hands afterwards. It was the same on the bus back to Sydney. I sat alone in the front seat because I didn't want to talk to anyone. But I could feel their eyes staring daggers into my back. That three-hour bus trip home was agony, possibly worse than the arduous ride to Newcastle with the Bulldogs a few months earlier.

For some reason, Ghosn stayed loyal and named me again. I couldn't believe it. Neither could the other players, who were furious and rightly so. Ghosn is also Lebanese and had a lot of faith in me. He told me that I couldn't turn into that bad a player overnight after winning man of the match in a grand final that featured virtually the entire Queensland State of Origin side less than a year earlier.

His faith inspired me. At the time, he was only 32 – easily the youngest and most inexperienced coach in the comp.

FIBRO WONDERLAND

Because he didn't have a reputation to fall back on, he needed results. If I played terribly again, he would lose a lot of respect in the club. I'd already been told that he had to convince a few directors to bring me to Wests. They knew about my reputation and Ghosn had to do some big-time persuading to keep my career in Sydney afloat after being sacked by Canterbury. I also knew the Magpies selectors had kicked his arse for refusing to axe me after the Seiffert Oval debacle. If not for my own reputation, I had to play well for his.

Ghosn didn't have the technical nous of a Warren Ryan, but he could pull tricks like that to motivate individuals. He was very good at inspiring players. I remember the following season in the sheds before our very first game at Campbelltown – where the club moved from Lidcombe in 1987 – he showed us a *Rocky* video. We were playing the premiers Parramatta and it was a huge occasion. He only showed the bit where Rocky's wife, Adrienne, was giving birth and told her husband: 'Just win.' Ghosn might as well have produced an ox's heart or had us slapping one another in the face, we were that pumped. I can recall big Ian Freeman sweating up before producing the game of his life. In one of the upsets of the season we beat the big-shot Eels 32–16 before going on to claim the wooden spoon.

Sometimes, however, his methods strayed a little too far into left-field. He must have been haunted by that 1986 flogging in Canberra, because when we ventured back to the ACT the following year he pulled an unbelievable stunt to try and get us up for the game.

At the time, Wests were bringing up the rear while the Raiders were headed for their first grand final appearance. To everyone's disbelief, Ghosn brought a hypnotist to training that week with the aim of convincing us that we would win. The bloke's name was Les Cunningham and the club forked out $2,000 for him to work his magic during the week and just before kick-off. Although he didn't have a swinging watch, Les performed all the other corny tricks like trying to put us to sleep and clicking his fingers to wake us up. I couldn't have been that far gone, because I can clearly remember lying flat on the floor in the dressing room before kick-off giggling with John Bilbiga. The hypnotist was doing his all to convince a bunch of rejects that they could beat Mal Meninga, Gary Belcher and co. You had to admire Ghosn for trying something different, but I thought it really missed the mark.

Before a footballer goes into battle, he needs to be pumped up and ready to kill. When I went to Balmain a couple of seasons later, Warren Ryan had an old trick of dialling Triple 0 moments before we took the field to call an ambulance. 'I think you'd better get one down here,' the Wok would tell the emergency operator. 'I'm predicting carnage.' That would really get us fired up and we'd start the game like men possessed. Not surprisingly, with us in a trance, Canberra repeated the treatment from 12 months ago.

My second game for Wests in 1986 was against Parramatta and the pressure was squarely on me to produce or else. Thankfully I had a big game, although we lost by a couple of points. That match proved a turning point in my relationship with the rest of the Magpies players and I stayed in first-grade for the rest of 1986.

By the club's standards in those days, we had a moderately successful season, finishing mid-table and just a couple of wins from the finals. Wests were the real battlers of the competition, a club whose roster always seemed to be made up from the players no-one else wanted. It was a genuine halfway house and everyone accepted that. It brought us closer together and I can honestly say the camaraderie was as good as any I've experienced, even if the scoreboard didn't always look pretty.

I was enjoying my football a lot more than at Canterbury, but still didn't have a job to fill those idle hours that would eventually turn to trouble. Each week until the end of 1986 it was always something – a delivery, a collect, a robbery. Around that time I also started to dabble in illegal SP bookmaking.

The idea was to provide punters with a service where they didn't need to pay until the following week. The odds were exactly the same as those offered by the TAB. I set up shop at the Punchbowl Hotel and also accepted bets over the phone at Mum's house. The wagers were nothing spectacular – no more than a couple of hundred at once. And neither were the results. I ended up breaking about even for 1986, neither recording a big win or a big loss.

But again, it wasn't the money that interested me. It was the thrill of knowing a big win or a big loss was just around the corner. By that stage I was almost 24 and had been gambling half my life. Setting up as a bookmaker seemed to make sense, but it needed to generate money as well if I was to drop the other stuff and make a real fist of footy.

There must have been something about black and white jerseys, because by the end of 1986 I had regained my form that won me man of the match in the Brisbane grand final 12 months earlier. During the 1986–87 off-season I recall Ghosn pulling me aside to say the representative selectors had their eye on me for the coming season. I don't think he was talking about State of Origin, perhaps City

Firsts. Nevertheless, I had never worn a senior representative jersey and saw it as something I still had to achieve in football.

Ghosn's tip re-ignited the fire in my belly for rugby league. It certainly wasn't the eternal flame of Olympus, was it? It would flicker on and off every year or so depending on outside influences. So I went back to Danny Karam and told him to cool it for a while, that I wanted to give footy my full attention. I was now old enough to realise that the game only gives you a short time to succeed, and I was nearing the halfway mark of my window of opportunity. As always, Danny was fine.

Ghosn was a good influence, another would-be father figure for this wayward soul. So I got worked up about 1987, doing extras during the summer at Burwood Police Boys Club as Wests moved their operations from Lidcombe to Orana Park in Campbelltown.

That was my best off-season ever. Ghosn took us on a bonding camp to Forster on the New South Wales mid-north coast, which was great. As well as being a top-grade league player, Ghosn was also a former Australian welterweight boxing champ. Players used to visit his backyard, where a ring was set up for them to spar. He had a favourite saying that went something like, 'If you don't like what I'm saying, I'll talk to you about it. If you still don't like what I'm saying, I'll take you outside.' Everyone ended up liking what he had to say.

Ironically, the Bulldogs also happened to be in Forster on a camp of their own at the same time. They ended up making the grand final again in 1986, but were narrowly defeated by their bitter rivals Parramatta 4–2 in what still ranks as the lowest-scoring decider in history.

FIBRO WONDERLAND

There was no bad blood between myself and any of the Bulldogs players, but I suppose I was getting a reputation as a bit of a journeyman for someone who'd just turned 24. I'd now played for six clubs in five seasons – Newtown, Avignon, South Sydney, Brisbane Souths, Canterbury and Wests. Someone should have checked our family tree to see if we were descended from Bedouin Arabs, because I was the ultimate nomad.

Looking back, it would have been ideal to be a one-club man and when I joined Newtown in 1981 that's how I planned it to work out. Little did I know their collapse would trigger such a transitory career. At the time, however, I didn't mind. I enjoyed picking up bits and pieces from different coaches. And at the end of the day I was a knockabout who got bored easily. My restlessness would have prevented me from staying somewhere too long.

Shortly before kick-off in 1987, my old reserve grade coach at Souths, Wally Watsford, rang to give me the tip about the rep teams. He told me if my form from the previous season held, I'd be selected for City Firsts at least.

Despite that stirring early win over Parramatta in our first game at Campbelltown, Wests struggled for success in 1987. Our team spirit and camaraderie remained intact, but we got into the habit of losing. There were several games we dropped by only a couple of points and that proved the difference between running last and a respectable finish. The most heartbreaking loss was a game at Brookvale Oval midway through the season. Ten years earlier Wests and Manly had enjoyed some thunderous clashes during the infamous fibro–silvertail years. Not that much time had passed since all those buckets of blood were spilt and there was still hype around the joint in the lead-up to games against the glamour boys from the northern beaches. In 1987, Manly were at the top of their game, beating all-comers to be flying solo at the top of the ladder. So when we made the long trek from the western suburbs to God's country one Sunday in June, it was the ultimate David versus Goliath battle.

We played our hearts out that day and ambushed the fancied Sea Eagles. With a quarter of the game left, the home crowd was gobsmacked with their heroes trailing 25–12 and looking no chance of winning. The upset of the decade loomed, but then our old habits slipped in. A dropped ball here, a penalty there. Manly scored and it made us nervous. Suddenly they got a sniff of blood. We were vulnerable, not sure of ourselves. They were on a roll where winning was second nature. They scored two tries in the last five minutes to secure an impossible comeback victory and went on to claim the premiership in comprehensive fashion.

Despite the team's poor showing, I was thriving at Wests. I won player of the year that season and would have had a rep jersey to boot had it not been for another brain snap. Just before the City teams were announced, we played Norths in the midweek Panasonic Cup. I was primed for a huge game that would leave the selectors with no choice but to pick me. Unfortunately, the red mist was a little too thick that night. I hit the big Bears prop Adrian O'Toole with a high shot and was sent off for the second time in my career. My brother George represented me at the judiciary the following night, but to no avail. I was rubbed out for a month, a suspension that signalled the end of my representative dream for 1987.

The timing was awful and it wasn't the first time. In later life I've thought about how incidents like that suspension have come up at precisely the wrong time to prevent me from getting ahead in the game. There was a pattern.

FIBRO WONDERLAND

When I was young, my booming off-season with Newtown ended with an ankle injury in the first trial. Then as soon as I climbed back into first-grade the club folded without warning. It always seemed that just as I was on the brink of doing something special in rugby league, when I had put in the required effort and toil, a setback would intervene. I've learned to be philosophical and see it as karma for my transgressions off the field. I probably didn't deserve a lot of good luck in footy and rarely got a break because to be honest, I did little with my life outside the game to warrant one.

Steve rushed me straight back into first-grade when the suspension ended and this time there was no animosity from the players. The team was really struggling at that point and we were drawn to play second-placed Easts at Orana Park. Somehow we lifted and won.

Better still, I earned myself a healthy collect after backing us with an eight-and-a-half-point start. From that day on, I would regularly back myself if we had the start at home and a decent preparation. Although some people might be shocked to hear about players betting on the outcome of their own games, I can't see the problem. As long as they aren't backing themselves to run dead, I actually see it as a positive. I always found there was more pressure – and more incentive – to play well when the big money was on.

Other players at Wests – and later on at Balmain – did it as well. The usual wager was about $1,000. Steve knew when I'd backed myself, because I'd usually win players' player. Putting my money where my mouth was proved a genuine incentive for me to play well. I loved nothing better than a collect in those days.

I stayed in first-grade for the rest of 1987, playing 20 out of a possible 24 games. I never played a single reserve-grade match at Wests, although there was one game later in the season that I couldn't finish.

Fellow cellar-dwellers Penrith had just debuted a firebrand back-rower by the name of Mark Geyer when we met them. Early in the game the towering tyro ran straight at me and lifted his knee directly into my groin. He got me flush and I recoiled in agony and had to be replaced. Back in those days there was no interchange – once you were off, you were off.

My teammates were livid at Geyer and bashed him so hard that the Penrith coach Tim Sheens had to replace him to preserve his safety. We won the game as well, 16–8. That was evidence of how tight-knit we were at Wests. As for Geyer, I never thought badly of the bloke. I don't think the kneeing was intentional and never held it against him.

As Geyer's career blossomed, I respected him as a fellow colourful character who was not scared to voice his opinion. Rugby league is so much poorer because of the demise of players like him. I'm sure the modern-day blokes have opinions, but their clubs won't let them say boo for fear of upsetting fans and sponsors. It's a man's game, for God's sake, and a free country – let people say what they please.

Things might not have been going well on the field at Wests, but I was in demand again off it. Much to my relief the interest was coming from my old buddy from Brisbane Souths, none other than Wayne Bennett. Wayne had moved to Canberra that season to co-coach the Raiders alongside Don Furner. As Queensland State of Origin coach, he still wasn't allowed to coach in the Brisbane competition because of the QRL's rules. When we travelled to the ACT to take on the powerful Green Machine in 1987, Bennett sent word that he wanted to see me – to stay in Canberra overnight and meet with him the next day. He wanted to sign me for 1988 and I was immediately keen.

Wests, however, were again thrashed (despite the best efforts of our own private hypnotist) and I was too embarrassed to stick around and meet Wayne. My pride can sometimes obscure my rationality. Although I was keen to catch up with Wayne and talk turkey for 1988, I was simply too ashamed to show my face after such a hiding.

That didn't deter him. A couple of weeks later Wayne was in Sydney for an away match when he organised to visit me at home in Punchbowl. I remember Steve Ghosn also came over for lunch that day and was actually asking Wayne for coaching pointers. Mum cooked and didn't pull any punches either. She really is an intense woman, but very funny. The whole time she kept bugging Wayne to help find her a husband, something she demands of every new visitor. Wayne just laughed and took it all in good humour. I think he enjoyed the chance to see where I came from and meet the Lebanese pocket battleship herself.

Wayne and I kept talking over the phone and we came to a loose agreement that I would join him in Canberra the following season. I still hadn't told Steve or anyone at Wests a thing. It was a hard decision because I liked and respected Steve immensely.

Earlier that year he had supported me through a controversy that threatened to split the team in two. Wests got me a job in their leagues club at Campbelltown, working the bar and stocking shelves. The manager in those days was our fullback Rod Pethybridge. Rod was a bit of a knockabout himself and gave me the OK to take home a complimentary case of beer every week. I didn't think anything of it because all the other employees were doing the same thing. But when Wests CEO Rick Wade discovered a near-empty cellar one day, it became a very serious matter. He soon found a witness who had seen me putting a carton in my car after work. He called Rod in and asked about who was flogging all the beer. Without hesitation, Rod hung it all on me.

This was a low act, given that he'd told me it was OK to take a carton each week and was also doing the same thing himself. Rod was the boss, but refused to take any responsibility. I told Rick this when he summoned me. The CEO was understanding, but still adamant that the matter had to be dealt with transparently. So the cops were called and I took the fall. I received a fine.

Once word got around that Rod had squealed, his name was mud among the other players. Steve stuck by me more solidly than ever. Even though Rod was one of the best in 1986, he hardly saw first-grade in 1987. And even though we were not going well, Steve refused to pick him unless absolutely necessary. If a teammate was not solid off the field, then how on earth would he bleed for the other twelve blokes on it? I respected Steve's philosophy immensely and trained harder than ever for the coach.

In the two years I played under Steve at Wests, I believe I only let him down twice – my first game against Canberra and a training session I tried to skip. The latter was because I'd just lost $10,000 on the punt the night before and my spirits were a little low.

Because of my loyalty to Steve, I initially felt torn when Wayne came to woo me away from Wests. But there was an unexpected twist. Unknown to me, Wayne Bennett and former international John Ribot, who once played for Wests himself, were in the crowd for our return clash against

Parramatta midway through 1987. They were there to cast an eye over players who might make suitable recruits for a new side that was poised to enter the premiership in 1988, the Brisbane Broncos.

The Broncos promised to be one of the best teams ever assembled in the history of rugby league. With the whole of Queensland to pick from, they would field a State of Origin strength outfit every weekend to compete against the Sydney teams. The creation of the Broncos signalled the start of a national competition, which would also include teams from Newcastle and the Gold Coast in 1988. Little did I know at the time, but Wayne had secretly agreed to leave Canberra to be the Broncos' first coach. Ribot was the CEO.

At 8 am the day after our game against Parramatta, Ribot phoned me to request a meeting. He told me about Wayne coaching the Broncos and how they wanted me to be one of the club's foundation players. I couldn't have been happier. Beautiful, I thought. I can finally go home and, better still, play amongst a team of superstars.

I couldn't believe my luck. I told Ribot to meet me at my brother George's office in Revesby. His two-year offer for 1988 and 1989 was considerable – a lot more than Canterbury had paid to wrench me out of Brisbane. I said yes straightaway but George was coy. I kept telling him to sign the contract – the papers were right there – but he was intent on playing games to secure more money. He told John that we'd consider the offer and return with an answer in a few weeks' time.

When Ribot left, I turned to George and asked why he didn't do what I wanted. 'John, they've come all the way down here to sign you,' he said. 'They want you badly enough to pay enough. If we hold out they will raise their offer. Trust me.'

I trusted him. The season was almost over by that stage and it became clear that Steve was not going be re-hired by Wests. The wooden spoon sealed his fate. I decided that I couldn't stay if Steve was being punted, so my days as a Magpie were drawing to a close no matter what happened with the Broncos deal. Wests had a made a decent offer for me to re-sign, but Brisbane's was much better. Even so, I still wanted to go back and play under Wayne. That's all I had wanted to do since I left.

Without any loyalty to Wests, Steve went in to bat for me with other clubs. He took a phone call from Roosters coach Arthur Beetson, who was hunting for forwards for the following season. 'Who should I go after from Wests?' Beetson asked. Steve told him to target me. I had no idea that Arthur and Steve had spoken when Roosters CEO Ronnie Jones phoned the house one morning. He told me he wanted to meet straightaway. 'Get a cab to the club and we'll pay for it,' he said and then hung up. Intrigued, I decided to go but didn't have time to tell George, so I just took a mate named Louie Boutros for company.

When we pulled up at Easts Leagues Club on the other side of town at Bondi Junction a completely different feeling came over me. As far as rugby league was concerned, this was how the other side lived. I'd come from training in the midst of housing commission estates at Campbelltown, 60 km from the coast, to the blue-chip realty on Sydney's eastern beaches. Money oozed from the Easts club, and a butler even came to meet the cab and escort me to Ronnie Jones's office.

It was like something out of a movie. The kid from the wrong side of the tracks who had somehow caught the attention of the big-shot, mega-rich executive. Ronnie's office was ridiculously big, as big as a pub. It also resembled one, complete with a fridge and bar. He was sitting at his desk, an intimidating presence. Here was a man with power, I thought. He didn't bow to people, he got whatever he wanted.

Ronnie didn't muck around. The first words he said were: 'What do you want, Mr Elias?' I replied: 'But you brought me here, you make me the offer.' He fired back with the same money the Broncos had offered. Then came the sweetener. 'There will also be some cash in it for you,' he added matter-of-factly.

The cash being offered was big. It was handed over in a paper bag from the bank once a year whenever I asked. It was no secret that most clubs did it. There was no salary cap back then, clubs could do what they wanted. I thought it was all part of the contract. Within 10 minutes of asking Jones for my 'bonus', the money would appear. His only condition was that I accept straightaway. 'If you don't, the offer is gone,' he said.

I told him I was hungry and needed to have lunch. He gave me an hour. I went downstairs and ate from the club buffet. As I tucked into the roast of the day, my mind was swimming. I was racked with feelings not unlike two years earlier when the Bulldogs had wrenched me away from Brisbane. I needed help, so I called George, who advised me to accept the offer immediately. The Roosters' deal, he argued, was too good to refuse. He told me that I only had a limited shelf life in rugby league and had to set myself up financially at all costs.

Then I rang Wayne. He was adamant that I had to come back to Brisbane. He always knew Sydney was no good for me. He simply said: 'John, come back here where you belong.' My heart agreed. Despite the big cash being offered under the table, I truly wanted to return to Wayne in Brisbane. I couldn't be bought – not this time.

Having made up my mind, I phoned Mum to let her know I was leaving home again to take up the Broncos' offer. It was the worst thing I could have done. She was hardly objective. As soon as I mentioned the possibility of going back to Brisbane, she started crying hysterically. She didn't want me to leave home again. Mum had just retired from her job and was looking forward to having me around the house. After not seeing me much during my youth, I think she saw it as a chance to make up for lost time.

What could I do? My mother was upset. I couldn't be the cause of that. So I went back to Ronnie's office and told him he had a deal for 1988 and 1989.

As soon as I signed, I regretted it. I felt like I had cheated myself. I knew I'd made the wrong decision, but that was somehow preferable to upsetting Mum. Again, I wanted to please someone other than myself. It's not a healthy way to live life, because you just end up unhappy in the long run. And when you are not happy, how can those around you expect to be?

I rang Wayne straightaway and broke the news. He was stoic. He said, 'Well, you've made your decision and the important thing is not to have any regrets. Just get on with it.'

But I couldn't. It's not easy to recover from the worst decision of your life.

CHAPTER 11
HEADLESS CHICKEN

How ironic – here I was before the start of the 1988 season feeling bullied and helpless. In the past I had threatened and intimidated drug dealers and criminals, belted Islanders and thugs and thumbed my nose at the police. I was nothing short of a stand-over man in every respect. And now it was me who felt I had no choice. Not a day goes by when I don't wonder what might have been had I not caved in and signed with the Roosters. The regret was particularly harsh during my third jail stint, where I had four-and-a-half years to reflect. It was by far the biggest stuff-up I had ever made.

The one consolation that I did manage to salvage was a bit of revenge on Steve Ghosn's behalf. By the end of 1987, I loved him like a brother and was appalled at his sacking by Wests. The club had done little to support him during his two-year tenure, recruiting only journeymen and rejects. What else did they expect but a wooden spoon? When I signed for Easts, I neglected to tell Wests for about a month that I was going elsewhere. Thinking I was still a chance to stay, the directors wined and dined me. I lapped it up with my fingers crossed behind my back. My duplicity was also personally motivated, because I knew a large number of these turncoats had tried to block me from coming to the club in 1986 when Steve approached them. They took me out for three or four expensive meals, thinking they could convince me to stay. I took great satisfaction when the time came to eventually break the news that I was headed elsewhere, even if it was to a club I genuinely didn't want to go to.

I don't want this to reflect badly on the Roosters. I'd be saying the same thing had I joined any of the other Sydney clubs instead of Brisbane. Although they had no juniors, Easts didn't have too bad a feel about them at the beginning of 1988. They'd finished one game shy of the grand final the previous season and confidence was high. There was a very solid, no-nonsense bunch of blokes at the club back then – tough guys like David Trewella, Trevor 'The Axe' Gillmeister and Hugh McGahan.

And then there was Big Arthur Beetson, our coach. I clicked with Big Artie from the start. Again, it was a case of two rogues finding one another. Big Artie loved a punt and owned the Big House Hotel at Darling Harbour back in those days. After trading hours ceased, he'd close the doors and selected people would head upstairs for all-night games of Manilla. I couldn't believe I'd found a coach who shared my passion for gambling. I was the only Easts player who joined in alongside the colourful characters who'd splash their money around. Unfortunately for Arthur, he wasn't the most accomplished card player. I can't remember him finishing in the black too many times.

HEADLESS CHICKEN

Those card nights were the worst thing I got into as I prepared for my first game in the tricolour. I was still on the straight and narrow, although Danny Karam and the nightclub owner were lurking in the background. I noticed that when I went out in the Cross or Oxford Street, I'd be ushered straight to the front of the queue and given free drinks inside. That was Danny and his mate looking after me, keeping me in the family. A few opportunities came my way but I knocked them back out of determination to make 1988 a success on the field. To Danny's credit, he never exerted any force on me to comply. Had he done so, I probably would have folded because I could be so easily led.

I first met Arthur at Centennial Park before the rest of the players had resumed training in October 1987. I was doing extra sprint training with another recruit from Wests, a young winger called Jason Williams, who would later go on to win a premiership at Canterbury. Beetson was impressed with our dedication and made his feelings clear. He was an excellent communicator, but also possessed a good grasp of strategy and planning. The Roosters also surrounded him with excellent people like the veteran conditioner Ronnie Palmer, who stayed at the club for another 20 years. Former dual international Russell Fairfax was the reserve-grade coach.

The expertise they provided was a reflection of how professional the Roosters were compared to their rivals. With an abundance of money from multi-millionaire chairman Nick Politis, the players wanted for nothing. We had the best equipment, the best training facilities. Everything was state of the art compared to the humble set-up at Wests. Politis, who still remains chairman at Bondi, made his fortune as a car salesman. But first and foremost he was a passionate

Roosters fan, willing to invest seemingly infinite sums of money to ensure his boys had the best possible chance.

I enjoyed the off-season until Artie came up and told me I was going to start the season at prop. I had never played anywhere else but second row or lock, so it was a big call. But I accepted the challenge and bulked up in preparation for my new position. Our first trial was against Balmain at Leichhardt Oval. Warren Ryan had moved to the Tigers that season, replaced by Phil Gould at Canterbury. There was always a little bit extra when I came up against one of the Wok's teams, because I knew how well drilled they would be.

And guess what happened? I fractured my cheekbone after 30 minutes. It seemed everything had come full circle from six years earlier when I did my ankle in that first trial for Newtown. Dr Neil Halpin was even on hand to treat me again. Talk about déjà vu. Dr Halpin said it was a bad fracture and ruled me out for eight weeks.

I should have known from experience that injuries and solitude eventually lead to trouble. But I elected to ignore previous experience. They say the definition of madness is doing the same thing over and over again and hoping for a different result. If that's the case, then I should have been declared a certified lunatic because I again took the easy option. Sulking and dirty on rugby league, I became bored and let the lust for excitement wash over me. I didn't need a regular job because the money at the Roosters was so good. Going back to working with Danny and his crew to fill in the free time seemed like a natural thing to do.

This time, however, I began to do my own work. I'd formed a crew with some of the people I met during my first stretch in Long Bay as a teenager. The intervening years had

HEADLESS CHICKEN

seen them follow a similar path to mine – one strewn with warehouse break-ins and even credit card fraud. I was more interested in collects and SP bookmaking. So I got some of the boys together and we started doing jobs on behalf of people who were out of pocket.

I had one personal rule in this line of work: never take the same crew twice. The rest I learned from Danny Karam, one of the best in the business. It was essential to be well prepared. So before we hit the road, I asked plenty of discreet questions about my target.

When we met them my manner would always start out reasonably. I'd say something like, 'Look, Mr X, we both know you owe this money so why don't we just settle it here and now and get the whole thing out of the way.' Rarely did the person agree straightaway. They'd usually deny knowledge or feign ignorance. At this point I'd up the ante slightly, but not too much. 'Look, Mr X,' I'd say, 'we're going around in circles here. There's a hard or an easy way of doing this. I know we'd both prefer the easy way, so why are we waiting?' From then on they'd usually gather that we weren't going away peacefully until a repayment plan had been finalised. An agreement was nearly always reached there and then. The only real trouble I had was from Con the Greek, who needed a trip in the car boot and a go at digging his own grave to be convinced.

I was again having the time of my life on the dark side, making big bucks and spending up even bigger at the trots or on the town. Football started to become irrelevant again.

When my cheekbone healed, Artie rushed me straight back into first-grade to take on the Sharks. My return straight to the top didn't come as a huge surprise, because the Roosters were really struggling by that stage. Like

Wests the season before, they just couldn't win tight games. We were competitive, but not winners. Injuries also played a role and Arthur rarely fielded the same team two weeks in a row. I played three more games before being wiped out completely with a knee injury against Illawarra at the Sydney Football Stadium. That afternoon summed up how dismal things were getting at the Roosters.

The club had moved into the newly-built 40,000-seater stadium that season along with Souths. But because we were playing so poorly, we'd be lucky to have 5,000 people come and watch. In such a huge arena, the atmosphere was soulless. It certainly didn't inspire you like a packed suburban ground and I can completely understand why so many of the games at ANZ Stadium these days are pretty much unwatchable. How on earth can the players expect to rise to the occasion with 75,000 empty seats staring back at them? It's soul-destroying.

My knee injury launched me back onto the streets with gusto. At the time it was kind of a blessing, because football had become secondary to my crew. All of a sudden I didn't care. The resentment and spite of being persuaded to join the Roosters against my will had manifested itself in ambivalence towards the club and the game. With the Roosters out of finals contention, my attention turned towards the other teams.

After a disappointing 1987 under Ryan, the Bulldogs were again challenging in their first season under Phil Gould. Knowing some of the players at Belmore, I was given a quiet tip that they were training harder than ever two weeks out from September. My old coach at Souths, Ron Willey, confirmed the good oil. Willey had moved to Penrith that season and his boys were also in line for a finals spot. He maintained the Bulldogs were a sure thing for the premiership.

That was good enough for me. I marched into Ronnie Jones's office and demanded a $20,000 advance on my contract for the following season. It was an audacious and somewhat arrogant request, but Ronnie didn't flinch. I remember he gave me the lot in crisp $20 notes. As soon as I got the money, I rang around a few SP bookmakers and managed to back the Bulldogs at 9/2. Because it was such a big bet, the bookie wanted the $20,000 up front. I handed it over without question. As the finals progressed, it was clear who the Bulldogs' main rival would be. Although Cronulla won the minor premiership that year, Balmain had hit form at the right time. They embarked on a golden run through September, qualifying for the finals in a midweek play-off against Penrith before winning three straight semis to make it to the decider.

The Bulldogs did it easier. They brushed past the toothless Sharks in the major semi to earn a week's rest before the grand final. I actually caught that game live at the SFS with my old mate Peter Rix and a few of the boys I was knocking about with. Peter had good tickets on the halfway line and invited me to go along with him. So when I arrived in the car with a load of crims, he looked a little bemused.

We got to the ground a couple of hours before kick-off and Peter made for the general entry gate. But I wasn't interested in doing things by the book. No matter what the occasion, I always wanted to buck the system. I got a kick out of going where I wasn't meant to be. Rules were made to be broken and I was on a mission to break every one of them, even if the result wasn't as desirable as playing it straight.

So instead of enjoying the match on halfway I grabbed

Peter and marched up to the bloke at the door of the members' area. I didn't even look at him as I attempted to barge straight in. This was my go in those days – I felt entitled to anything. I was reckless and didn't care, despite being a well-recognised footballer. The bloke on the gate knocked us back and I gave him a bit of a gobful. No worries then. I just went straight to the next gate – still on crutches from my knee injury – with even more bravado.

This time we swanned straight in, with Peter complaining the whole way about why I couldn't be content to use his perfectly good tickets. I ignored him and led the group down to the fence and onto the field. Peter was white as a ghost but no-one stopped us. Because the SFS was the Roosters' home ground, I knew my way around. I marched the boys up the tunnel, at the end of which lay a private elevator that could take us up to the members' area.

For me, it was all about conquest, about proving people wrong. When the bloke on the door barred us, it only made me more determined. Once there, instead of staying in the members' bar, we climbed the top deck and perched ourselves behind Russell Fairfax, the Roosters' reserve grade coach. He was on duty at the time, with Easts having made the second-grade major semi. As soon as we sat down I made Peter get coffees for Russ and me. The look on Peter's face was priceless.

Even though Balmain was everyone's fairytale team and had Ryan on their side, I was supremely confident of Canterbury's chances on grand final day. The Bulldogs were short-priced favourites and there was a temptation to lay off on the Tigers at 2/1. I spoke to Ron Willey and he said I'd just be wasting my money. He remained adamant that Canterbury were sure things. But when Benny Elias scored

HEADLESS CHICKEN

the first try to put Balmain ahead I wasn't feeling so good. I was watching on TV at Mum's house and started calling my own namesake – who would very soon become a close mate – every name under the sun. The Bulldogs, however, were too well drilled. Balmain had done their dash just getting there and fell away as the match wore on. Final score: Canterbury 24, Balmain 12.

A $90,000 win for yours truly, by far my biggest at that stage of my life. The things I could have done with that amount of money in 1988 were mind-boggling. I could have bought two houses outright. But that was too easy, too straight. At a glance, I reckon I gave half of it back to the bookies at the races and trots in the ensuing months. The rest was squandered on partying and prostitutes for my mates. It was easy come, easy go. I did it for the buzz and, once the money arrived, the thrill disappeared, leaving only a desire to get rid of the cash as soon as possible and start all over again. I thrived on life on the edge, and if I had too much money then I would be too comfortable. I'd get bored, something I was easily prone to do but found impossible to tolerate.

By that time gambling was beginning to control my life. It was more important than football, more important than collects. The only crossover between rugby league and gambling were the weekly card games at Artie's hotel. Poor old Artie. He was the nicest bloke and the best Gin player I've ever seen, but whenever we played Manilla poker he was no match for the sharks that swam through his saloon door. And pretty soon he would be gobbled up by the Roosters as well.

Nick Politis didn't become a successful man without making hard decisions along the way. The Roosters' performance in 1988 – a near-bottom finish – simply wasn't acceptable. Artie became the fall guy and was sacked in favour of Russell Fairfax for 1989. Another coach I admired and respected had fallen by the wayside. Artie was a great motivator and had some unique methods. As a big man, his appetite was famous and he'd bring doughnuts and coffee for us to enjoy after training on Saturdays. He might not have been as professional as a Warren Ryan, but there wasn't a bloke at the Roosters who didn't respect or listen to his instructions. He was naturally pretty bitter about the way things finished up and I couldn't help but feel the same.

Artie's sacking was the final straw in 1988. I ended that year more disillusioned with rugby league than ever. I didn't even care if I played another game. I was possessed by the punt and couldn't think about anything else.

Finally, I had discovered a way to beat the bookies at their own game.

CHAPTER 12

HOT TO TROT

As I told my friends who owed other people money, there's always an easy and a hard way to do business. It's simply a matter of choice. The same applies to making a quick buck. Since I entered the world of crime, I had made my living off robberies and collects. Both provided the thrill I lusted after along with wads of easy cash that funded my crazy lifestyle and gambling habit. But they carried a high risk of being caught and sent back to prison. A safer, more calculated option was out there. In fact, it had been sitting under my nose since I started going to harness race meetings with Peter Rix's old man as a kid.

By the time I joined Easts, I was a diehard at Harold Park trots on a Friday night. I had plenty of cash thanks to the Roosters' generosity and the proceeds of my other line of work. But it was money I didn't respect. In short, I was a terrible punter. Through the connections I had made as an SP bookmaker, I thought I had some inside knowledge on the trots. I'd load up on certain tips I thought were certainties and more often than not I'd be left with a big hole in my pocket that could only be repaired by selling suits from the back of a truck outside after the last race.

I seemed to be donating all my money to the bookmakers and it pissed me off. As I got really immersed in the trots, I started to realise that the bookies had information about certain runners whose chances had been influenced by a prohibited substance or a bribe. In my eyes, they were profiting from a rort at my expense. I figured if it was good enough for them, then it was good enough for me. Two can play at this little game, I thought.

In 1988 I had begun to get close to the former Dragons star Harry Eden. Everyone in rugby league knew Harry was a bit of a knockabout. He had done his fair share of SP bookmaking and had a much better idea of how the trots really worked than I did. He held bets for none other than Robert Trimbole, the notorious Mafia figure from Griffith. While other punters used SPs to bet on credit, Trimbole paid up sums of $50,000 in cash. Harry made a great earn from Trimbole's custom, skimming the top whenever he obtained bigger odds than the agreed rate. In time, Trimbole uncovered Harry's game and there could have been drama. The Italian, however, couldn't care less because his tips always won.

Harry and I also did a few debt collections together and after a while we decided to go 50-50 in any SP bookmaking work we conducted. In a very short time, he taught me the ins and outs of how trots races were corrupted. Back then, there was a ridiculous amount of rorting that went on. Everyone was in on it – trainers, drivers, bookmakers and stewards. The only poor bugger who didn't know any better was the good ol' punter doing his hard earned cold at the TAB. I truly feel sorry for anyone outside the loop who bet on the trots in those days. They were being taken for a very expensive ride.

I can still recall the night the crew and I met for dinner and decided that enough was enough. We had enough connections to beat the bookies at their own game and we decided to blow them away. Over the next three years I'm certain we were responsible for reducing the number of bagmen at Harold Park from 50 to five.

In my eyes, the bookmaker who seemed to be really cleaning up was a bloke called Tony Gorman. He was a smug bastard who thought he knew everything about the game. He was the first bookie to use the computer form that is commonplace nowadays, but I was later to learn that he also organised help in different places. Most of my money ended up in Gorman's satchel and it seemed like I was not alone. An owner by the name of Glenn – we nicknamed him Shami – and a trainer called Balmain Greg were also filthy on Gorman. It seemed that every time he won, he'd smile and be smug. But as soon as the punters got one over him, he'd rush off and have a whinge to the stewards.

Over time, Shami, Balmain Greg and I decided to form a little syndicate and make some money. This sport was corrupt to the core, with up to four or five runners dosed up to the eyeballs with performance-enhancers in a single race.

They were known as 'milkshakes' in the industry. The mixture was based on a combination of bicarb of soda and water, but different chemicals were thrown in for greater impact. A common one was Palfium, which was a narcotic analgesic used to treat cancer patients. It was a primitive form of EPO, the new buzz drug all the stewards are on the lookout for these days. Stanozolol – the same substance disgraced Olympic sprinter Ben Johnson tested positive for – was another favourite. The milkshakes made the horses impervious to pain and exhaustion, so they simply kept running. They didn't go any quicker, but they didn't tire either, which meant that if your runner got the lead it was almost certain to win. Back then there was hardly any testing and the procedures were so antiquated that a simple masking agent could be used to get around the blokes in lab coats.

The milkshake, or 'elephant juice', as it was also known, was fed to the horse through a tube into the nostril as near as possible to the start of a race. On one memorable occasion a certain trainer was on the way to the course when he pulled over to administer the milkshake in the float. A passing steward saw his car pulled over and stopped to give assistance, thinking the trainer must have broken down. The steward then saw what was going on in the float and a huge penalty resulted.

But penalties were exceptions rather than the rule in that era, because most of the stewards were being paid off to lay off. The winner of every race was swabbed, but there were all sorts of rumours about stewards tampering with the evidence or urinating in vials themselves. When the levels of rorting were finally exposed, several stipes were hauled before an ICAC (Independent Commission Against Corruption) investigation and sacked.

Because Shami owned horses and had been part of the scene for some time, he had plenty of contacts. While there's no such thing as a certainty in gambling, there were ways to stack the odds in your favour.

With a good connection to a particular chemist you could

get the best drugs available, new and exotic substances that the stewards didn't even know existed. If they were unaware of the drug, then how could they test for it?

But doping horses alone was not enough, as so many trainers were doing it. Another key was to get the lead, because doped-up horses didn't tire. This could usually be secured by paying off the driver of a fancied chance to allow your trotter to take up the running. Drivers in the city could usually be bought for between $300 and $500 a race. In the country, it was considerably cheaper. They'd settle for a steak dinner instead of their usual Vegemite sandwich at the local RSL afterwards.

Our gang eventually grew to about 10 and once we got control there was nothing that could stop us. We had some very profitable years at the trots between 1988 and 1993. But things tightened up with the ICAC inquiry, which signalled the end of our party.

During the heyday, however, the money was so good that I didn't need to do any other work. I hardly did a debt collect in the years that I was frequenting the trots. We fixed up so many races and pulled off so many results it wasn't funny.

Arguably the most memorable came on Miracle Mile night at Harold Park in 1992. Back then the trots were huge and there was a crowd of 25,000 on course to witness the biggest race of the year. More importantly for us, there were also dozens of bookmakers ripe for the picking. The horse we fancied that night was having its first start for Balmain Greg in Sydney, a nag called Levin Helm. Greg had the poor thing juiced up to the eyeballs with who knows what and let us in on the secret. Levin Helm had terrible form leading into the race and was posted at odds of 7/1.

We had to be careful about not making a plunge look too

obvious, because it never took bookmakers long to realise who we were and what we were up to. So our little trick was to personally throw $2,000 on something that couldn't win and then get our girlfriends or an anonymous scab to lay the real big money on the one we knew was going to salute. That smug Gorman thought he was taking my money, but little did he know that his mounting losses were coming back to us.

That's exactly what happened with Levin Helm that evening. The poor thing raced three wide and then dashed away in the straight to score a commanding victory. All things being equal, it's simply not possible for a trotter to race three wide and win pulling away. I recall that Ray Hadley was commentating that night and made mention of us celebrating as Levin Helm saluted. 'And there's Johnny Elias and the boys cheering down on the fence,' Ray yelled across the PA. We bumped into Ray upstairs afterwards and he gave us a wink as if to say he knew exactly what had happened.

But we weren't the only ones trying to fix races. The bookmakers were just as determined and when a race came up that saw us in a bidding war to bribe a driver, that's when things got really interesting. Such an occasion arose at Penrith one Thursday night. A couple of days before the meet, Shami approached a certain driver and offered him $1,000 – big money – to hand up the lead to our horse. The driver was known to be close to Gorman, but agreed. Unknown to us, Gorman then offered him money to attack our horse. The bloke, being loyal to Gorman and not wanting to arouse his suspicions, jumped ship.

When we arrived on track just before the race, another bloke came over and said the driver wanted to tell us something urgently. He was obviously trying to relay a message for us not to have a bet, but we ignored the messenger because there wasn't much time left to get on. So, none the wiser, we each had $15,000 on our horse thinking we had the driver in our keeping. You don't need a vivid imagination – or vocabulary – to imagine our reaction as the driver proceeded to do the opposite of what we paid him to do. Instead of handing up the lead, he attacked our horse. It tired from the early pace and fell away badly at the finish. Furious does not begin to describe how we felt. In short, the driver would be lucky to get away from Penrith alive.

We were sitting in the bar looking very mean when he approached us. 'You got my message, didn't you?' he asked. 'They told you I was going to attack and not to have a bet, didn't they?' We looked at him and shook our heads. His face went white and he immediately tried to rectify the situation. He gave us a 'certain' tip for the next race in return for the mix-up. Fortunately for this fellow, his tip came good and we got our money back. But it was a close call for him that night.

As you can see from that story, there's never a sure thing in racing – even when you go to all that trouble to fix a race. Greg was notorious and received a couple of big suspensions when he eventually got caught. He has since been run out of the game.

There were other trainers who were even more brazen. We knew a guy who took a horse to Maitland one night and gave it cocaine. And he gave it a good whack. He acted so brazenly because he knew the steward who was overseeing the meet was in his pocket. But disaster loomed when that steward got sick and another stipe turned up instead. By the time he found out that his man was not at the meeting, it was too late. The horse had been well and truly coked up. It won by a country mile and was routinely swabbed.

The trainer was beside himself with worry. The results would reveal cocaine, which was sure to deliver him a three- or four-year suspension. He was left with one option. At the end of the meet the stewards would carry the samples to their car and lock them in the boot. Somehow, he had to steal the swab and destroy the evidence.

We were at the meet and he asked for our help. Because the guy had been good to us, we agreed to help and try to steal the swabs. When the steward left Maitland we followed him all the way home to Sydney. He lived in Five Dock, near former world champion boxer Jeff Fenech. Because it was a night meet, he didn't get home until well after midnight. We waited for the steward to go to sleep and then broke into the boot. Thankfully, the swabs were still there. Our friend's problem was solved.

But it would never happen like that again. The theft caused such a huge controversy that the Harness Racing Authority ordered all swabs to be transported by security guards from then on.

Within a year, our notoriety at the track was beginning to grow. We kicked about with all sorts, including a promising young player from Souths called Terry Hill, the boxer Jeff Harding and a rich kid in his early 20s from the Central Coast called Eddie Hayson.

The latter has gone on to become one of the biggest punters in Australia and shot to fame when he pulled off an ingenious betting plunge on a greyhound race in Adelaide in 2005. Eddie is now one of Sydney's more colourful characters, with his big-betting lifestyle, and owns one of the city's finest brothels, Stilettos at Camperdown.

But back then Eddie was only a kid looking for a buzz. There were plenty of them around, but the difference with Eddie – who also came from a Lebanese family – was that his mother was loaded. She made her wealth from a couple of shopping centres in Fairfield and Northbridge. Eddie never wanted for money, but always wanted to be one of the boys. He was hooked on the punt and I believe he was also fascinated by the gangster lifestyle.

We liked Eddie not for his money but for who he was. He shared our values – when he said something it was the truth, he didn't squeal and he could party hard. He also started out as a mug punter like the rest of us. When he first hit the scene, Eddie would think nothing of losing $10,000 at a meet. The next day he'd be scrounging about for $50 to buy petrol. It was a rollercoaster we had all ridden, so we took Eddie into the group at Harold Park and he remains a mate to this day.

Balmain Greg used to direct most of our betting and at times I found his methods a little infuriating. For example, I hated going to far-flung country towns for a bet. I found the seven-hour drives boring and what's more they increased the pressure for us to win big. Time, after all, is money. Looking back, however, I can appreciate why Balmain Greg had to spread his risk. Things were already a bit dicey with us hitting Harold Park so often. We needed to spread out a bit and visit bookies that didn't have a clue who we were.

One day Balmain Greg told us we were off to Dubbo to back a thing called Meggsy Campbell at the Western Derby. I whinged because it was a long, hot drive but Greg said: 'Mate, money is money – whether it comes from the bush or in town.' We arrived in Dubbo before the race on a Saturday and Greg paid one of the drivers $500 to hand over the lead to Meggsy, which was also geared up on milkshakes. We backed the thing in from 5/1 to 6/4 and were certain it could not get beaten. I just wanted to get the money and go home.

Meggsy rushed straight to the lead and things were looking sweet until one of the back tyres blew towards the end of the first lap. It wrapped around the axle, and all hope appeared lost. I started cursing and swearing because we'd come all this way just to lose a whole lot of money. Meggsy was racing on a steel rim, digging up dirt and dust as she dragged the sulky along. It was an appalling sight but somehow she was still in front at the 600 m mark. Her lead was cut to a nose at the 400 m and I was still certain she couldn't win. Then at the 200 m she was a half-head in front. Surely this couldn't be happening? My spirits were resurrected and we cheered like giddy schoolgirls as Meggsy won by a head.

I don't know what Balmain Greg put in the milkshake that day, but it sure was some potent stuff to make a horse break the course record on rims. Four bookmakers had to pack up and go home straight after that race because they were stone broke after our sting.

It didn't take long for our reputations to precede us wherever we went. When we turned up at a track the bookmakers would be ready for a sting. One night at Newcastle, Balmain Greg had this pacer Mercy Dash ready for a hit. Its recent form was terrible. On that alone it should've opened up at 25/1, but instead the starting price was 5/1. This was simply unacceptable, because although Greg had trained the horse hard as well as having paid off another driver to hand up the lead, it was no certainty to win.

Sensing a sting, the punters kept coming for Mercy Dash and with five minutes to go its price was totally prohibitive – something like 2/1. We went onto the track and Shami told the driver: 'Not tonight.' That was a signal for him not to hand up the lead to Mercy Dash because we weren't going to have a bet.

There must be a lot of loose lips in Newcastle, because somehow word got round that the fix was off. All of a sudden there was a huge plunge on another horse, pushing Mercy Dash's price back out to 8/1. The bookmakers didn't know what to think – they'd never seen anything like it. Suddenly, the odds were long enough for us to have a go. All we needed to do was get word out to the driver that the fix was on again. With a minute left, we rushed out to the track but only one horse was still warming up near the fence. It was driven by a bloke called Daryl. Shami called him over and promised $300 just to relay the 11th-hour change of plans to our driver before they started. Daryl agreed and we raced back to the ring to lay our bets. Mercy Dash won by 20 lengths.

Stacking the odds so that our horses won wasn't the only way to make a buck. Sometimes other owners or trainers would approach us to hand over the lead. One example involved Levin Helm, once again at Harold Park. A big punter called Carlo got in Shami's ear about one of his horses, Guitar Of The Law. Carlo was planning to have a huge go at Guitar Of The Law at 10/1 and wanted Levin Helm, the 2/1 favourite, to back down at the start. Because Levin Helm was so short, it represented no value for us, so we were happy to agree to Carlo's request. He told Shami that his boys would back Guitar Of The Law before we got on. Shami agreed, but in truth, all bets were off. As soon as the odds were posted we sent our touts in to have big money on Guitar Of The Law. Had we waited for Carlo, its price would have halved. We owed him nothing, and he was filthy when he only got 4/1.

We were pretty smug as the race began, knowing our driver had been paid to pull Levin Helm up. He did a good job, too, easing it to the back as Guitar Of The Law took up the running. Then disaster struck. It was late in the day and shadows stretched across the track. Pacers often get spooked by the shadows and try to jump them, so at this time of day most trainers will equip them with a shadow roll. But for some reason the dope who trained Guitar Of The Law neglected to do this. When it reached the first shadow, Guitar Of The Law reared and began to break up. The sting had collapsed because of some trainer's idiocy. Levin Helm ended up winning and I couldn't blame our driver when he leaned over the fence after the race and whispered: 'Johnny, three cheers is better than three years.'

Generally, though, it took something extraordinary like that for us to lose. It really was a golden period that saw me become a bit of a punting genius among my teammates. I'd occasionally tip the boys off, but I never told them what was really going on. After a big win we'd regularly go and celebrate at the Leichhardt gambling den owned by one of Sydney's more notorious characters of that era, Bruce Harding. Bruce was bald and wore glasses, but his looks were deceiving. On one particular evening I suggested to one of his many glamorous female friends that Bruce must be a very generous sugar daddy. 'Don't let the glasses and bald head fool you,' she replied. 'He's the best lover around.'

But good times can't last forever and things began to tighten up around 1992 when the ICAC stepped in. More than a decade later two stewards, Roger Nebauer and Paul

Archer, were forced to stand down when evidence emerged that they were dealing with a suspended trainer.

Balmain Greg's tricks had also caught up with him and he was suspended for four years. It was obvious the party was over, a party that had raged well beyond what we could have dreamed. By the time we left the scene, our old mate Gorman was a mess. We had really cleaned him up. Whenever one of our horses led into the straight, we'd all start yelling 'Get it ready, Gorman! We're on our way, Gorman!' Towards the end he became desperate and started to accompany us to dinner, begging to be let into the crew. But it was never going to happen.

I did, however, come extremely close to doing him a favour of another kind. Gorman used to field at Penrith on Thursday nights, a meeting that was extremely popular with the local league side, the Panthers, in 1991. A lot of the players used to go for a bet, but their bets were not as big nor as frequent as those laid by their coach during that season, the one and only Gus Gould. Gus would prance around the track in 1991 – his first season at Penrith – wearing his liquorice all-sorts Dahdah Uniforms tracksuit. He bet big and regularly with Gorman, but started to get behind on his repayments. Every time we saw Tony he would complain to us about Gus's debts and how the famous coach refused to settle.

I remember one night at Penrith seeing Gould and then immediately hearing Gorman yelling out to him. The tiny bookmaker – who was so paranoid that he even carried a gun on course – chased Gus and fronted him for the money. 'Pay me what you owe,' Gorman yelled in front of everyone. 'Or I'll go to the papers.'

Gus continued to fob him off and Tony was at his wits'

end. Then the offer came through Shami. He went over to Gorman and mentioned my other line of work – debt collection. He said, 'If you want we can get Johnny to pay Gus a little visit.' Gorman thought about it and told us to give him a week.

I would have had no hesitation in putting the hard word on Gus. After all, we needed Gorman to stay in the game for our own profits. Bookmakers were dropping left, right and centre because of all the rorts those days and the lack of competition meant shorter odds all round. Tony never did ask me to do the deed because Gus finally paid him back after landing a huge collect on the gallops soon after. He also got the trifecta in the Melbourne Cup 10 times over.

But my showdown with Gus was still to come. In 1995 he moved from Penrith to Bondi to coach the Roosters, where a good mate of mine, Nat Wood, was playing. During that off-season Nat and Gus became very close. Gus would put his arm around Nat and tell him how much he thought of him as a player and what a big season they were going to have together.

Just before the 1995 season started I was out with the Rabbitohs rogue Darrell Trindall, when we decided to meet Nat at Bondi Junction. He'd been drinking with Gus and Roosters supremo Nick Politis. We all headed to a bar called Archies. When we got inside, Gus took Nat aside for a very private heart-to-heart.

But little did he know I was sitting close behind and could hear every word he said. Gus was also facing a mirror, so I could watch him speak as well. Gus proceeded to again tell Nat how much he admired him and what great things they were going to do together. Then he said: 'But there's one condition: you have stop hanging around that John Elias.

He's bad news.' I could see everything Gus was saying and the red mist began to rise. Nat protested, saying that his social life was off limits. 'Gus,' he said, 'I'll do whatever you tell me to do on the field, but I'll choose my own friends off it, thank you very much.'

Not impressed with the response, Gould sulked to the other end of the bar. I immediately went up to Nat and grilled him about what Gus had said. I was fuming, ready to belt the bloke's lights out. After all, Gus and I had played together at Newtown. I had never bad-mouthed him. Nat begged me to calm down, pleading that he had a three-year deal with the Roosters. He didn't want any trouble with the coach he'd have to play under for the next three seasons.

A couple of weeks later I bumped into Gus outside the Palace Hotel at Coogee. He greeted me with open arms and cried: 'Johnny, my brother!' I decided to cut to the chase. I demanded to know about him bad-mouthing me to Nat Wood. I was seething, because he wasn't man enough to tell me face-to-face about his concerns for Nat. Although it wouldn't have pleased me to hear that Gus didn't want us to be mates, I at least would have respected him for telling me straight. But he didn't have the guts.

I took off my jacket, squared up and said: 'Don't let fear hold you back.'

But Gus was too smart to throw one. He is a scholar, not a fighter. Looking back, I wish Gorman had given me the green light to pay Gus a visit. Maybe it would have changed his outlook and deflated his ego. He went about making Nat's life a misery at the Roosters in the conviction that Nat had given him up.

Although Gorman got paid by Gus, his days were

numbered. A couple of years later his body was found in the Royal National Park, south of Sydney. People said it was suicide, but people don't usually take their own lives in the middle of the bush.

CHAPTER 13
INTO THE EYE OF THE TIGER

Having discovered the easy money available at the trots, football became less and less relevant. Every time I put in the hard work, injury or suspension seemed to undo it all in a split second. It seemed such a randomly unfair way to make a living. At least with the trots, I was able to have a large degree of control over the outcome. With football, it seemed there was too much left in the lap of the gods. And the gods had no reason to smile on a sinner like me.

Towards the end of 1988 I became very laissez-faire at Easts. I remember playing cards at Arthur Beetson's pub all night and turning up for training with little or no sleep. I just didn't care and when Artie got the boot my last shred of motivation evaporated.

All of a sudden I saw the Roosters as the transit lounge club that everyone says they are. They had no juniors, no grassroots culture. All they had was a lot of money which enabled them to try and buy premierships. But it didn't buy spirit. I felt the club lacked the essential soul of the others I had played for, which had their own real identity. The Roosters lacked that special something that made you strive to put in that all-important extra one per cent.

Perhaps we were too pampered. Perhaps the spoon-fed lifestyle didn't suit me. I had always been a battler and that's why I enjoyed places like Newtown, Wests and Souths so much. Russell Fairfax took over as Roosters coach in 1989 and he was very inexperienced. I liked Russell – as all the players did – but in my opinion he was pitched into first-grade before his time. We had another poor season, never threatening to make the top five at any stage. I struggled to make any first-grade appearances and by the time May rolled around I was warming the bench for reserve grade for the first time in five years.

I should have been ashamed, but I didn't give two hoots. Our good times at the trots were all that mattered and I would have been more than happy to live, eat and sleep in the stables at Harold Park. I felt more like a professional gambler than a professional footballer.

Just before the cut-off date for mid-season transfers, Ronnie Jones summoned Jason Williams and me to his office. Jason was one of my companions on the bench for reserves. How funny it was to think how keen we were just 18 months earlier, doing voluntary sprint sessions at Centennial Park. I had changed into a different footballer – undisciplined, ambivalent and complacent.

Ronnie Jones knew it and wanted us both out of the place. He said we were taking up import spots and offered us a pay-out to go away. I couldn't say yes quickly enough.

I walked out of Easts Leagues Club feeling great. I was a free man – free to play the trots and not worry about football. I could have retired then and there. I was still in this blissful state when the phone rang a couple of days later. On the other end was Brian Slattery, the football manager at Balmain. Brian and I are still close – he even testified as a character witness in the Supreme Court on my behalf when I got into real trouble more than a decade later.

My old coach Warren Ryan, who was coaching at Balmain, had heard I'd been released from the Roosters and was interested in picking me up before the transfer window closed. I figured I had nothing to lose and signed on for incentives for the rest of 1989, with an option in my favour for 1990.

Balmain was a strong club in those days. They were runners-up the previous season and on course for another high-placed finish as autumn turned to winter. Their forward pack was one of the best in the league, featuring a host of representative stars like Steve 'Blocker' Roach, Wayne 'Junior' Pearce, Bruce McGuire, Paul Sironen and my old namesake Benny Elias.

I knew what to expect from Ryan, who was probably the most astute coach I've ever played under. But I didn't have much of an idea about the culture at Balmain. It was therefore a pleasant surprise to see that the joint was full of scallywags and knockabouts like me. OK, not quite like myself – but they appreciated a bit of fun and didn't turn their noses up at my reputation.

I felt like I belonged at Balmain more than any other club. The area was renowned for its knockabouts in those days before gentrification inundated Sydney Harbour's inner western peninsula with organic vegetables and hand-woven wicker baskets. The directors and CEO Keith Barnes – a great bloke I eventually would call Dad – didn't even mind when I occasionally sold a truckload of suits at training.

I immediately became close with Blocker and Sironen. Blocker is the toughest man I've ever seen play. The amount of punishment he withstood and then returned in those days was incredible. Off the field, he loved a laugh and a good time. He seemed to understand what I was about, revelling in the post-training 'excursions' I'd take the players on to an illegal casino down the road from Leichhardt Oval. I loved the man's honesty. If Blocker was mad, he couldn't contain himself.

I recall one time we were at a fundraiser when this comedian was getting some cheap laughs at Blocker's and my expense. He'd poke fun at Blocker's weight, pointing out that his wife should practise their lovemaking by hugging the fridge. The comedian then said, 'Thank God we're all safe tonight – John Elias is here. If anyone wants a suit, go see him in the car park afterwards.' I wasn't too bothered, in fact I found it rather amusing. But Blocker was fuming because the guy kept having a crack at his weight. After another gag, he couldn't take any more. The big fella jumped to his feet in front of what was a very well-dressed, high-class audience and began yelling and threatening the comedian. I was certain Blocker was about to get up on stage and flatten him in front of the whole room. I'm pretty sure the comedian felt the same because he ran off stage mid-routine and got out of there quick-smart.

Undoubtedly the player who inspired most respect was Wayne Pearce, our captain and lock. The man they call Junior was disciplined before his time. In fact, even if he was coming onto the scene in today's overly regimented era, I'd still call him a fitness revolutionary. In an age of drinking sessions and partying, Junior refused to touch a drop of alcohol. Instead, he'd have all these vitamin pills and supplements that he insisted were the secret of his success. Although he was a squarehead in a club comprised predominantly of jokers and knockabouts, everyone respected Junior because of his dedication and consistency.

Football really can be a great leveller for people from all walks of life, provided everyone gives it their best shot. That's something I regret. There were plenty of times in my career when I was content to sail through. Looking back, I let my teammates down on several occasions. I feel awful about this now, because the reason I started playing rugby league was for the camaraderie and mateship. During the periods that I strayed, I not only let down the other players but also myself. There's no shortage of people who now tell me how good a player I might have been if I'd applied myself properly. When your chance is over, nothing hurts more than knowing you didn't give it your all. Although I ended up playing nearly 150 first-grade games, I have to be honest and admit that I blew it. There's no-one else to blame but myself.

Warren Ryan knew me well when I started at Balmain. He'd coached me at both Newtown and Canterbury and immediately pulled me in to say he wasn't going to take any shit. He knew what I was capable of and demanded results. I took his rev-up as a show of faith and my inner switch again flicked on to football mode. Despite my laziness over the previous 18 months, I was now inspired to channel my energies into the game.

Within a few weeks Ryan drafted me into first-grade to cover for the big-name forwards on State of Origin duty. I performed well but could not keep the likes of McGuire, Pearce, Sironen and Edmed out of the side. So I played most of that season in reserve grade under Graham Murray, who would later go on to lead the Roosters and Cowboys to grand final appearances as well as coach New South Wales. By the end of the season I was sitting on the bench for every first-grade game. Ryan gave me the occasional run, but when the semis came around I couldn't get a look-in because everyone was fit.

Unlike the previous season, the Tigers didn't need a fairy-tale run to reach the grand final. We finished the season in second place behind Souths and were favoured among the bookies to avenge our 1988 grand final defeat. We accounted for Penrith in the first final and then upset Souths in a cracker at the SFS, 20–10, to earn a week off before the big one. The Rabbitohs were tipped to bounce back and force a re-match by beating Canberra in the preliminary final but they again lost, meaning we'd have to beat the Green Machine to win Balmain's first title in two decades.

The experience against Canterbury from 12 months earlier helped everyone to remain calm and Ryan, with an abundance of grand final experience, was an excellent influence over the younger backs like Tim Brasher and James Grant. Brasher was still in school back then and had set the media alight with his maturity during the finals series. Off the field, Tim was also well advanced for his years. He quickly cottoned onto what I was about and we've stayed close friends until this day. There was a feeling of destiny during the week leading up to the decider. We'd done our homework, left no stone unturned, and felt that victory was painted in the stars.

Game day. The first half went according to plan. We stuck to Ryan's strategy of playing the game through the middle, and held a comfortable 12–2 lead at the break. We were dominating the Raiders in every aspect and, if anything,

INTO THE EYE OF THE TIGER

we should have been ahead by more. Despite the scoreline, there was no sense of complacency in the sheds. The players were simply determined to go out and put their opponents to the sword over the next 40 minutes.

Then fate turned on us. Sitting on the bench, I had a front-row seat to arguably the best grand final finish in history. I'm certain we were the better team but external factors gave the Raiders a sniff. For one thing, we couldn't take a trick from referee Bill Harrigan. Every call seemed to go against us, including a big one to penalise Bruce McGuire while he was in possession. Canberra scored to make it 12–8, before a penalty goal gave us some breathing space. As the clock wound down we were still sitting pretty, so Benny Elias decided to take a field goal to give us a seven-point cushion. It hit the crossbar and rebounded – that was the first indication that it simply wasn't to be our afternoon. Then our five-eighth Mick Neill made a bust and looked certain to score and wrap up the game. Somehow, he was ankle-tapped by a fingernail and stumbled with the line wide open. That was the second indication that glory for Balmain was not part of the grand plan upstairs.

But the moment that created most debate was Ryan's decision to replace Blocker and Sironen, our two best forwards, with 20 minutes left. History and the weight of public opinion have forever condemned Ryan to damnation for taking them off. But, being part of the club at the time, I'm adamant that it didn't cost us the game. The thing that most people conveniently forget is that Wok had replaced both Sirro and Blocker at the same stage for our previous two finals appearances. No-one complained about it then, so there were definitely no surprises when they came off on that last Sunday in September.

I can't deny, however, that both players weren't happy. Who would be? It was, after all, practically the biggest game of their lives. The criticism of Ryan is unfounded. In my book, games are seldom won and lost on a single decision. I also recoil when people blame Anthony Mundine for costing St George Illawarra the 1999 grand final by dropping the ball over the try line with his team ahead 18–6 in the second half. Again, that was a lead that should never have been frittered away. Every member of the team has to take responsibility for letting it slip. Rugby league is a team sport and on that day the 17 players didn't do enough to ensure we went on with the job in the second half. The simple fact is that we should never have been in a position to lose from 12–2 up at halftime.

The shift in momentum that swept across the SFS that afternoon felt eerily tangible as the clock wound down to the final 10 minutes. On the bench, I could sense the game slipping away even though we were still ahead by six points. The boys began to panic, with our British import Andy Courier over-calling a bomb from bulletproof fullback Garry Jack. Courier proceeded to spill the ball, giving Canberra the chance they were waiting for. The invitation was accepted, with my old Newtown teammate John 'Chicka' Ferguson crossing to send the game into extra time.

Ryan tried his best to get the boys up for the extra 20 minutes, but we had Buckley's. Although I loved the boys to death and desperately wanted us to win, I knew deep down they were gone. Our best two forwards couldn't return and Canberra had all the momentum. In hindsight, we probably did well to hang in with a chance until the final few minutes, when unheard-of Raiders replacement Steve Jackson dragged what seemed like our entire team across the line to seal an epic 19–14 victory.

In the aftermath of such a famous game, much has been written about the devastation that hit Balmain Leagues Club in Rozelle that evening. We went back and mixed with the fans before sulking onto the Bourbon And Beefsteak in Kings Cross to drown our sorrows.

I remember Blocker getting angry at Garry Jack, whose wife kept ringing the bar asking for her husband to come home. Unable to contain himself, the big fella arced up at Jack and told him to ring his wife and tell her to quit calling. Jack went over and picked up the phone and began speaking. I thought nothing of it, but Blocker obviously knew him a bit better. He strode over and ripped the receiver out of Jack's hand. There was no-one on the other end.

Garry Jack was a funny sort of guy, whose relationship with the team was hard to describe. You couldn't help but respect him for the wholehearted way he went about his football. The bloke was pretty much the best defensive fullback ever to play the game. If our line was broken, no player got past him one-on-one. He was a freak in those situations.

But he did himself no favours with his penny-pinching ways. I've never met a bloke so obsessed with not spending money. He was so extreme that it got funny – even going as far as borrowing 40 cents to make that fake phone call to his missus after the 1989 grand final loss. Players who went on Kangaroo tours with him said he kept a stash of complimentary sponsors' beer in his hotel room that he would raid for his shouts at the bar.

Then there was a time when we caught a dodgy light plane to Canberra in 1990. One of the engines blew just after we took off and there was a fair bit of panic among the passengers. Garry, however, could see a buck in it. He sold life insurance at the time and began handing out the forms, trying to sign up blokes as they said their Hail Marys and uttered their final penances. I've got to say that spun me out a little.

I had an option to stay in 1990 and was keen to exercise it. Keith Barnes felt the same way about me, perhaps because he was suddenly very well dressed at a good price. Again, the warm feeling of home descended on me. I was more settled than I had been since my Brisbane Souths days. Off the field I had fallen into a routine at the trots, albeit a dubious one. Our chronic gambling, however, was less of a distraction than coming home from a collect at 4 am and then going to training.

Although most of the club was still in mourning when preparations began for 1990, I was raring to go. Because I didn't play in the grand final, I was spared the scars many of the players battled to heal before the 1990 campaign. Ryan handled things well that summer, taking us to Hawks Nest on the mid-north coast for a boot camp with an ex-SAS army dude. The 1980s were over and rugby league was starting to get very serious. There was more and more training and less and less time for blokes to hold jobs outside of footy. On that trip to Hawks Nest I recall playing practical jokes on the other players and officials with Benny and Blocker. I was really starting to feel at home and stamp my personality on the team. I had pretty much become the unofficial social co-ordinator, thanks to my mates at the casino and various card joints around town.

When the 1990 season began Ryan started me in first-grade for the opening match against Manly, a game I'll take to the grave with me. In fact, everyone who played that day will. It still goes down as the only time I've ever seen the referee offer both captains to abandon the match. On that steamy March afternoon a fierce lightning storm lashed the ground just after halftime, sending what was a capacity Leichhardt crowd in brilliant sunshine at kick-off fleeing for the exits. In no time hailstones were rocketing down. It was by far the worst storm I'd ever witnessed and here were 26 blokes trying to play a game of first-grade footy in the thick of it.

But there was never any doubt about continuing. Rugby league players are bred to soldier on. Even a player of average constitution prides himself on withstanding pain and some of the best stories revolve around guys who defy extraordinary injuries to stay on the paddock. Who, for example, can forget John Sattler leading Souths to grand final victory in 1971 with a broken jaw? I know of no other sport that stands testament to such bravery. That's why it always makes me shake my head when I watch a game of soccer and see those European and South American fleabags feigning injury for the sake of a penalty.

That day, however, we ended up losing narrowly to Manly, and followed up with another defeat in the second round. People inevitably started talking about a hangover from two straight grand final defeats.

But I couldn't see any signs of disillusionment and was convinced we had what it took to atone and proceed to snare victory in the grand final. Our season finally got on track with a win over Penrith in round three, a game in which I won man of the match. My form was suddenly back to near-best and all of a sudden the newspapers were taking notice.

Veteran league journo, the late Peter Frilingos, rang me one day for a story on my form reversal from the previous season with Easts. I always shot straight with reporters and told Peter my Mum had threatened to kick me out of home if I didn't have a big season in 1990. It was a true story. Mum could see I was wasting my career and at 27 I was now closer to the end than the beginning. Peter was rapt with the yarn and sent a photographer to the house to mock up a picture of Mum hitting me over the head with a frying pan. It ran on the front page the following day – a nice change from the usual stories linking me to notorious activities and criminals.

But the real headlines came after we played Wayne Bennett's Broncos at Leichhardt in round four. I was still mates with Bennett but by that stage the ship had sailed on me returning to Brisbane. It was a big game personally because a lot of the players I had lined up with or against in 1985 were part of those early Broncos teams. King Wally was still going around that season, although there were plenty of rumours about a rift between him and Wayne. Wally had been stripped of the captaincy that season and everyone was saying his days at the Broncos were numbered.

A huge crowd flocked to Leichhardt, partly because Balmain had never been beaten by the despised Queenslanders. During a tightly fought first half I remember taking the ball up and being met in a solid tackle by three Broncos players – Greg Dowling, Gene Miles and Wally Lewis. As I was trying to get to my feet I felt a finger gouge my eye. I was certain it was Wally. I must admit that I didn't see his finger, just felt it hooking into my eyeball. But something just told me it was him.

I got to my feet complaining about being gouged. Quick as a flash, Benny Elias demanded that I lodge an official complaint with the referee. Benny hated Wally from their

INTO THE EYE OF THE TIGER

clashes in State of Origin and would have loved nothing better than to see his nemesis be tainted with a suspension for gouging. I went through with the complaint because I was angry. I'd never been gouged in Australia before and felt it was off limits. In France, that kind of stuff happened regularly but it was a different set of rules. There was no tolerance for grubby acts like gouging, spitting and biting in Australia and that's the way it should be. The complaint was a huge deal, even for the rest of the match. Wally was usually verballed mercilessly at the best of times, but our boys went at him with unprecedented venom after that.

Then something very strange happened after halftime. Broncos forward Mark Hohn lodged a complaint to the referee that I had eye-gouged him. It was about as true as those charges for stabbing that bus driver all those years ago. Video evidence would later show that I was nowhere near the tackle in which Hohn claimed to be gouged. But he still made the claim. We won the game, but I walked off in a foul mood. Why would Hohn lie?

Then it became apparent. As all the players walked up the tunnel, Wally trotted up alongside me with an offer. 'If you drop your complaint against me, I'll get Mark to drop his against you,' he muttered.

I laughed and told him to get lost. There was no way I was willing to play such a game because I knew I had never gouged Hohn. I can honestly say I never gouged anyone in my entire career. But the significant thing about my little chat with Wally was that it convinced me he was the gouger. My loose suspicions had set to a firm belief because he had taken the trouble of trying to strike a deal. He obviously had something to hide.

When the story about Wally's offer broke, it was massive

news. His iconic image was suddenly at stake. There are few worse slurs on a footballer's reputation than being branded an eye-gouger. Wally was one of the all-time greats and, if he was found guilty at the judiciary, it would have tarnished his standing in the game. The hearing was set down for NSWRL headquarters in Phillip Street on the Tuesday night following the game. It was the only story the newspapers were talking about. Reporters called me incessantly and I continued to maintain that Wally had eye-gouged me.

Of all the phone calls I received in those two days between the match and the hearing, the most telling came from Wayne Bennett. He had one question: 'John, tell me the honest truth – did Wally do it?' I told him the truth about the tackle and Wally's offer afterwards. As always, Wayne gave very little away after fielding my response. He just said thanks and hung up. I don't know what he was thinking, but his silence led me to believe that he was doing a bit of due diligence on Wally's character. The rumours were stronger than ever that Queensland's favourite son was on the verge of parting ways with its beloved Broncos.

There were enough cameras at the judiciary hearing to look as if the paparazzi were there. My charges against Hohn were immediately dismissed when the panel watched the video and couldn't sight me in the tackle. Then came Wally's moment of truth. The tackle on me was replayed numerous times, but in those days there were only limited camera angles. None of the angles conclusively showed him eye-gouging me. It came down to my word against his. The panel simply could not find him guilty based on my testimony alone – they needed either a witness or some conclusive footage. They had neither, so Wally was exonerated. I had to accept the result. I've sat in front of my fair share of real hearings, and have learned a little bit about what standard of proof is required to declare someone guilty. The proof obviously wasn't there, so Wally is innocent. And I didn't hold a grudge against him. The man still remains the best player I've ever seen play.

I played the first 11 games of that season as we kept pace with the competition front-runners. Because I was beginning to get on a bit of a roll, I should have known that something bad was about to happen to bring me down to earth. And so it did. Midway through the season we travelled to Cronulla, where I had to go off the field with a mystery injury to my groin. I didn't think a whole lot of it until the following morning when I simply couldn't walk. It was one of the most painful things I've ever felt. Every movement below the belt resulted in agony. I was stranded.

What I didn't tell the Tigers medical staff was that I had spent some time between the sheets with a young lady the previous evening. I'd had a funny feeling that might have exacerbated the injury, although there was no warning of what was to come when we hopped into bed the night before. My new female friend also happened to be a masseuse and her hands tried everything they knew the following morning. But it was to no avail.

The pain was so bad that I resorted to visiting my old pal, Dr Neil Halpin, at Auburn. The doctors at Balmain had no idea. Neil was the first one to tell me I had an inflamed pubic bone. The condition is known as osteo pubis and required seven weeks rest in bed. I was out for the year. Great, I thought. I can't even get out to the trots, let alone play football.

Those seven weeks that I was housebound were the hardest I've experienced outside prison and suffering from cancer. I was trapped at home with Mum and a million chattering relatives as my teammates continued their push for the finals. Worse still, I had to watch while the starting spot I'd worked so hard to earn was taken by somebody else. The only training I could do was a bit of upper body work. Inevitably I lost fitness because I could hardly walk, let alone run. But thanks to Mum's Lebanese delicacies, I didn't lose any weight.

After only a week, I was going insane with boredom and began hunting about for alternatives. I spoke to Keith Barnes, who advised me to go and see a masseur by the name of John Guttenbeil. Keith reckoned the bloke was a miracle worker who had privately helped world champion boxer Jeff Fenech with his aches and pains.

John was 70 years old, but his hands had the strength of a man half that age. He put me in so much agony that I, a non-drinker, needed to skol a schooner of beer before every treatment. I remember John asking me if it hurt as he applied pressure to the affected region. Even if it didn't, I'd always say yes because I was petrified of him going even deeper and inflicting maximum discomfort.

But it was a case of no pain, no gain. There was plenty of pain, but John's hands got me back within 11 weeks when the doctors had written me off for the season. I had two matches in reserve grade against Norths and Wests before Ryan put me back in the top side. But I was not ready. Despite John's miraculous hands, my groin was still playing up. I had lost at least five yards in speed and couldn't maintain my place in a side that was still challenging for a place in the top three.

It was depressing to go back to reserves after such a good early season run, but if there was one bloke who could lift my spirits it was the Tigers' biggest fan: Laurie Nichols.

Laurie was more than just a supporter, he was as important to the club as the CEO or captain. By the time I joined Balmain he was well and truly eligible for the pension, but age refused to weary the man who famously wore a training singlet everywhere no matter how cold the weather. He came to every session and got on great with all the boys.

It was impossible not to be inspired by his commitment to the club. Laurie made up rhyming slang nicknames for all of us and mine was 'John Elias, come and try us'. Other ones I liked were, 'Sirro, you're my hero' and 'Paul Davis, can he save us?'. In every way, Laurie was part of the team. That meant he'd accompany us on drinking sessions after games and training. To this day, he is the only bloke they've let into the Bourbon And Beefsteak on a Saturday night wearing a footy singlet.

I regained my form before the end of the premiership rounds and managed to earn a place in the starting pack for Wayne Pearce's last game at Leichhardt. It was a real privilege to spill blood for Junior that day. We were playing Parramatta and needed a win to secure third spot. The occasion of Junior's farewell, however, got to us and the Eels, with nothing to play for and nothing to lose, sprang an upset.

The competition was so close that season that losing spelt a sudden-death play-off for fifth against Newcastle. The game was played on Tuesday night at Parramatta Stadium, with the winner to progress to the sudden-death semi-final against Manly four days later. Having been admitted to the competition three years earlier, the Knights were jousting for their first finals appearance. They played hard but our big-game experience proved decisive. We got the cash thanks to a late intercept try to winger Steve O'Brien, meaning that Junior would finish his decorated career on the big stage no matter how far we progressed in the finals.

He got another 80 minutes and that was it. Everyone was tipping a 1988-style run from the Tigers, but Manly accounted for us easily on the Saturday. We just found it too mentally draining to back up from the torrid play-off a mere four days earlier.

Although our elimination was disappointing, the game was a personal highlight for me. It was the first time I'd played in a Sydney semi-final (off the bench) and it was an incredible thrill. After warming the bench at the same venue, the SFS, 12 months earlier with no prospect of getting a run, I was proud of how far I had come that season.

CHAPTER 14

KEEPING UP WITH THE JONES BOY

It would be fair enough to speculate whether I was a bit of a curse on Warren Ryan's career. Every time I arrived at a club he was coaching, the Wok would be gone the next season. It happened at Newtown and Canterbury and at the end of 1990 he was on his way from Balmain, this time headed for my previous club, Wests.

During the off-season when I took Con for our little grave-digging expedition, the players were kept in the dark about who our next coach would be. To me, however, it wasn't a concern. I had contract negotiations to worry about. I was 28 and nearing the twilight of first-grade football. My next contract could conceivably be my last and I needed it to be a decent one. Things were going well away from football, with some handsome collects both on and off the track. But my big-spending lifestyle was terribly high-maintenance and there never seemed to be enough money.

For example, I was and still remain addicted to buying

expensive clothes. I will only wear the latest fashions and only the best brands. This habit meant I was spending a couple of hundred bucks a week on clobber. The wardrobes at Mum's house were overflowing so she introduced a rule – for every new item I bought, one had to be thrown out. I would have happily consented had Mum policed the rule correctly and discarded my old clothes. But more often than not she'd grab the brand new ones and have them for sale at the local St Vinnie's in no time. It infuriated me. Mum, however, had a soft spot for donating to the poor given the charity handouts she had relied on to feed us as kids.

When the time came for me to negotiate with Balmain, I reckon I gave Keith Barnes the most harrowing four-and-a-half hours of his life. We finished up with a handshake for a two-year deal for 1991 and 1992. Realising this was probably my last real shot at rugby league, I trained extremely hard that off-season – even 'borrowing' the club's rowing machine for extra sessions at home. Mentally and physically I felt good, but the coaching situation had still not been resolved. When Balmain finally announced who Warren Ryan's replacement would be, it caused one of the biggest sensations in years.

Alan Jones was best known in Sydney as a top-rating talk-back radio broadcaster, a role he still pursues with relentless passion and vigour all these years later despite a recent cancer scare. In 1991, however, he had also just completed a mostly successful stint as coach of the Australian Wallabies rugby union side. Under Jones, the Wallabies completed a memorable grand slam of Europe in 1984.

Jones had never coached rugby league at any level. Before getting his break in the media, he started out as a top rugby coach at private schools in Queensland. The idea of him crossing codes was never seriously contemplated, so it came as a huge story when Balmain announced that Jones had been signed as head coach for the next three years.

I was more caught up in my own challenge of playing well that year than being swept away by the hype. But I do remember Jones's first proper address to the playing squad. He took the stage in the auditorium at Balmain Leagues and spent an hour outlining his vision for the club. It was clear from his speech that big changes were in the wind. Jones kept stressing how he had taken on the role not only for the challenge of revolutionising Balmain, but also the way rugby league is played.

He passionately believed in attack. If Jones truly had his way, teams would fling the ball wide on their own goal-line. During that off-season we spent an unprecedented amount of time on ball work. Under normal circumstances it would have represented a major change, but this new playing style was a stark contrast after three seasons under the man who reduced rugby league to defensive wars of attrition during the mid-1980s – Warren Ryan.

Unsurprisingly, Jones had a bit of talent for motivating people. He could probably convince you to run through a brick wall. On one hand you wanted to do it for him, because he was generous and concerned about the players on an individual level. On the other, you'd probably do it because Jones's rhetoric was so good that you were convinced running through a wall was logical.

After a lacklustre end to 1990, the club was undergoing a changing of the guard. Junior and our Pommy whiz Andy Courier had moved on. Jones replaced them with some players from rugby, including former Wallabies playmaker Brian Smith. Big things were expected from Smith, who came to Leichhardt with a close working relationship with Jones.

I enjoyed the off-season, but things between Jones and me weren't running as smoothly as they might have. Although he was a great talker, I felt there was very little communication between us. I didn't know what he wanted from me and in turn struggled to reach solid expectations and goals for the upcoming season. From early on, Jones made it clear he did not tolerate smartarses. That spelt trouble for me, the self-appointed team scallywag. I'd crack crude jokes and make fun of the officials and opposition coaches. I'd take the players to illegal casinos and out in the Cross. Everyone at the club had come to enjoy my humour and not be offended or concerned. But for Jones, I believe my ways were a bit of a culture shock that he thought might undermine his authority if left unchecked.

For no reason in particular I could divine, Jones started me in reserve grade. Again, I didn't rise to the challenge. Dropping my bundle and not caring was the wrong way to respond. But that's what I generally did when a coach kept me in reserves. There were too many distractions happening off the field to devote energy to anything below the top level. If it wasn't first-grade, I wasn't bothered. I felt insulted because I knew I had what it took to make the side, particularly when they couldn't win a game for the first two months of the season.

Eight losses had the Tigers tethered to the bottom of the ladder, despite fielding a team containing rep players like Roach, Benny Elias, Sironen and Jack. There were injuries, but such a shocking run wasn't acceptable for the fans and media. Already under pressure to justify the hype, Jones was being devoured on a daily basis by the papers and the team waved goodbye to any chance of finals football with April yet to finish.

Adapting to Jones's style was a major reason for the slump. There were very few set plays, something guys who had played long careers under prescriptive coaches like Warren Ryan found difficult to digest. But another problem was Jones's abrasive relationship with our new captain and halfback Gary Freeman. Whiz was a cheeky, opinionated player who didn't hold back. After a few losses, I felt the strain between him and Jones deepening. Another factor was the presence of Brian Smith, who many felt was being given an inside run by his former Wallabies coach.

In round nine, Jones produced a major shock and dropped Whiz to reserves. It was unheard of for a coach to axe his number one halfback, but Jones must have felt that desperate times called for desperate measures. And they must have been desperate, because he recalled me to first-grade the same week.

The timing was perfect because we were drawn to play the Broncos at home, a match we always enjoyed. During Brisbane's early years, Balmain had an incredible sway over Wayne Bennett's men. It took them years to finally beat us. When we maintained the hoodoo with a 14–4 win, it was hailed as the upset of the season.

Losing teams can forget how to win and that game stirred our memories of victory. We won more games than we lost for the remainder of the season, but our terrible start meant anything better than a mid-table finish was always out of reach. Our best victory after the Broncos game was a win over high-flying Manly at Leichhardt. It was in that game I witnessed one of the most brutal attacks ever committed during a first-grade game.

Our fullback Garry Jack was bringing the ball back from his in-goal when he was met by giant Manly second-rower Ian Roberts. For reasons unknown to the rest of the players, Roberts got to his feet and started throwing punches. He was a fearsome sight, a 6 foot 4 inch (1.93 m) frame chiselled out of granite striking without mercy into the hapless Jack. To make matters worse, Manly's fullback Matt Ridge had rushed over to restrain Jack while Roberts pounded him. The incident happened in the far north-eastern corner of the ground, a long way from where the rest of the players were. By the time we arrived to help Jack, his face was a bloodied mess. Roberts had a crazed look in his eye, a look that would have made even the hardest inmate at Long Bay think twice.

Many theories have been tossed up about why Roberts snapped that day. The most popular one was that he responded to a gay slur. At the time, however, there were no rumours circulating about Roberts' sexuality. They didn't start until a few seasons later, just before he bravely came out in public. There was also talk of a long-running feud between the pair that ignited on the 1990 Kangaroo tour. Whatever the case, Jack must have done something extraordinary to upset the big cyborg and earn a mugging no less savage than the ones I'd witnessed in prison.

I remained in first-grade – either off the bench or starting – until the end of 1991. My elevation thawed the freeze between Jones and me and we began to understand and appreciate one another. He later told me that it was none other than Wayne Bennett who inspired my return to first-grade against the Broncos on that cool May afternoon. Jones was speaking to Bennett about certain members of the side when my name came up. Drawing on the experience of our clashes in 1985 at Brisbane Souths, Bennett told Jones that

I was no use to any club in reserve grade. He basically told Jones to get rid of me if he didn't intend playing me in firsts. Thankfully, Jones listened – he was a great listener – and gave me a chance I made sure he didn't regret.

Jones divides opinions, but in mine he was a tireless and giving worker who would do anything to see the team succeed. Perhaps more than any coach I've played under, he cared about his players as human beings. Maybe even more than Wayne Bennett did. While this was obviously appreciated by us, it may have been part of the reason why Jones never excelled at Balmain. Despite his apparently limitless reserves of energy, the coach's attentions were commonly distracted by helping players with their personal problems rather than focusing solely on what the team had to do to win that weekend.

I've got no doubt he has a brilliant football mind, probably one ahead of its time. But if he had one flaw it was spreading himself too thin. His more calculating predecessor, Warren Ryan, managed things better in this respect. Ryan was very football-orientated. He wasn't there to be your mate, he was there to be your coach and that was it. To most of the players at Balmain, Jones was both friend and coach and maybe our football suffered because of that.

There were also players at the club who took advantage of Jones's generosity. They knew his influence could be called upon to help with personal sponsorships or a mortgage, maybe even a weekend in his flat on the Gold Coast. Some players didn't hesitate to sound him out, with nothing else on their minds but milking as much as they could. Jones was extremely fond of helping young players from the wrong side of the tracks, guys like the rookie centre Jacin Sinclair, who burst onto the scene in 1991.

At Balmain, Jones was a faithful replica of the man behind the microphone. He was a self-appointed champion of battlers, the poor kid made good who was now fighting for the hapless souls on Struggle Street. This is why he enjoyed rugby league. He'd tell us the union boys he used to coach were 'pampered'. They had mostly come from rich families and private schools. In that sport, his crusading had no cause. But at blue-collar Balmain – as it was back then – Jones was suddenly surrounded by the very people he went in to bat for every morning on the radio. He threw us seafood barbecues and took us to a training camp at Joey's, one of Sydney's most exclusive boarding schools.

But arguably the biggest thrill that we experienced under Jones was a visit to the late Kerry Packer's horse stud in Scone, northwest of Sydney. I remember being taken into Packer's office for a one-on-one meeting, at the mogul's request.

He just sat in silence, staring at me for what seemed like ages. I began to feel slightly unnerved, so I quipped: 'What's the matter Kerry – does someone owe you money?' He let out a laugh and then spilled his heart out.

'Do you realise, John, how many people in my position would give everything to be where you are?' he asked. 'How many people in my position would give everything to play team sport at the highest level? I might be rich and know a lot of people, but how many of them really like me for who I am – not my money?

'Team sport is not like that. You trust and like one another because you've got a common goal. I'd love to be part of that camaraderie.'

We chatted for another 15 or 20 minutes. Packer was all too aware of my activities on the streets, but only mentioned them in passing. The last thing he told me was: 'Be good to your mum.' I walked out surprised that a man with so much power and wealth could still have unfulfilled desires. Our talk was perhaps the most sobering reminder of how lucky I was to play rugby league – and how irresponsible I was not to make the most of that gift.

Jones and I were becoming closer, but our friendship was sealed once he discovered my family's past. I approached him one day after training in 1991, but he shooed me away. 'John, I've had enough of talking to you after every match,' he said. 'You played poorly on the weekend and that's the end of it.' I smiled and said, 'But Alan, I came to invite you to dinner at Mum's house this week. She's been nagging and nagging me for weeks. If I had it my way, do you think I'd be inviting you?' A warm change swept over Alan's cold, hardened expression. 'Oh, really?' he asked a little sheepishly. 'I'd be honoured.'

The sight of Jones's private car – driven by his personal chauffeur – cruising through Punchbowl must have turned some heads. Jones, however, had the common touch because of his humble upbringing in rural Queensland. He and Mum got on famously. In fact, it's probably the only time he has been shouted down over such a sustained period. Mum put on one of her best performances that night, cooking up a storm and haranguing Jones about whether he was single and interested in dating her.

It was a good thing that I had earned his trust by the end of 1991, because if I hadn't had his confidence I would have been back on the scrapheap after getting into trouble during the 1991–92 off-season. My main activities at the time were SP bookmaking and the trots, but I'd still take on the odd collect if it was worth my while. I had teamed up with the former Dragons star Harry Eden for a few jobs. I had a friend who was owed a very old debt by someone we'll call Bill. The word on the street was that Bill was a real lowlife. And I'm not talking your normal criminal stuff. The word was that he fancied kids.

I did my research on Bill in preparation for paying him a visit and most of the innuendo seemed to stack up.

At the time I was also in possession of a police badge that I purchased on the black market. There was nothing I couldn't get back in those days. Let's say it came in handy for access to certain venues, but I also had some fun with it. I'd use it to pull drivers over and scare them a bit. It was extremely juvenile, dangerous and irresponsible behaviour, but I had such disdain for authority after being sent to Long Bay as a 16-year-old. Instead of trying to erase it to lead a better life, I dined out on that anger. I now believe that the challenge for me – after three jail stints – is to control those feelings, something I haven't made enough effort to do thus far.

I was casing Bill's house and followed his movements. I had no intentions of bashing him, just scaring him into thinking the authorities were on to his activities. Once he believed that, he would be in no position to refuse to pay back the debt.

Bill was suitably frightened when I approached him and he agreed to pay back the debt, so I left it at that. The next step was to have my good mate Georgie Boy or some of the guys pay him a visit for the collect proper.

I didn't give it much thought the following day until there was a knock at the door. Standing at the front of Mum's house were two cops who had come to arrest me on charges of demanding money with menace and impersonating a police officer. I didn't have a leg to stand on. Bill had recognised me as the footballer John Elias and gone straight to the cops. They had a warrant to search the house and dug up a toy gun that belonged to my nephew. Bill had also claimed I pulled a piece on him – which was rubbish – and the cops wanted to believe it was that toy gun.

I was taken away and charged and a small story appeared in the next day's paper. Thankfully it wasn't like these days, which would have seen my arrest plastered all over the front page.

When Jones found out, he called me to Leichhardt Oval for a confrontation. I told him the real story behind my arrest and he looked at me suspiciously. 'If you're lying I'll rip up your contract right now,' Jones said. 'You'll never play at this club again.'

Jones was judge, jury and executioner. The Tigers board had given him unfettered power over disciplinary matters. It was he alone who would decide whether I was sacked or not. Because of his connections with the police, Jones was quickly able to test the veracity of my story. It stacked up. He came back to me and said: 'John, thank you for telling me the truth.' And that's the last thing he or anyone else said about the matter.

He accepted me for who I was and only judged me as a footballer. I'm sure Jones was smart enough to realise I wasn't going to church in my spare time. The truckloads of cheap suits and clothes that were hawked at training told him that much. But to his credit, Jones didn't stick his nose in. He had excellent judgement in that regard, knowing when he was and wasn't required to ask questions.

The charges, however, were still to be heard. I didn't face

court until more than a year later – in early 1993 – when I was sentenced to three months weekend detention and community service.

Our late flourish at the end of 1991 had everyone primed for a big 1992. There was a meeting of the minds between Jones and rugby league. I think he realised that he had tried to be too innovative in his first season and began to have us working on set plays. This gave us more confidence and we started like a bull at a gate, winning five games in a row early on to share the competition lead with big guns like Canberra, Brisbane and North Sydney. Our best victory during that run – and possibly my entire time at the Tigers – was a stirring comeback over St George at Kogarah. They led 16–0 at halftime and were still ahead 17–16 with a minute to play. Then our backs produced a thrilling passage of play to score a stunning last-gasp try. We won 22–17 and anything seemed possible from then on.

The real test came the following week at Penrith Park. The Panthers had just won their first title the previous season and were still regarded as the benchmark. They were still coached by my old friend Phil Gould, whom I'd see swanning around Penrith trots in those days. Brad Fittler, Greg Alexander, John Cartwright and Brad Izzard were the nucleus of a very strong team – but unfortunately they were brought undone by the tragic death of Greg's little brother Ben in a car accident later that year.

Our clash against Penrith was one of the most titanic games of the 1992 season. With minutes left the scores were locked at 12–all. This week, however, it was our turn to suffer a last-gasp defeat. The home side was awarded a dubious penalty on halfway, leaving former Wallaby ace Andrew Leeds with a 50-metre penalty attempt to win the game after the siren. Leeds was deadly accurate and didn't flinch. Final score: Penrith 14, Balmain 12.

Team sport is a strange thing. Some losses hurt infinitely more than others, and this one left us bleeding. We had travelled to the foot of the mountains with huge expectations and come as close as possible to fulfilling them. To be robbed in those circumstances was heartbreaking. We just struggled to accept the result and couldn't recover. Before we knew it we'd dropped three games straight and were plunging back down the ladder. Our momentum stifled, the semi-finals proved a step too far and we finished a couple of wins away from the fifth-place cut-off.

Another season of wasted opportunity renewed calls for Jones's head. Accustomed to so much success during the previous decade, Tigers fans went into overdrive for his sacking. Jones's position was the subject of constant media speculation, but I can honestly say he had a great rapport with the players. That was a big thing in his favour in the face of two seasons in the doldrums.

But I would not be sticking around to find out whether Jones survived the final year of his contract. I had spent much of the season thinking about playing in England. My time in rugby league was running short and I again had itchy feet. I spoke to Keith Barnes about the prospect of playing the 1992–93 off-season in the Old Dart, but he point-blank refused to release me. I would have loved to stay at Balmain, but my desire to experience the British game trumped any loyalty to the Tigers.

There was also another opportunity from Wests, who had agreed in principle to allow me to play over the summer months. My old coach Warren Ryan had moved out to Campbelltown and was keen to have me on board for 1993, with the Magpies fielding one of the most intimidating forward packs in the league. Wok had decimated his old club Canterbury to rebuild the Fibros, who now boasted the likes of David Gillespie and Andrew Farrar. They had made the finals the past two seasons and were tipped for bigger and better things the following season.

I travelled to Campbelltown to meet Warren and new Wests CEO Steve Noyce. We agreed on a one-year contract for 1993, with the deal signed on a piece of notepad paper. I thought it was a little amateurish, but took a copy nevertheless. I knew from my brother George that a contract was a contract – no matter how fancy the paper it was printed on.

I left happy – it was always a privilege to be chased by a coach of Warren's calibre. I still regarded him as the best in the business in those days and he obviously had a high opinion of the way I played the game, having signed me at every club he had coached since Newtown. The only condition of the deal was that I report for training on 1 February 1993. But for the next few months, the northern hemisphere was my oyster. I stocked up on winter woollies and began to do a bit of research on a town called Leigh, whose footy side had just signed me for a short-term deal.

CHAPTER 15
TICKET TO ROAM

As soon as we landed in Manchester, it became apparent what the next three months of my life would be like: cold, drab and dreary. From the sunny Sydney spring, I'd landed on the doorstep of a ferocious English winter. There would be no respite. There were a load of Aussies playing in the 1992–93 competition, including my Tigers teammates Garry Jack and Bruce McGuire. Both were playing for Sheffield Eagles and Jack had actually helped me secure a deal with their rivals Leigh.

A stint in England was one of the final things I felt I had to do in my rugby league career. But there were also other things in Sydney that made it good sense for me to leave then. For one, our exploits at the trots had slowed dramatically after our trainer was caught doping horses and warned off tracks and TABs. Then there were the charges arising from my confrontation with Bill. I knew the case would be heard the following year and a guilty verdict might jeopardise my chances of travelling overseas. As it was, I was a touch-and-go proposition with the UK authorities given my rap sheet as a teenager. Thankfully, though, there were no hassles obtaining the correct visa.

I don't sleep on planes, so when my new room-mate laid eyes on me it would not have been a pretty sight. The club was putting me up in a furnished townhouse with another Aussie player, Scott Mahon, a promising young fullback who'd played a few seasons at Parramatta. Scott was almost 10 years my junior, but we hit it off handsomely from the moment we met because he was a bit of a larrikin and was always up for a good time. His blond mullet should have been a dead giveaway. The jetlag was really messing with me and I hardly got any sleep on the night I arrived.

As fate would have it, my first game for Leigh was the next day – against English champions Wigan. I knew I would be starting on the bench, but struggled to see how I was going to acquit myself properly on such a limited preparation.

I didn't meet the rest of my teammates, or coach Dennis Ransdale, until our team lunch a couple of hours before kick-off. While this might have seemed strange to most players, it wasn't a big deal to me because I'd played for so many clubs already. The challenge of fitting into a new team and meeting new players was the norm for me by the time I'd turned 30. I didn't fare as badly as I expected when I was thrust into the game with 20 minutes left. Leigh were the real battlers of the league and given no chance of beating Wigan, even before a packed house of 8,000 chanting home fans. We gave it everything that day and went down by something like 16 points, a margin that probably didn't reflect our effort.

The routine after matches consisted of drinking, drinking

and more drinking. Apart from its abundance of pubs, Leigh was a very nondescript town. There were no coffee shops or trots courses there. Nothing else to do, apparently, but go to the pub and sink pints of warm lager with your mates who worked in the local mines. It was simply too cold to do anything else. The thing I couldn't understand, however, was why the pubs shut so early. By 10 pm during the week and midnight on the weekends everything was closed. For a night owl like me, it was a shock.

It sure put the pressure on the boys to get a result with the ladies nice and early in the evening. On that matter, Scott and I had some epic nights out. We made a very effective team with the local lasses, who were always very accommodating and interested once they heard our Australian accents. It also didn't hurt that we were stars from the local footy team, which everyone in town supported and recognised. We had a running bet about who was going to fall in love first and, as luck would have it, we both slipped up at the same time.

I fell for a girl called Barbara Prescott. Ironically enough, she worked at the local jewellery store. I'd just emerged from an on-again, off-again relationship in Australia and was getting to the age where marriage probably would have been the best thing for me. But my lifestyle was not conducive to giving girls the attention they need from a proper relationship. While I was always generous and kind, it's fair to say my attention was elsewhere a lot of the time and this proved a killer blow to potential relationships.

In Leigh, however, there were no distractions so Barbara and I progressed quickly. Like most girls from that part of the world, she had a tough and uncompromising streak. She'd stand up to me and I'd respect that. No-one ever said no to me, but Barbara was never afraid to disagree. She also didn't mind being one of the boys. And when you are one of the boys you are loyal. In that respect, I had as much confidence in Barbara to stick by me as I did any of the boys I rode with in Sydney. There wasn't another woman I could say that about until then.

Scott fell for his own lady and was rarely sighted at our townhouse from then on. His extended absences, however, made little difference because I never saw him before noon anyway. Scott was a legendary sleeper who would face every new day with a freshly lit cigarette. He smoked an incredible amount for a footballer – at least a pack a day. I was amazed how he played so well every weekend.

While Scotty slept through the mornings, I'd do extra weights at the gym before afternoon training. That was the main difference between English and Australian clubs back then – there were no individual fitness routines for the players. Away from training with the rest of the team, you were expected to take care of it yourself.

As expected, we struggled to win many games and by the new year Ransdale was sacked in favour of Aussie coach Steve Simms. Steve cut his teeth in the lower grades at South Sydney and fancied himself as a bit of a Warren Ryan clone. But he was no Wok and we didn't improve much. The English game was played in a different style to Australia, with an emphasis on ball movement among the forwards. We were encouraged to run two wide of the ruck and use the width of the field. Simms's poor imitation of Australian coaching blueprints simply didn't make the grade.

But like the other battling teams I'd played for, the spirit was still good. I particularly liked our big front-rower Tim Street. He was a beast of a man who copped some incredible punishment. Once again, my attraction to him was based on a common dark streak. It was not until later that I discovered he'd spent six months in jail for assault. We were kindred spirits from opposite sides of the globe and got on well.

Tim also didn't mind a bit of a gag. One night we were finishing up at the pub when Tim arranged a little stunt with a few of his copper mates. The police in England were so different from the ones in Sydney. They talked to people like human beings, not their underlings. As long as you behaved, respect went both ways. If you strayed, then they didn't hesitate doing their jobs. But there were no unnecessary suspicions, no copper who was always on the hunt to make a name for himself by abusing his power.

Tim convinced the cops to load us all into the back of a paddy wagon and drive to Barbara's house in Salford. They were then to knock on the door and tell her I had been arrested and was handcuffed in the back. We drove to Barbara's house and the cops were so good they even flicked on the sirens for added effect when we got close. The look on her face was priceless and she broke into tears and became hysterical. But being such a great girl, she laughed when we told her the truth.

Another stunt we enjoyed came at the expense of an Aussie journalist, Matthew Gunn, who was travelling around England catching up with expat players for *Rugby League Week*. He didn't seem like a bad guy when he arrived to interview Scotty and me, so we decided to take him with us on a bit of a pub crawl that night. I remember my old mate from Souths, Craig 'Tugger' Coleman, tagging along as well. Tugger played for Salford and we caught up a fair bit, usually at Ladbroke's for a punt on the races.

It took Matthew a couple of pints to turn from a decent guy to believing he was a superhero.

We decided to put a stop to it and amuse ourselves at the same time. There was a certain local girl who didn't have much luck socially. Why? Well, let's just say she'd be one of the last people you'd want to sit next to on a plane. But she was a knockabout and would always agree to a bit of fun. So I approached her and asked if she wouldn't mind taking care of our annoying guest for the evening. It had been many moons since her last man, so she couldn't agree quickly enough.

We all went back to our townhouse and on the way I convinced Scotty to hand up his bed to the happy couple. There was no way I was going to have either of them in my bed. Scott, Tugger and I were downstairs when the noises began. We expected it to only last a few minutes but they went on all night panting and groaning like a couple of elephants on heat. But when our friend awoke in the morning he was smug and triumphant. Matthew thought he was some sort of stud and must have really taken a liking to Big Bertha because he extended his stay another two weeks to move in with her. Each to their own, I suppose.

I was having a great time in Leigh by the time it came for me to head back to Sydney. I was contractually obliged to be back at Wests training by 1 February 1993. Although I was keen for another season in Sydney, I made a romantic compromise that I hoped would keep Barbara in my life. I planned for 1993 to be my swansong in Sydney. After finishing up with Wests, I'd return to Leigh and play a few seasons and then retire with a nice superannuation. Along the way I might shake the bad elements and settle down with a girl I truly loved.

TICKET TO ROAM

The plan seemed completely reasonable, but it was doomed just one day after I returned to Sydney. Wests had changed their mind and didn't want me any more. The bastards tried to claim that I returned a day late, but it was an outright lie. I was back before 1 February, something they would later concede in mediation.

The real story was that a couple of Wests board members were dirty on me for leaving the club in 1987. They were a bunch of dinosaurs with no qualifications to sit on a board and deliver results for a top-grade football club. They were people like butchers and gear stewards who felt they knew how to run a business, but simply ended up costing the Magpies a substantial pay-out.

The matter went to court, which was an embarrassing experience for Magpies CEO Steve Noyce. The judge couldn't stifle his laughter when he saw the piece of paper that Wests had used for my contract. He immediately told them: 'You need to reach a settlement.' We did just that and I was very happy with the pay-out, a figure I'm still obliged not to disclose.

I had my money, but no team. It was a disastrous time of the year to be stranded, with everyone's roster full just before the season started. I rang Keith Barnes at Balmain in desperation, but he couldn't help. Then I got on to Jack Gibson, who was coaching director at the Roosters. I hammered Gibson on a daily basis, fast realising that my final season in Sydney might be remembered as 1992.

Gibson finally dismissed me with the following words: 'John, it's not your football ability I'm worried about – it's what's in the car boot.' He was making a veiled reference to my activities off the field, which was fair enough. But I did find it a bit rich coming from Jack. Without wanting to disrespect the great coach, he wasn't exactly an angel off the field either. Like me, he was good friends with Harry Eden, with whom I had begun debt collecting again, this time on behalf of an overseas betting agency in Vanuatu. Gibson knew his fair share of SP bookies and stand-over men during the 1970s and 1980s, let's put it that way.

I was shattered. It was like bad déjà vu of the time Newtown collapsed – all your best-laid plans shot down by something you can't control. I could only think of karma at the time. My criminal lifestyle hadn't exactly encouraged the gods to smile on me. I could hardly complain about a bad break when I did myself no favours. As they say, you make your own luck.

The only interest I had was from my old coach at Wests, Steve Ghosn, who was now at Metropolitan Cup side Guildford. The Metro Cup was a lower standard than reserve grade, played on suburban grounds before a handful of people and their pet dogs. If I had planned to finish up at that level, I wouldn't have minded playing for Steve. But I wanted to end in first-grade. I knew I belonged there.

Nevertheless, I agreed to play for Guildford because I simply had no other options. It was a mistake. I didn't want to be there and I didn't give 100 per cent. As an athlete, you should always give 100 per cent, especially in a team sport. There's no greater crime than letting your teammates down, knowing the bloke next to you is busting his arse while you're in cruise mode. For that entire season I gave about 50 or 60 per cent and Ghosn knew it. He must have had a lot of time for me because he never said anything, although he would have known I was playing nowhere near as well as I could. For this, I still feel awful. It was the only time in my career I had not re-paid someone's faith – something I'll regret forever.

TICKET TO ROAM

As was the case at Wests in 1986, he had to do some swift talking to convince his superiors to give me a chance. And I did his cause little help after upsetting the directors by fencing hot gear from the car boot at training. Although this was tolerated at Newtown, Wests and Balmain, the small fry at Guildford didn't want a bar of it and Ghosn was forced to tell me to stop.

I was also derailed by weekend detention. My charges for police impersonation were heard in February 1993. At a sentence indication hearing the judge said I would get two years fulltime detention if I was found guilty. My lawyer John Korn said I'd only have to do three months weekend detention, if I pleaded guilty. Knowing I was culpable and not wanting the bad publicity, I raised my hands and swallowed the punishment. After serving 18 months at Long Bay, weekend detention was an all-expenses-paid holiday. I was placed at a facility in Silverwater, not far from Punchbowl. I'd go in at 4 pm on Wednesday and be released at 5 pm on a Friday, meaning I was free to turn out for Guildford on the weekends.

But the truth was I could have walked out any time I pleased. None of the doors were locked. There was only one screw. We'd do community work like feeding elderly people during the day and at nights we'd sit up and play cards. There was no bedtime. There were no rules, no regimen. It didn't feel like punishment. Instead, it was a waste of taxpayers' money. Low-level criminals would be better off on home detention wearing a tracking bracelet than mixing with other undesirables in such a lax environment. It was certainly no deterrent to me and everyone else there seemed to be doing it pretty easy.

Despite my attitude, Guildford performed well enough to be a certainty for the finals. The prospect of the big games lifted my spirits and I began to improve. Until then I had been taking it easy both on and off the field. Harry and I were starting to make a bit of money from the SP business, which made up for our dwindling returns at the trots. The good times at Harold Park had just about died off by then, with stewards and trainers being nabbed left, right and centre for rorting.

Again, timing did not smile on me. In the final round before the semis I was cited for a high tackle. The judiciary showed me no mercy and I was suspended for three weeks. The fact my season with Guildford was effectively over didn't really bother me. It was more the fact that my football career in Sydney was done for that upset me. I was resigned to heading back to Leigh and finishing there when an unexpected opportunity came up.

Balmain have a traditional old boys' reunion at the final home game every year and, with my weekends free thanks to the judiciary, I turned up for the 1993 bash. Blocker, Junior and all my old mates were there, having a great time on the drink. The game was to be Alan Jones's last in charge at Leichhardt.

If 1991 and 1992 were bad at Balmain, then 1993 was a disaster. The Tigers finished second-last and had no choice but to punt Jones, who was headed to Souths the following season. In a surprise move, Balmain went with sentiment and appointed Junior as coach for 1994. It was seen as a bold gamble, because Pearce had only retired three years earlier and was being asked to coach many of his former teammates. But the Tigers board felt they had nothing to lose. Also, after having an outsider like Jones in control for so long, it was felt the club needed to get back to its roots. And there was no prouder Balmain boy than Junior.

After the game, Paul Sironen approached Junior and told him to get me on board for 1994. Having played alongside me for a season and a half, Junior knew I was capable. But he also knew I'd sat an entire season out of first-grade and could not afford to risk offering me a contract. 'We'll give you a run in the trials and see how you go from there,' Junior said. 'But I want you to put on some weight because I want to see how you go at prop.' I trained the whole 1993–94 off-season with the Tigers.

It was just like old times. I'd turn up with suits in the car boot and lead the team on some interesting expeditions. On one occasion, the whole side went to watch a Billy Joel concert at the Entertainment Centre. Not used to paying for anything, I marched up to one of the guys on the door and said, 'G'day mate, here's your security team – what do you want us to do?' He looked puzzled and said to head inside and talk to the venue manager. So the whole Balmain Tigers team walked in and saw the Piano Man from the dance floor for free.

The difference from my previous stint at Leichhardt was a young rookie by the name of Nat Wood. Nat was a ball boy at Newtown when I joined the Jets in 1981 – an unwanted reminder of my age (now 31). He remembered me from those days and we clicked immediately. Nat grew up in rough-and-tumble neighbourhoods around Redfern and could hold his hands up. In fact, he would have made a great boxer.

The earliest proof I saw of his pugilism came later that year on Melbourne Cup day at Randwick racecourse. A group of players and I were trackside when Nat came across this bloke who was bad-mouthing me. It was late in the day and the big fella was fired up with Dutch courage from all the beer he'd sunk. Nat was not impressed and told him so. Now Nat is only a small bloke, despite being lean and muscular. But he has no fear, which is a critical advantage in these situations. The bloke thought he was in for an easy kill until Nat threw one of the cleanest right crosses I've ever seen. It knocked the big fool out cold.

Because it all happened so quickly, security were none the wiser, so we sat the bloke's unconscious body on a chair. Then we placed some sunglasses over his eyes and a hat on his head. To anyone who didn't know better, it looked like he was sleeping. But to us, it looked like a remake of the hilarious film *Weekend at Bernie's*, where the characters dress up a corpse and pretend he's alive. After we arranged the bloke I turned to Nat and said: 'Welcome to the family, buddy.' He's been a member ever since and ended up marrying Neddy Smith's daughter, Jamie.

But that wasn't the only scuffle that sticks in my mind from 1994. On another occasion, I was out with a few of the boys at the General Bourke Hotel in Parramatta when we came across North Sydney halfback Jason Taylor in a bit of a blue with a Lebanese bouncer. The police were called and the bouncer wanted Jason charged for king-hitting him. Wanting to avoid Jason's name being splashed across the front page, I spoke to the bouncer in Arabic and convinced him to drop it.

I didn't expect any thanks, but I also didn't expect Jason to return the favour like he did a couple of weeks later. Surprise, surprise, it was another late night out on the town with my mate Shami – this time at the old Bourbon And Beefsteak in Kings Cross. But on this occasion, Jason was fancying himself as a lover rather than a fighter. He decided to have a go at a girl I'd been putting the hard word on. He leaned across and said to her, 'Why are you talking with him – he's a criminal.'

Jason had conveniently forgotten that this criminal had prevented him from being charged just a few weeks earlier. If it hadn't been for me, he would have been a criminal as well. I reminded him with some colourful language and was tempted to impress it further on his memory with my fists. If there's something I can't stand, it's hypocrites.

As a player, Wayne Pearce was a fitness freak. He was also fanatical about diets and pills. So it wasn't surprising that he forced us into the same routine as a coach. I remember leading into the 1994 season we were all given boxes of vitamins to take at regular intervals. Junior would constantly check in, saying, 'John, have you been taking your vitamins? Do you need any more?' I'd always say yes, but never bothered with them. To me, that kind of thing is all mental.

But I did listen to Junior's tips about eating right. He broke new ground by insisting we eat six small meals a day and taper off eating carbohydrates at night, two things I continue to do. I've found it's a surefire way to raise the metabolism. Junior had us very fit, but our skills and strategy probably weren't on par with teams playing under the more experienced coaches. That's completely understandable, because the poor bloke had no blueprint on this coaching caper.

Wayne brought in a few people to help him out, including his former coach Bill Anderson and freshly retired St George captain Michael Beattie. Little did I know then how Beattie's arrival at the club as defensive coach would change my life just a few months later.

Junior was obviously thrown in too young and the first couple of seasons were very tough, particularly 1994 when

Balmain finished last. But Junior hung in there and eventually got the team in the position to make the semi-finals a few years down the track. He also coached New South Wales for two seasons, including the memorable 3–0 whitewash of 2000 that culminated in the Blues' record 56–16 drubbing of the Maroons at Homebush.

During 1994, however, there were far fewer highlights for the Balmain Tigers. I won an incentive-based contract with a solid performance against Manly in the trials but had to sit out the first two matches because of my Metro Cup suspension from the previous season.

Because the Tigers had lost their opening two games, Junior rushed me straight into first-grade for our round three clash against lowly Gold Coast at Leichhardt. This match stands out because during our warm-up behind the grandstand I was approached by my old teammate from Souths, Rick Montgomery.

Knowing I was in the SP business, he told me there had been a massive go on the Coast to win that afternoon. Rick said several of their players had outlaid big dollars on themselves, including their new signing Craig Coleman. Betting on football was illegal by that stage, but definitely not unheard of. In my SP bookmaking, however, virtually all the wagers were for trots and races. And even so, the idea of players betting on their own team didn't seem a problem. If anything, it provided them with further incentive to win.

The only thing I saw wrong with what Rick was saying was that people were so confident of the Gold Coast's chances. He said he wanted to have $5,000 on the visitors. I couldn't accept the bet quickly enough. I was sure we'd account for them that day. It was an even-money bet and I was very confident of collecting.

However, you can never be too confident. To insure myself, I approached a couple of our players and offered them $500 on themselves to win. I remember Tim Brasher, Martin Masella, Benny Elias and Mick Neil all being happy enough to have a dabble. We really didn't think anything of it because we were betting on ourselves, not running dead.

We went out and smashed the Gold Coast by 40 points, earning myself a nice payday even after paying off my teammates' winnings. But a far bigger – and darker – wager awaited.

CHAPTER 16
THE FIX

You don't forget faces like the one that belongs to Dave. Mean and reckless faces with unforgiving eyes that give nothing away. The last time I had looked into those eyes was 15 years earlier at Long Bay jail. I was a teenager and he a brutal kingpin of the yard who terrorised anyone who threatened his supremacy. He was holding a bloodied shiv, having just stabbed another prisoner on the oval. He didn't so much as see me witness the attack, he saw through me. I was terrified and refused to say a word, even when the cops offered me an early release to give him up.

I knew Dave appreciated my silence and now, a decade and a half later, he had found me. I saw his face and was transported back to the Bay. The sweat of the gym, the odour of the shower, the sterility of the detergent – these smells struck me at once as he looked down upon me one cold night in August 1994. Moments earlier I was relaxed. So relaxed. Lee, my favourite masseur, had just started his weekly foot rub as I sipped on a glass of watermelon juice. Lee had incredibly strong hands that could elevate you to another level, a place that felt good the night after a game. I visited him every Monday at Chequers in Chinatown, a massage joint that offered the full range of hands-on services. My friends would often order from the *other* menu, but I always played it straight and opted for a simple foot massage followed by a spa.

I don't know how Dave found me. It didn't matter. You don't ask a man like him unnecessary questions. The fact was that he had walked in the door with three goons minutes after Lee's hands started going to work. The recognition was immediate. Dave smiled and said 'Hello, John.' I could tell by the tone of his voice that he still respected me after all these years. My silence had saved him an extra 10 years in jail, a decade that had served him well on the streets. Although I had never seen or spoken to Dave since leaving the Bay in early 1981, I knew he was doing well. We moved in the same circles, but he moved faster and generated much more money. Put simply, he was still the bigger fish.

Dave had a presence. I could feel it as he sat on the couch next to me. He leaned low so Lee couldn't hear and whispered: 'John, I've come to see if you are interested in making a very big earn. I've got 50 large for one afternoon's work.'

My first instinct was to decline. By this stage, I was old and experienced enough to survive on my own. I had my own crew and didn't need jobs from anyone else. I didn't need the obligations or sense of debt. My problem, however, is that I rarely follow my instincts when there's any hint of danger involved. And Dave was dangerous. Although I didn't know the details, I felt sure that what he was offering would be something beyond the usual jobs I took. In these circumstances, my instincts give way to my curiosity. It has always got the better of me, especially when there's an easy $50,000 on the line.

Given Dave had taken the trouble of seeing me personally, I owed it to him to at least listen. But not here. Chequers was frequented by all sorts, including detectives. Its old walls sprouted ears a long time ago, so I suggested to Dave that we meet for dinner across the road at my favourite Chinese noshery, BBQ King.

It was just the two of us. We exchanged pleasantries over salt-and-pepper lobster before returning to the subject at hand when our ice cream dessert arrived.

'Whatever it is that you're offering . . . I will only agree if it's a one-off job,' I began. I didn't need the potential hassle of getting in deep with someone so unpredictable.

Dave looked back at me with those eyes and stuck his right hand out. As we shook, he said: 'I promise John . . . it will be a one-off.' His word was good enough for me. 'I'm involved with some boys who wanted me to visit you tonight,' he continued. 'Some of them are guys you once knew in prison and they are very proud of how far you've gone in rugby league. It's been a big effort to play so many first-grade games from where you were as a teenager.'

I knew this spiel was a sugar-coated prelude to something that wouldn't sound so sweet, but I didn't utter a word. He went on: 'John, the thing is that you aren't getting younger. I'd say this is probably your last season and it's your final couple of games that I want to discuss with you.'

At this stage I was playing for South Sydney, having secured a mid-season transfer from Balmain. There was no ill-will in the move. Alan Jones, who had switched to Redfern that season, sounded me out in May with a good offer for the remainder of the season. I was playing well for the Tigers, but the team was running dead last. The Rabbitohs, on the other hand, were having their best season in five years. Not only had they won the pre-season competition, but they were also finals-bound on the back of a youthful team of potential superstars headed by halves Craig Field and Darrell Trindall. Appreciating that it was probably my last season, the Tigers were incredibly understanding when I approached them. The transfer was completed immediately and I had been playing off the bench for Souths for seven weeks. Unfortunately, however, the team's form had dipped over the past month and the finals had disappeared from reach with three matches to play.

I still didn't put two and two together when Dave raised football. I stayed silent and waited for him to resume. 'My people want to offer you $50,000 to pull up against Wests in two weeks time,' Dave said. 'And they are also offering to give you another $100,000 to buy whatever players you need to pull off the fix.'

The fix. They were two words I had uttered plenty of times in trotting circles, but never in rugby league. The thought of running dead for an earn had never crossed my mind. Honestly, it had not. Suddenly, a jolt of adrenalin struck my temples. Was there guilt as well? There might have been, because I didn't say no straightaway.

Instead, I started thinking how it could possibly be done. Even if I wanted to fix a game – and I didn't want to – it was a huge risk. I was only a hard-working second-rower who occasionally started the game. What influence could I possibly have on the outcome? I put this to Dave and he replied: 'It's not your influence on the game, it's your influence over your teammates.'

I still didn't say no. Bloody hell, I can never say no to these scallywags. I should have shut it down then and there. Realised the sheer stupidity of even entertaining such an offer, which not only raised serious questions about my commitment, but could also bring the credibility of my teammates into serious doubt.

But again I allowed myself to be swept up. For that moment I was the central character in a *Looney Tunes* cartoon, with a devil on one shoulder and an angel on the other. Both were shouting to be heard. The angel kept saying over and over again: 'You can't do this to your teammates! You can't do this to your coach! You can't do this to your fans! *You can't do this to your fans!*' Then the devil countered: 'What does it matter? Neither Souths nor Wests can make the finals and no-one will know the difference. You've worked hard to get where you are in rugby league, think of this as one final pay-out.'

The devil was holding his own. I told Dave to give me two days to think about it.

How differently I felt the following day at training compared to 24 hours earlier. On the Monday I showed for our weights session untroubled and content. I was in the final month of my Australian career and playing well. I felt satisfied that I would go out on my own terms after staring embarrassment in the face at Guildford in 1993.

But by 4 pm on Tuesday I was nervous and agitated. My mind was so heavy. Or was it my conscience?

Over the course of the previous evening it began to make more sense – perhaps because I wanted it to. It wasn't the $50,000 that kept me interested, it was the thrill. It always came down to the allure of the excitement, the anticipation of the electricity – regardless of the circumstances. Morally and fundamentally this was wrong. But I was blinded by the challenge of pulling off something unthinkable, even if it meant putting myself through gut-wrenching anguish in the meantime. As a matter of fact, I think I enjoyed the stress. My devious mind just needed to be occupied, and it was drooling at this prospect.

The previous night I thought hard about which Souths players to approach. I decided that I needed four to make it happen. They were equally important, meaning that if one declined then the fix would be off. It was a case of one-in, all-in.

For months and years later the big question would always be: who were the players? No-one said a word but the media reported Craig Field, Darrell Trindall, Tyrone Smith and Jacin Sinclair. They and I were the obvious ones because we were the knockabouts in the side. The four of them later sued for defamation and won. The media outlet that made the accusation – Channel 7 – had no proof they were involved in anything suspicious.

So who were the players? I will not say. I get asked all the time, but have never told a soul. It is something I promised then and there to take to the grave with me. I expected the same from them when I made the approach and, as far as I know, they've all kept their end of the bargain. What I will say is that people should never assume the obvious. Everyone has their price, including squareheads. Money is a great leveller and there was $25,000 in cash for each player who agreed to go along with the plan. That's a very good earn for 80 minutes work, especially in the last days before footballers' wages exploded with the advent of Super League the following season.

One of the oldest photos of me as a kid: with my brothers Joe and George and sister Jennifer.

My first junior footy team – St John's Lakemba – in the Canterbury district league. I am kneeling on the far right. My childhood friend Mark Cronk, who was later killed, is in the white hat on the left.

Me and a few young mates getting up to our usual mischief as teenagers.

A very young Wayne Bennett acting the gangster at Brisbane Souths.

Our 1985 premiership-winning team at Brisbane Souths. That side contained some of the true greats including Mal Meninga, Garry Belcher and Peter Jackson.

Chris Phelan was probably my best mate at Brisbane Souths. Here we are together at the team's mad Monday celebrations after our 10–8 win over Wynnum-Manly.

Eddie Hayson wasn't always such a street-wise dude, but he's always been a good friend. Here we are together with another mate, Alex Shalala, during the years that we terrorised the trots bagmen.

Mum threatened to throw me out of home if I didn't play better – and her cooking was a good enough reason to lift my act.

At a black-tie function with Arthur Beetson, who coached me at the Roosters and still plays a mean hand at cards.

Playing against Penrith in 1992. The player in the background, Brad Izzard, also later spent time in prison at Oberon.

My time in England with Scott Mahon was a blast – I take my hat off to him.

Playing for Souths against Wests, in the game of the infamous alleged fix. At Orana Park, Campbelltown, late 1994.

A screen-grab of me being interviewed by Ray Martin on *A Current Affair* during the police investigation into the Souths–Wests fix.

These are the gun parts the police impounded that led to my arrest with ex-Dragons skipper Michael Beattie.

Elias jailed over drugs, gun deal

By BRAD LAWSON

FORMER South Sydney rugby league player John Elias was jailed yesterday for a minimum of nine months over drugs and firearms offences.

Elias's mother, Susan, broke down and wept as the sentence was handed down in the District Court — and later outside the court — where witnesses had described her son a "rascal" but a "very warm, loving man".

Judge Joe Moore said Elias acted as a middle man in transactions with an undercover police officer involving military bullet-proof jackets and submachinegun parts.

Elias, 31, was also charged with supplying amphetamines to the officer.

But Elias had claimed he only became involved with the firearms to help out his mate, former St George captain Michael Beattie.

Judge Moore said Elias was a "naive" man who "liked to be liked" or in the words of his former coach, Alan Jones, was at times "silly".

Elias pleaded guilty to 13 charges including supplying amphetamines and possessing prohibited weapons and military style bulletproof vests.

He admitted he was to receive $100 from each of the two drug deals on September 15 and 21 last year.

Elias was arrested on September 21 in a storage shed at Tempe where he met the undercover officer to pass over the guns.

The items were given to him by Beattie, who was sentenced to 250 hours' community service for his part in the scheme to sell the gun parts and the vests.

Beattie said he found the gun parts and vests in a park while on a training run eight years ago.

The five dismantled F1 submachineguns were to be sold to the officer for $1500 each and the vests for $400 each.

Judge Moore said he took into account positive aspects of Elias's character in imposing the minimum nine months term.

He said Elias at first believed he was not breaking the law when he was supplying the gun parts and vests to the officer whom he thought was a firearms collector.

Elias claimed the officer told him he would not proceed with buying the gun parts and vests unless amphetamines were also provided.

Judge Moore said he was satisfied Elias was told the amphetamines had to be provided if the rest of the deal was to go ahead.

He said he also accepted from Elias that it was Beattie who initiated the transaction over the gun parts and vests in the first place and had told Elias he was in financial straits.

Elias told the court Beattie begged him to help get rid of the items for him because he was bankrupt and in a bad financial position.

Judge Moore said Elias's evidence was that he was being pestered by both sides, by Beattie to assist him in the sale of the weapons parts and vests and by the undercover officer who refused to take part in the transaction unless Elias made available the drugs.

Beattie was not involved in the amphetamines aspect of the transaction.

Judge Moore said Elias, who also played for Balmain, came from a culture with a strong abhorrence of drugs.

He said Elias had not been involved with drug offences before and he accepted Elias would not do so again.

He said part of Elias's punishment he had already received was the shame and dishonour inflicted on his family with his mother hurt by taunts and publicly humiliated.

Judge Moore said Elias "feels genuine guilt and remorse particularly for allowing himself to be duped into supplying amphetamines."

Judge Moore recommended that Elias serve his term at a minimum security prison.

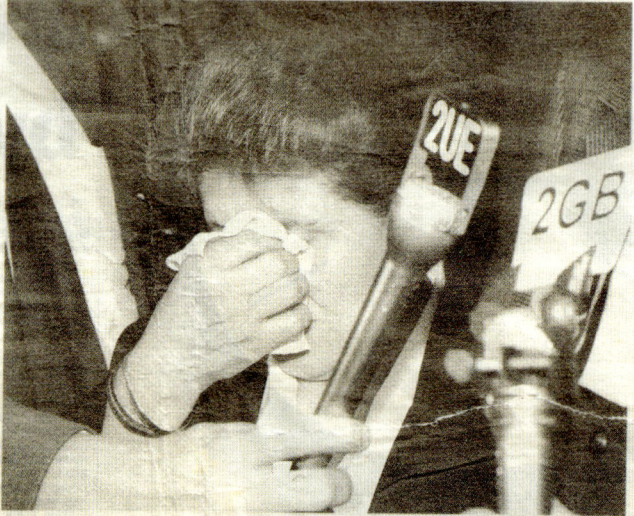

A mother's tears . . . Susan Elias at the District Court yesterday

John Elias yesterday

Mum was distraught to see me sent back to prison again.

On my way out of court after being charged for illegal firearms trading in 1995.

There aren't many bright days in prison, but this was one of them. Some of the biggest names in league at the time including Jim Dymock, Shane Walker, Nathan Wood, Gorden Tallis and Darren Senter took the time to visit me in Oberon.

When I got out of prison, I came back to what I knew – rugby league. This is me in the weights room preparing for a return for the Newtown Jets in the old Metropolitan Cup.

At Jets training in the week leading up to our 1996 grand final win over Balmain Ryde–Eastwood.

One of the proudest moments of my life – representing Lebanon while playing with cancer in 1999.

My battle with cancer reduced me from a fit and strong athlete to a scrawny bag of bones.

My ex-girlfriend Lisa was a rock during that time.

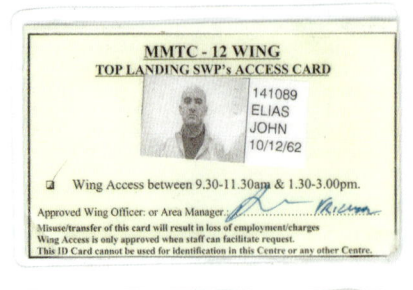

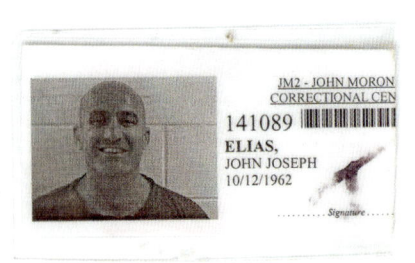

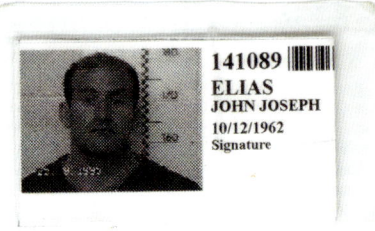

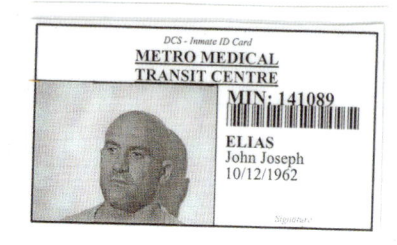

My various ID cards from prison.

12 WING SWEEPER DUTIES:

10. Maintain Stores
11. Mop Floor Daily
12. Empty Bins Daily
13. Clean Dinning Room
14. Polish Locks
15. Clean Landing office (Toilet, Mop and Bins)
16. Clean windows and vents.
17. Supervised and work as directed by Correctional Officers
18. Pay $15.75 daily every Wednesday

Contract of Understanding ....
                                    Inmate Sign

A duties card listing our responsibilities.

Back in jail – with plenty of spare time to pose for the cameras.

With a dear old friend, Elisabeth, who visited me regularly.

With Robbie Farah, who I had the privilege of coaching during the inaugural Lebanon vs France Test Match in Tripoli in 2002.

Little Al, known around the streets as 'the peacemaker', as he would rather put out a fire than start one.

My Kings Cross family – John Ibrahim (right) and John's minder Tongan Sam.

Who says super-coach Wayne Bennett does not smile? Catching up in 2009.

My good friend Nathan Wood and I, preparing for another torturous workout.

Blocker, Alan Jones, myself and Benny at Alan's 66th birthday celebrations.

Sydney's colourful identities, my mates Bruce Harding (left) and Olympic boxer Rick Timperi having fun on my recent birthday.

Wendell Sailor, myself and player manager Sam Ayoub during a day out at the races, 2010.

THE FIX

I approached the first player before training began on Tuesday afternoon, because the opportunity presented itself. I didn't have long to act. He was warming up alone in the middle of Redfern Oval when I made my way over. I didn't muck around. 'Listen, I've been asked to approach you on behalf of some boys who want to pay you $25,000 to play poorly against Wests the game after next,' I said. Naturally the player was surprised, but not as taken aback as I had expected. I could see his mind holding court between the same angel and devil I had been deliberating with the night before. He asked for a week to think about it, but I could only wait two days. I then made him swear not to tell a soul.

The next player was told after training as he walked through the car park. My routine was exactly the same, but this time we spoke openly about the fact that the match had no bearing on the finals. Like the first player, he hesitated but I could see the pause was just the result of a natural reaction. There was an overwhelming urge in both cases to take the money. I left training feeling that delicious tingle of adrenalin and electricity.

I was truly shocked by both players' reactions. I was fully expecting them to knock me back, because what I was suggesting went against everything we stood for. It would have been completely understandable if they had told me to get lost. I was now 50-50 about going ahead. The thrill was beginning to consume me, blocking out all sense of reason and conscience.

I spoke to Dave on the phone on Tuesday night and from that moment I believe he thought he had me. It was then he introduced a new element to our scheme. 'I'm also going to give you $50,000 to pay the Wests players to have the game of their lives,' he said. Approaching them would be a lot easier, because it didn't carry the stench of asking blokes to run dead on their teammates. In those days footballers backed themselves to win regularly. It was nothing out of the ordinary. Being paid extra to ensure you played well was simply an incentive, albeit this one was coming via a member of the opposition. Still, I reasoned there was nothing wrong with inducing the Wests players to perform above themselves. After all, it was Dave's money – not mine. I was just the middle man.

I phoned a certain Wests player I considered was critical to their chances of beating us. We knew each other and spoke every now and then. 'Listen, mate, there's a group of guys who are planning to have a go at Wests next weekend and they've asked me to offer you $15,000 to have the game of your life,' I told him. This little Magpie couldn't agree quickly enough. And why wouldn't he? It was simply a bonus to do what he was supposed to do – play to the very best of his ability.

I still had two Souths players left to speak with before the fix could be seriously contemplated. Wednesday was our day off and I made arrangements to meet both for coffee during the morning. The first was in Surry Hills and the second in Balmain – I always go for coffee in Balmain. They both baulked, but then I said: 'There's a lot of money involved.' I was getting better at the routine. Interested, despite themselves, they replied: 'How much?' When I mentioned the figure, their attitude changed. It was a stack of money and I've no doubt many players today would be swayed if they were in the same position.

The fix was starting to go from a possible to a probable. What had seemed ludicrous and morally incomprehensible just two nights earlier was suddenly very real and within reach. Feasting upon the illegitimate thrill, my mind raced ahead of my reason.

That evening, a plan of my own came together like pieces of a jigsaw falling from the sky to magically complete a puzzle. Dave was willing to outlay $200,000 to ensure players from both sides did their job. If that was his investment, then how much money was his crew actually betting on Wests? It had to be considerably more – millions perhaps. I suddenly realised I was at the centre of the plunge of the century.

It was then that a very dangerous possibility emerged, more dangerous than even entertaining this idea in the first place. Why should Dave be the only one to get a collect out of this? I was making all the arrangements, assuming a lot of risk and had intimate knowledge of who was involved. If everything went to plan and Dave was so confident, then surely I could have a bet with the same certainty. It suddenly ranked as a must-take opportunity to earn much more than $50,000. This was the chance of a lifetime to clean out the SP bookies and make more money than I could ever imagine.

My mind never stopped racing during those frantic days. But on that Wednesday night it whirred faster than ever with this newfound possibility. Everything began to line up. I felt like a professor who had just cracked a new mathematical equation, or a scientist who had made a landmark breakthrough.

Although Souths were falling away in late 1994, we were still placed much higher on the ladder than Wests. That meant we would start the game warm favourites. I estimated the bookies would give Wests a six-and-a-half points start at the line, or $1.90. Backing Wests with the start meant we could still win the game and collect, so long as we didn't win by more than six points. Yes, yes . . . this felt right. We could still win and collect. I could have it both ways – make a motza without having to deal with the guilt of running dead.

I was so swept up in the plan that I picked up the phone and redialled the Wests player. Then and there I offered him another $25,000 to find some teammates to play well. I kept up the story about some guys having a big bet who were Wests fans. He didn't question me and I honestly think he didn't see me as anything more than a go-between. My conscience felt like it had been released from a vice. I woke on the Thursday morning feeling like I had solved world poverty. My next step was to shore up my four teammates and then meet Dave. I spoke to each of the players at Redfern Oval that afternoon. Each one of them said he was willing to go ahead.

That night Dave and I met at Chequers. He was wearing a big grin even before I told him about the players agreeing. Not much more needed to be said, aside from emphasising the proviso that all players come through that weekend's matches uninjured for the fix to finally be locked in.

I didn't say a word to Dave about my plan to have a bet. It was a tricky operation, because I couldn't lay the bets on Wests myself, given I was a member of the opposition. Someone else needed to put their face on show.

Who else but my loyal mate and accomplice Georgie Boy? Georgie Boy and I did everything together and when told of Dave's arrangement he agreed to lay the bets.

But these just weren't any bets. This was the blitz to end all blitzes. Because we thought Wests winning with the start was a sure thing, we decided to hit every SP bookie for as much as we possibly could. The problem, however, was that we only had contacts with about three or four illegal SPs. There were many more operating but none that knew or trusted us well enough to hold the type of money we intended on betting.

There was only one man who could bring them into our grasp: Neddy Smith. In 1994, he was back in prison after a couple of fleeting releases since my stretch 15 years earlier. Unable to put my head on show I arranged for Georgie Boy to meet a contact of Neddy Smith over the weekend for a leg-up with every SP bookie in town. Georgie Boy returned with instructions to talk to a bloke called Willy. Neddy had told Willy to recommend Georgie Boy to the bookies, who would then accept his bets. Willy had contacts with about 17 bookies, which, including my handful, made 20 all up.

It was a nice even number that demanded a clean bet. On the following Monday, Georgie Boy and I decided on an insane figure to bet – $1 million. The plan was for Georgie Boy to whack all 20 bookies at once as soon as betting opened on Tuesday morning. He was to place $50,000 with each bookie on Wests to win with six-and-a-half points start at $1.90.

We were betting $1 million to win $900,000. Suddenly, my $50,000 cut from Dave seemed inconsequential. The fact neither Georgie Boy nor I had $1 million was a major concern. All the bookies bet on credit, meaning we wouldn't have to pay until the following week if the bets lost. But that didn't enter my mind. I was sure we had everything covered, with the four Souths players agreeing not to play well and the Wests players primed to do the opposite. There was also the ring of confidence that radiated around Dave. If his boys were in, then it couldn't lose.

All the players from both sides came through their respective matches on the Sunday unscathed. I remember doing a rapid check of the four Souths boys in the SFS dressing room after our 30–28 loss to Illawarra. They told me they were all sweet, both physically and mentally, about what was to happen in seven days time.

Monday was hectic. At recovery, I told the players that we could still win the game and collect. They understood that the bets were being placed on the start, meaning that all we had to do was win by less than seven points. This came as a huge relief to them. No player I've ever met would feel comfortable about running dead and trying to lose. We were still determined to win – just not by too much. Although the margin for error was tight, I felt comfortable there were enough key players in on the plan to ensure we didn't score more points than necessary if things went down to the wire.

At this time none of the players knew who the others were. In fact, they had no idea there was anyone else involved. I didn't tell them a thing. Even after stories emerged that a group had been approached, some of those players came up to me wanting to know who the others were. But I swore never to utter a word, pointing out that I had equal respect for their involvement.

Georgie Boy was doing it equally tough that day, running around all over town with Willy to meet SP bookies. By nightfall, however, we were ready. All that was left was for the betting to open and my meeting with Dave. It had now been a week since our first meeting and I was sitting across from him feeling much more assured. I had taken this scheme much, much further than I ever thought possible when it was first suggested. We were now on the verge of pulling off something unprecedented and I couldn't foresee a hurdle that would stop us.

At BBQ King, I told him about the line betting without mentioning my personal plunge. Instead, I said the players had only agreed to be in it if the fix was to win by no more than six-and-a-half points. I said no-one would agree to lie down and lose. Dave understood their attitude and agreed to back Wests on the line. All he said was: 'Just make sure you keep quiet.' Referencing my previous favour to him in jail, I replied: 'You of all people should know my lips are sealed.'

'It's not you I'm worried about,' Dave said. 'It's the other players.'

When the odds came out on Tuesday morning Wests were given a six-and-a-half points start, just as I had predicted. Georgie Boy didn't waste any time. Within 10 minutes he had spread $1 million worth of bets among 20 illegal SP bookmakers at $1.90. We were set. The pressure was now on, because either way that sum of money can represent problems.

If Souths somehow won by too much, we had no idea how to pay. In my line of work, I understood the type of trouble this would lead to. But winning $900,000 in illegitimate cash also had its pitfalls. How on earth were we going to launder that amount of money? My first thought was a friend I had in the Commonwealth Bank, who I hoped would come to the party if needed.

Aside from those doubts, I was relatively calm considering what was at stake. I had been in plenty of high-pressure situations during my time, but these were uncharted waters. I don't know if my imagination was vivid enough to conjure up what consequences might await if the fix came unstuck.

We'd be in debt for $1 million and then there'd be Dave to contend with. Crazy, unhinged Dave.

The rest of Tuesday and Wednesday passed without incident. I was happy, particularly because our coach Ken Shine had named me on the bench. The less game time I had in this match, the better. The other players weren't saying a peep and everything was heading for the big moment, like a motorcycle stuntman who's had the perfect ride to the lip of the Grand Canyon. He's done everything to ensure he gets to the other side, but nothing is certain until his tyres hit terra firma on the other side.

Up until then, we'd had the perfect ride. Then the bloody phone rang. It's 10 am on Thursday. Dave is on the other end. Oh shit. Even before he spoke, I knew it wasn't good news. 'John, I need to meet you in Balmain asap.' This was an order, not a request. Racked with uncertainty, I drove from Punchbowl to my coffee shop of choice and found Dave waiting. His eyes didn't give anything away. He still looked relaxed. But I wasn't, particularly when he opened with the words: 'John, there's been a change of plans. Forget the handicap betting, my boys have backed Wests straight out to win at $2.60.'

I froze. I folded my arms in silence, sat back and let a world of pain descend on me. This was not good news. Not good at all. Just as the Souths players and myself had found the perfect medium between making an earn and not compromising victory, it had all fallen apart. We were being told to run dead. I began to speak quickly, telling Dave that the players had only agreed to the six-and-a-half point handicap.

Dave looked at me and smiled. Right at that moment I felt embarrassed to have insulted his intelligence. 'John, I knew you'd have a go with the bookies, but you got in before us,' he said. After Georgie Boy had smashed them, the bookies wouldn't take a cent more on Wests with the handicap. They had obviously spoken to one another and sensed a fix. That left Dave and his mates in a tight spot. Their only option was to back Wests straight-out at bigger odds.

The reality was crushing my lungs, squeezing the air and forcing me to gasp. I felt like choking. Wests had to win the game and that was that. It was what Dave wanted and people like Dave got what they wanted. I now had the horrible task of going back to my teammates and telling them to run dead. Sensing I was in strife, Dave said he could guarantee extra money for the Rabbitohs players to run dead instead of winning by less than a certain margin. It was little consolation.

I trudged to training that afternoon a hollow man. I felt drained and worthless. Panic and fear had robbed me of the thrill I had felt all week. I now saw the situation for what it was: a dirty, grubby scheme. Nevertheless, I couldn't afford to pull out. I felt that between Dave and the bookies, my very life could depend on convincing the players to stay solid.

I spoke to each of them before training and they were bemused. I could feel them quietly freaking out, wanting to scream. It made me feel like shit. Here I was, a senior player and a bloke who had been brought to the team for his experience, putting them in this position. It was feeling less and less worthwhile, no matter what I risked personally. Rugby league, after all, is a team sport. I realised how wrong I had been to put myself first.

The fix began to collapse after training on Thursday night when one player approached me to say he was pulling out. 'It's just not worth the drama,' he said. 'I can't bring myself to run dead.' Secretly I agreed, but my outward emotions were still on autopilot. 'A deal is a deal,' I fumed. 'You can't back out. How much more money do you want?' But he was adamant. And what's more – he was right. 'We never had a deal to run dead – the deal was to win but by less than six-and-a-half points. You're now asking me to do something else.'

The plan was always contingent on all four players agreeing. If one pulled out, it was over. And so it was over as far as the Souths guys were concerned. I couldn't have felt a more extreme mix of emotions at that point in time. On one hand there was an incredible relief because we weren't going ahead to lose the game. Looking back, if I had cheated Alan Jones and the team it would have been something I couldn't have lived with. But then again, I might not live that long. All of a sudden there was no certainty. The Souths players were now determined to win and on form there was no reason why they shouldn't. If that happened, I was a dead man walking.

By Saturday all four players had told me they wanted no involvement. I accepted their decision. They were entitled to pull out, because the rules had been changed midway through the game. What's more, rumours had started around town about an orchestrated sting on the Souths–Wests game. It was far too hot for these players to handle.

When I told Georgie Boy about our decaying situation he suggested we could send in some of our Islander acquaintances to convince my four teammates to change their minds. It was a ludicrous idea, given they were on my side, but Georgie Boy was the one being exposed to a $1 million debt. He was desperate and willing to contemplate anything. The next bright idea was to contact Dave and tell him. But we quickly realised this was out of the question

THE FIX

for precisely the same reason. If he knew the Souths players had reneged, Dave would send his own heavies their way to force a change of heart.

We were in deep strife. Only two options remained – the Wests players and Neddy Smith. On the eve of the game I rang my man at the Magpies and offered him an extra $50,000 to spend as he saw fit to ensure Wests played the game of their lives. This player must have thought I was Father Christmas, throwing money at him just to play well. He said he'd been in touch with another four players who were primed to cash in with big games.

At 8:30 am on Sunday, less than seven hours before kick-off, Georgie Boy went and saw Neddy Smith's contact again. He needed to ask for Neddy's help with the bookmakers in the event of our bets losing. He told the contact he would need extra time to pay the money. When Georgie Boy pulled up at my house around 10 am I was a human wreck. I had slept like a damned man the night before – not a wink. I felt like I was about to face the firing squad that very afternoon at Orana Park. There was no chance of a pardon, no prospect of escape.

To top everything off, the Sunday newspapers had published a story detailing the rumours about a suspected fix on that afternoon's game between Souths and Wests at Campbelltown. The stories said that bookmakers were wary of Souths players running dead after a huge plunge on the Magpies. No names were mentioned, but it didn't matter. My ordeal was now being played out in broad daylight. There was nowhere to hide.

When I went outside to meet Georgie Boy, my heart skipped a beat. Sitting in the passenger seat of his car was Dave. Fuck! The last thing I needed Dave to know was where my family lived, particularly given what was likely to happen if Wests didn't win that afternoon. Once again, Dave looked at ease. In fact, he was even smiling. It turned out Neddy had told Georgie Boy to get in touch with Dave asap. My old friend in prison knew exactly what was going on. I should have known better.

'Neddy was filthy that you beat him to it,' Dave joked. 'He wanted part of the sting.' I couldn't bring myself to laugh along. Dave was still smiling as he continued. 'Now look, John, about these SP bookmakers, you and Georgie Boy don't have to worry because I've bought the debt. I still remember what you did for me in Long Bay all those years ago. I would have got an extra decade if you hadn't stayed quiet. The last 10 years have been kind to me and I owe that to you.'

My eyes widened. I couldn't believe Dave was willing to cover us, but was still wary of being in his debt. Nevertheless, I didn't have a choice. 'Will my family be OK?' I asked, still petrified about the consequences of anything but a Wests victory.

'They will be OK,' he promised. 'But if Wests don't win you will have to leave the country. I'll have a passport organised for you within a week.'

It was simply too much for me to process. I felt like I was going to collapse. I was out of the frying pan and into the fire. The fix was now well and truly off, with Dave also withdrawing my $50,000 fee. Georgie Boy and I were saved from a debt that could have had us killed, but the price could be leaving Australia. What was going on? Was it worth it? I couldn't tell. I didn't know. I couldn't think rationally.

And I had a game of football to play. The Souths team bus was due to leave Redfern at noon for Campbelltown. The prospect of driving myself to Redfern from Punchbowl was like being asked to walk to Perth. I simply didn't know how to do it. I relied on a dozen years of first-grade experience to see me through. I was in such a daze that I could have started drooling.

The only thing that jerked me to attention was Ken Shine's fury before we boarded the bus for Campbelltown. Ken was brandishing the newspaper articles about the fix. He screamed that if any player planned to lie down, they should get off the bus immediately. No-one moved a muscle. Several players denied any knowledge and insisted the story was bullshit.

I didn't say a word.

During the 45-minute drive west I sank into a conscious 'coma'. My mind drifted away to places like Lebanon, France and the UK. Which would be my new home? Would I even have a choice? A media circus greeted the bus when it arrived at the ground. There were journos and cameras everywhere, hitting us up with questions about the rumoured fix as we tried to rush to the visitors' dressing rooms. Ken Shine and Alan Jones did well that day. They shooed the reporters away and allowed us to prepare in peace.

By complete coincidence, I ended up bumping into the Wests player I had been speaking to about 30 minutes before kick-off. I'll never forget his words. 'John, we're treating this game like a grand final,' he said. It didn't make me feel any better. I had the chance to speak with the four Souths players I'd tried to pay off. I told them the fix was off – to go out there and play the game of their lives. It felt good deep down because I can at least sleep at night knowing I didn't induce anyone to lie down. I felt like an evil man who had repented all his sins on his deathbed and been absolved.

Then I went back into my coma. I felt like telling Ken that I wasn't well enough to play, but decided it was too hard. Just before kick-off I decided to accept whatever happened. From then on my mind went blank and the next 80 minutes passed as if I wasn't there.

All I knew afterwards was that Wests had won. I read in the paper the next day that the score was 34–26. I can't remember anything about the game, who scored when and what happened at halftime. I played the final 20 minutes, but the result was sealed by then. At least that was some consolation. Disaster had been avoided, but I felt no reason to rejoice. I should have been exultant, but I only felt emptiness. I now recognise this as guilt for ever contemplating such a thing.

Thankfully, Dave was off my back. He was also $900,000 richer – money Georgie Boy and I would have collected if not for the change of plans. My street sense told me that we might have been the victim of a double cross, but it was all academic now. The truth was that Dave had probably been too smart for us. When we met the following night at Chequers, he told me: 'Don't worry, John, I was never going to make you go overseas because Wests were never going to lose that game.'

I didn't ask any questions. There was nothing more I needed to know.

CHAPTER 17

THE FIX-UP

Monday passed without incident. One day was all I had to reflect and absorb the shock of what had just happened over the past fortnight. Then, on the Tuesday after our match against Wests, a fresh wave of controversy broke. One of the SP bookmakers that Georgie Boy had bet with decided to contact every media outlet in town and finger me as the ringleader of the fix. Newspapers and talkback radio went into meltdown. Gotcha! Their suspicions had all but been confirmed.

That afternoon at training, Alan Jones approached me for a private chat. He looked me in the eye and asked, 'John, I want you to tell me the truth – did you have any part in a fix?' What do I say? Truly, in my heart, I felt absolved from the moment I approached the four Souths players just before the game and told them to play well. I also did my best on the day. I had harboured no guilt about running dead, because we didn't.

Or at least that's what I thought. There was a nagging suspicion that Dave might have organised something from his end in secret. He just seemed so relaxed and confident the whole time. And I'll never forget his final words – 'Don't worry, John, Wests were *never* going to lose that game.' It couldn't be denied that I was guilty of arranging money for the Wests players to perform well. I assumed Dave had organised the final payment to them, as the Magpies never complained about being owed money. In my mind, this did not constitute foul play. It was nothing unusual for players to back themselves or accept incentives to have a big game.

But it could never be denied that I'd set off a potentially disastrous chain of events. I'd been guilty of putting my teammates under enormous personal strain. My own internal struggle was evidence enough. Although we didn't end up playing poorly, I'd still gone a fair way down a very murky road that would have shattered the faith of the coaching staff and fans if they knew. Out of all the mistakes I'd made, this was arguably the worst because I'd endangered the reputations of others who were like brothers to me on the field. I'd also come within an ace of destroying the very essence that maintains professional sport's very special place in society: the absolute belief that every contest is a genuine one and that every competitor is trying their very best.

'There was no fix,' I replied to Jones. He looked at me and walked off. It was the last time we spoke about the incident.

The papers, however, were not done. The story grew enough legs to walk to China, headlining the front and back pages for a week. My phone was under siege from journalists wanting answers. I gave them the same one I gave Jones – there was no fix. While I was being bombarded, the real pressure was directed at Jones. Because he was a tall poppy, the media wanted his scalp. They felt that if his players were involved, then he should accept responsibility as coaching director and take a fall.

After a week of unrelenting pressure, Jones finally spoke to me about doing a proper interview to put the controversy to bed. As an experienced broadcaster, he knew the media would not stop braying until it got a public inquest. I decided to go for Ray Martin on *A Current Affair*. Ironically, Ray was also a big Souths fan. The interview was to be aired live across Australia. I was given no briefing about the questions before we went on air. It was just 'Bang!' Ray asked all the same old questions and I kept challenging him for proof. No-one had any.

But he did reveal something new that evening. He told me the National Crime Authority (NCA) had evidence of my involvement and had frozen my bank account. While this piece of information obviously intrigued me, I couldn't afford to show any emotion before a national audience of millions. I just nodded and said, 'That's their prerogative, but I'm innocent.'

Freezing my bank account was of no great consequence because I always had access to large sums of cash. But being tailed by the NCA was a worry. At the time, I was still finishing my community service from the previous charges of obtaining money with menace from Bill two years earlier. I had been placed at Newtown Police Boys, helping underprivileged youth with the great boxing trainer Johnny Lewis. Johnny took to me straightaway, saying, 'If a person has good in them, I like them. If a person has a lot of good in them, I befriend them.'

On the weekend after the Wests game I went to Redfern Oval with a couple of the other Souths players to watch the local A-grade grand final. Terry Hill and Jim Dymock, a Souths junior who went on to star for Canterbury and Parramatta, were also there. During the match I spotted a couple of blokes on the hill wearing binoculars that weren't aimed at the field. Instead, they were fixed in my direction. I'd been around long enough to realise they were undercover cops trailing me.

This was not a problem in itself, so long as I didn't do or say anything stupid. That was left to someone else. An old friend of mine called Mick was also at Redfern Oval that day. When he spotted me he came up and sat next to us in the grandstand. As luck would have it, Mick was carrying $14,000 cash in a paper bag. He put the paper bag down between us and the cops jerked to attention straightaway. I saw them start our way immediately. I told Mick to get out of there. But he was too slow, he didn't realise what I was going on about.

Within seconds the cops were on to us. They grabbed Mick and the bag and took him away. I remember yelling at him to take all his clothes off so the cops didn't plant anything on him. Given the fact they were gunning for my head, this was probably too cheeky. But I could never help myself whenever an opportunity to be a smarty presented itself. The circuit between my mouth and brain would conveniently lose transmission.

When the NCA finally summoned me for an interview at their headquarters, it came as no great shock. By then it was the week before our final game of the season against Cronulla. Even though it was shaping as my Sydney swansong, the game couldn't come quickly enough. I was sure that once Souths finished playing, the media circus would pack up and leave town. Two coppers greeted me in an office deep inside the NCA building at Surry Hills. They had a particular look about them. A determined look. It would mean a lot for their careers and reputations if they could score an arrest in a high-profile case like this one. I suddenly felt like the white whale in *Moby Dick*.

The two cops had nothing. They knew it and I knew it. They questioned me for about two hours, but it was no tougher than being pumped for information by Ray Martin. These situations just didn't faze me. From the day I survived Long Bay as a teenager, I felt steeled for anything.

I was released and played off the bench in our final game of 1994: a 42–0 loss to Cronulla. After climbing into the top five on the turn for home, Souths compounded badly in the straight that season. We dropped our final six games to plummet down the ladder and finish 10th out of 16 teams. It was a disappointing end to a season that had promised so much.

Personally, however, it was a decent season. Although I switched clubs midway through, I'd played almost every game in first-grade. If this was the end, then it could have been worse. My thoughts turned to heading back to Leigh for a final fling, but there was also a slight nibble from the Gold Coast for me to head up there and join Craig 'Tugger' Coleman in 1995. Wayne Bennett had been speaking to his former coaching partner from Canberra, Don Furner snr, about my possible signing. Don was CEO of the Gold Coast at the time. As the 1994 finals kicked off, he was thinking about signing me to an incentive-based deal.

There were suddenly no commitments for me to honour in the meantime. I could easily have run wild, but the NCA shadow kept me cautious. I had to lie low for a couple more weeks before it cleared. During those early spring days I frequented the races with former St George captain Mick Beattie. I'd played against Mick on many occasions, but only got to know him well when he joined Balmain as defensive coach at the start of 1994. Although I only played half that season at Leichhardt, we quickly became good mates. Mick wasn't a scallywag or anything, but he did enjoy a punt. He was also good mates with Harry Eden, my SP bookmaking partner. We hit it off pretty well, and stayed in touch even after I left for the Rabbitohs.

It was on a deserted Wednesday afternoon at Canterbury racecourse that Mick caught me by surprise. 'I've come across a load of bulletproof vests and machine-gun parts,' he said suddenly. 'Do you think you could help me get rid of them?'

Mick wasn't dumb. Although I'd never told anyone the full story about my double life, he knew I was well connected. I was mildly surprised that our friendship was moving into this territory, because Mick was clean as far as I knew. But who was I to judge? After all, they were only bulletproof vests – items I truly didn't think were illegal to sell. As for the machine-gun parts, he told me there were no firing mechanisms. I couldn't see the risk, but in hindsight I also blinded myself. Again, I was infatuated with the lure of black money and whatever adventures its solicitation might bring. Although I'd done worse previously, it was sheer recklessness to sell guns and vests given the proverbial bullet I'd just dodged. Either way, I'd put myself right back in the firing line.

I'd never dealt with firearms. I had no contacts in the area. I told Mick to give me two days to think about it. Mick informed me there were as 'many vests as you can sell'. I didn't ask him where he was getting them from. I don't seek answers I don't need. But I suspected he might have had a contact in the army. It was obvious who would buy the vests. Bikie gangs loved them. But I had nothing to do with bikie gangs. I needed a middle man.

That man was a very old friend of mine called Sam, whom I had met in Long Bay jail 15 years earlier. He had a wife and two children, but family life hadn't blunted his edge. Sam was still very well connected to all sorts. I could trust Sam. The NCA spooks had me a little paranoid and what I was doing was risky given my name had just been dragged through the mud in connection with the fix. I had to be very careful who I spoke to and what I said.

Sam and I went back a long way. He told me that selling the vests and gun parts wouldn't be a problem. And so it proved. For the next couple of weeks we moved a heap of vests, hundreds perhaps. Mick's supply seemed to be endless and Sam's bikie mates couldn't get enough of them.

About a fortnight after I first talked to Sam, he told me about another contact who was particularly interested in the gun parts. This guy, Tony, wanted to meet me. It wasn't the usual practice to deal directly with a buyer if I didn't know them. That was left to the middleman, in this case Sam. But because I knew Sam well and he asked me to meet the guy, I agreed. Tony was heavy-set, with a long ponytail shooting out the back of his otherwise bald head. When we met at Sam's house Tony told me he was a gunsmith. He collected and stored gun parts in a warehouse and was very interested in what Sam had shown him.

As far as I was concerned, Tony was just an innocent gun collector. He was buying the parts for personal use, not for anything illegal. I was selling them. The possibility that we were doing something wrong didn't cross my mind. Over the coming days I sold four sets of gun parts to Tony. We always met at Sam's house to do the business. He wasn't such a bad bloke either. In time, Tony and I got on. I liked his sense of humour and genuine interest in the products.

For the fifth transaction, Tony asked me to meet him somewhere else. Then he asked for some additional merchandise – an ounce of speed. I had never sold drugs before, because I was against them. My only contact with drug dealers was collecting money from them. The request took me by surprise a little, but Tony was developing into a very good client. He was paying big money for the gun parts and had bought a few vests as well. I suddenly had a financial stake in keeping him happy. So I agreed to fix him up with the ounce of speed.

Once again the dreaded blinkers had descended and impaired my better judgement. I was still vaguely aware of the NCA and the risk, but I was more caught up in the thrill of making quick money. Tony wanted to meet in the SFS car park on the Tuesday night before the 1994 grand final between Canterbury and Canberra.

As always, I arrived first. Tony then pulled up in an old blue Datsun. This was the first thing that made me think twice. If he was a gunsmith with all this money to purchase parts, why the hell was he driving a jalopy worth no more than $500? It didn't stack up.

Tony got out and immediately asked: 'Have you got the speed?' There was no greeting, he got straight to the point. But what really irked me was the fact he referred to the drugs directly. This was never done. Because of the risk of police wires, taps or microphones it was commonplace to say: 'Have you got the stuff?' But Tony had gone out of

THE FIX-UP

his way to mention the drugs, which sent my paranoia into overdrive.

It was the first time I thought I could be dealing with an undercover cop. Sure not to make a sound, I put my left index finger over my mouth and reached out with my right hand and placed it gently on Tony's chest. He was only wearing a T-shirt. As soon as my hand touched his chest I could feel what I thought was a wire. It was pure instinct that made my hand reach out and touch his chest and I was very thankful for it. 'What's this?' I asked, groping gently. 'A wire? Are you a cop?'

Tony didn't flinch. 'What are you carrying on about, John?' he said with an incredulous look. 'Of course I'm not a cop. It's a gold chain my father gave me before he died.'

His manner was convincing, but I had too much to lose to believe him straight up. 'If it's just a chain, then take off your shirt and show me,' I ordered.

He now looked slightly offended, eyeing me as if I was some sort of lunatic. 'John, be serious. I'm not a cop, OK? Relax.' Maybe I was going overboard. After all, Tony had been introduced to me through Sam, a lifelong friend I could trust no matter what. Surely Sam would never double-cross me and set me up with an undercover cop.

Still, I wasn't willing to take any gambles unless he was willing to take off his shirt. Because of my faith in Sam, I decided to go through with the deal – but in code. 'I've got those grand final tickets you wanted,' I said, in reference to the speed, which I handed over very quietly.

Tony's demeanour didn't change, despite my accusations. He accepted the ounce with a smile and thanked me. 'See you soon,' he said. I was left alone in the darkened car park, the huge white sails of the SFS looming over me. In a few days time it would be packed with 45,000 screaming fans for the biggest game of the year. But at that moment it was just me, my thoughts and my suspicions.

I was still troubled the next morning. If Tony wasn't wearing a wire, why didn't he just remove his shirt and prove it? I had to see Sam. 'What are you going on about?' said Sam, his face wearing the exact same expression of ridicule that had crossed Tony's features the previous night. 'Tony's father gave him that chain before he died. He's been dead for a long time.'

My gut instinct told me not to see Tony again, but he was in touch with Sam soon enough. By the following week he had put in an order for more machine-gun parts. And this time, he wanted two ounces of speed as well.

And this is where I keep stuffing up. I just can't say no. Mick was making a good earn out of the vests and gun parts and I was happy to be helping a mate. If I turned away one of our best customers, we would have struggled to move so much gear so quickly. I hated dealing drugs – never had done so before – but thought the speed was essential to keeping Tony's business. He always paid up in cash and on time. The money was easy, too good for a blinded fool like me to refuse despite every instinct within telling me to stop. I wilfully ignored them and pushed on, like a deranged poker machine addict doubling up his winnings on red or black, convinced that the inevitable loss will never arrive.

Again it was the SFS – this time during the day about a fortnight after our first one-on-one in the car park. Because the previous season I had played for Souths, who were based at the SFS, I still had membership to the stadium's gym. I'd go there on most mornings to work out and keep fit in the event of the Gold Coast making me an offer for 1995.

THE FIX-UP

This time I didn't have to ask Tony twice to take his shirt off. He unbuttoned it straight away, revealing a gold chain. 'See, it's just a chain. You happy now?' he exclaimed with a smile.

Perhaps sensing I was still uneasy, he then showed me something else in his wallet. It was a licence – a gunsmith's licence with his full name, address and photo. Tony then told me about his workshop in Tempe, near the airport. He said he was storing all the gun parts and vests there, along with other items he had collected over the years.

'I want you to get me as much as you can – as many vests and parts as you can fit into a truck,' Tony said. 'Come and check out the warehouse tomorrow, so you can see how big it is.'

The uplifted shirt, the non-existent wire, the sentimental gold chain . . . it all had me feeling more relaxed. Not convinced, but still relaxed enough to let my curiosity off the leash. It was extremely hard to restrain at the best of times.

By the next day I felt little trepidation as I was let through the gates of the industrial complex that housed Tony's workshop. The friendly-looking bloke on the gate waved me straight through as soon as I mentioned Tony's name. It was obvious which warehouse belonged to Tony. Above the roller door to his storeroom was a massive sign bearing his name and occupation. I suddenly felt silly for being so paranoid about his identity. This guy was obviously fair dinkum.

Tony must have heard me pull up, because he opened the door before I could reach it. I didn't have any items for him on this occasion. It was just a reconnaissance for next time. The warehouse was huge – lined with shelves bearing antique guns and firing mechanisms of all descriptions. Because they were tools of my trade, I had a general idea of different makes and types of guns. But Tony's collection dwarfed my limited knowledge of what weapons were required to scare people. He had firearms from all over the world, from different periods in history. Tony led me through the warehouse with the devotion of a mother showing off the sleeping infants in her nursery. He also recounted an amazing amount of knowledge about each item.

As intriguing as the tour might have been, I wanted to talk my business – not his. Tony's eyes widened when the topic changed to the upcoming deal, his arms flapping to emphasise the free storage space available for our merchandise. 'Bring as much as you think will fit,' he said. The warehouse could have accommodated several truckloads, and we had no shortage of vests and gun parts.

But Tony's eagerness bugged me as I drove out of the estate and waved goodbye to the smiling gatekeeper. I also couldn't help thinking about his request for another 'couple of ounces' of speed. It seemed an unusual combination, so I decided to supply only five vests and five lots of parts as well as the drugs. I'd simply tell him our man had got caught up and that the rest was on its way.

Mick Beattie and I were still in regular contact. He was pleasantly surprised with how well trade was going, especially Tony's custom. Mick wanted to meet our number one buyer, so I told him that I'd arranged to drop some gear off to Tony's warehouse in three days time. Mick was dead keen to accompany me. It would be the first time we worked together.

On the morning of the deal – a Wednesday – I got a phone call. That simple dial phone in Mum's sitting room was like a tolling bell. I'd lost count of how many times its beige receiver had conveyed news that would change my life or freeze my veins. This time, it could have done both had I been thinking more clearly. But I wasn't. I was a non-questioning believer. On the other end was an old mate called Adam. Like Sam, he was very well connected – even with corrupt police. He didn't get in touch often, so just the sound of his voice already had me interested.

'John, I don't know what you're up to but I want you to be extremely careful,' Adam warned. 'You've just been connected with trying to fix a game and it would be a good idea to lie low.'

I told Adam that everything was fine, that I was keeping a close eye out. I knew the NCA was on the lookout and had been careful not to expose myself. I'd given Tony the treatment and convinced myself he was the real deal. He came recommended by Sam, who I knew would never dud me. Unperturbed by Adam's call, I drove south to meet Mick in Blakehurst, on the corner of King Georges Road and the Princes Highway. There we loaded the car with five vests and five bags of parts. I already had the two ounces of speed packed down my pants. Mick looked excited to finally be getting a first-hand look at the way this business worked. And he'd brought along a surprise item for us to sell.

It was a .44 Magnum, just like the one Con's gang had held to my head four years earlier. That gun belonged to Mick's good mate and former centre partner at St George, Brian Johnson. Brian also captained the Dragons at one stage and was a real squarehead, going on to be CEO of the club before a battle with cancer. Brian owned the gun legally – he had a target shooting licence – but had no need for it anymore. He passed it on to Mick, believing it would be sold to a legitimate gunsmith.

When Mick and I pulled up, the same bloke was at the

gate as three days ago. He recognised me and waved us straight through before I had a chance to stop the car. It was midday and the weather radiated summer's advance. It was warm and humid, especially inside Tony's warehouse. Mick was utterly fascinated with the goodies on the other side of the roller door. After meeting Tony, he got lost in his own infatuation and wandered around the room picking up different guns and caressing them.

Tony seized his chance. He shepherded me to a corner and asked about the speed. Thinking I was smart I replied, 'What speed? I don't know anything about any speed?' Then I handed him the bag without another word.

I thought I was so smart. I thought I had it all covered. Then the sunlight appeared. It rushed through the darkened warehouse like a cool change on a stifling summer day. It made my eyes burn and the world went white. The only thing I could hear was the final echo of the roller door – WHOOOOSH.

Then came the yelling. It seemed like hundreds of male voices: 'Get down on the ground NOW!' they shouted in unison. The words hit us from behind face shields and gas masks. This was the New South Wales police riot squad speaking.

We were surrounded by blue overalls and black steel-capped boots. Machine-gun muzzles trained themselves on our foreheads, guided by infrared beams. If I remembered anything from those terrifying couple of seconds, it was those beams. I recall how they led straight to my chest and face, the two kill zones a sniper is trained to aim at.

As I hit the floor, I blamed myself. I had seen the signs and ignored them. I had listened to others over my own instincts. This was no different from the time I'd allowed

THE FIX-UP

George and Mum to convince me against playing for the Broncos. Just another regret of the worst kind, the kind when you make the right decision only to forsake it for someone else.

I'd been done a beauty. I'd been played like a fool. Tony was on the floor as well, but I knew he wouldn't be compromised for long. In a couple of hours he would be the toast of the force, while Mick and I rotted away in anticipation of our fates.

For someone who rates themselves as a serious player on the streets, this was the ultimate humiliation. I'd been set up. I'd been played like a fool. I thought about how Sam introduced me to Tony and defended him. Sam, my good mate. Sam, who had now better be hoping they find him a good safe house. I thought about the bloke on the gate. How he was there both days and recognised me earlier on. I thought about his smile, which I mistook for a friendly welcome. But all along it was a smile of knowing contempt. *Just like the one Tony wore when I accused him of being an undercover cop.* I've got to hand it to Tony – he put on a fantastic performance. I should have been flattered. In reality, the police had spared no expense or effort to net me. All these old weapons, the fake gunsmith's licence, the warehouse – they were all props in a reality movie in which I was the unwitting protagonist.

As the world came back into view, I could sense at least 20 riot police in the warehouse. This was a huge operation in honour of yours truly. To go to such lengths, the police must have wanted me badly. It wasn't hard to guess why. The NCA had been left red-faced after beating its chest about having evidence linking me to the Souths–Wests fix. Instead of following through with what should have been a routine arrest, they got nothing. Ego thrives on both sides of the thin blue line. They weren't going to give up so easily. They'd get their guilty verdict – even if they had to manufacture it themselves.

Still, it was a hollow victory for the cops. They only had me for two ounces of speed and a small quantity of vests and machine-gun parts compared to what we had previously moved. I know the way set-ups work. They aren't pulled off at two ounces. The police prefer to wait until they've got you dealing kilograms before they pounce. The heavier the weight, the longer the sentence, the bigger the salary bonus. Isn't it beautiful?

I was stony-faced as they handcuffed me and led me to the paddy wagon. Although the police sting was a shock, it had nothing on being sent to Long Bay at 16. Something died inside me that afternoon in 1979 inside the children's court. It left me numb. From that moment on my spirit died, leaving me impervious not only to fear and pain, but also to love and warmth.

Mick Beattie was somewhere else when we pulled up at Newtown cop shop. I hadn't seen him from the moment Tony ushered me away to hand over the speed. I spent a couple of hours in the lock-up before being allowed to make my solitary phone call.

I rang my brother George. He already knew. The bust was a huge story on TV that night, probably as a result of the self-righteous police media department blowing their own trumpet. My older brother was shattered and arranged for John Korn, the solicitor who had defended me on my previous charges of obtaining money with menace, to come straight to the station. He advised me to say nothing and that's exactly what I did during the two-hour interview with the Newtown detectives. They were yet to lay charges,

THE FIX-UP

which I was told would be revealed in court the following morning.

I also learned that Mick was in another lock-up at the same station. John Korn was representing us both. At least I was an old hand at this caper. Mick, a first-timer, must have been petrified. I'd be lying if I said I wasn't concerned. I was yet to finish my community service from the previous charges, an overlap that would not help when it came to sentencing. Although the charges would not be too serious on the criminal spectrum, I had a sinking feeling that my freedom would again be taken away.

The cops treated me OK, handing me a takeaway sandwich for dinner and green pyjamas to sleep in. But I was given no fresh clothes, and had to front court in the same casual outfit I'd been arrested in.

Our game plan was to make no plea when the charges were announced in court. John Korn was a specialist in obtaining bail and said Mick's case would be heard first. He was certain Mick would be awarded bail because of his clean record and the fact he wasn't involved in dealing the drugs. Once Mick had bail, John would then use the precedent to try and secure my temporary release at the next hearing.

George told me our arrest was a big story on the news, but nothing could have prepared us for the number of cameras outside the courtroom at 10 am that Thursday. If anything else of note happened that day it must have gone unreported, because I'm sure everyone with a notepad or microphone was there that day. John Korn cruised through the pack like Moses parting the Red Sea, but my face felt like it was going to explode from the heat of camera flashes as I entered Newtown courthouse.

Mick and I were both charged with the illegal sale of

bulletproof vests and gun parts, as well as two ounces of speed. The prosecution would later drop the drugs charge against Mick, after John convinced them I was dealing on the side without his knowledge. Although it was Mick who had dragged me into this situation, I felt sorry for him. The cops wanted me and if I had been smarter, they wouldn't have got either of us. I was the one who got fooled, not Mick. But he was paying the penalty, particularly from the media, who were stunned at his involvement in such a scene. I think they had come to expect it from me by then.

Mick got bail and was led out of the courtroom and back to his family. He would later plead guilty and receive community service. But the real penalty was the slur on his reputation. All these years later, strangers are still fascinated by his involvement.

John delayed my bail application and the matter was held over until the Friday morning. That booked me another night in the slot at Newtown. On this occasion, however, it was easier to tolerate because the duty officer was a nice-looking female copper who took a bit of a liking to me. She brought me a change of clothes, cups of coffee and even magazines to flick through. Her biggest concession, however, was visitors. Apart from lawyers, outsiders were strictly prohibited from going downstairs. So that's why I couldn't believe my eyes when I saw Mum march up to the bars with a Tupperware container of her homemade tabouleh and kibbee. I ate well that night, which ended with me and the female copper talking for hours about footy. She was a big league fan and obviously fancied me because I was a player. I wasn't complaining.

The media redoubled its efforts the following morning, packing in so many reporters that the magistrate had to boot some of them outside. Those who were made to leave missed an amazing testimony from my brother George on the witness stand that morning. George had decided to be my character witness only on his way to the court. Before then John was going to ask for bail on the basis that Mick had been allowed to go home.

My older brother – the straitlaced solicitor – let it all out that day. He told the judge about our upbringing and how I was effectively left to run wild. He confessed his guilt at not being a better influence because of his preoccupation with his studies. At one point he started crying, but I can vouch it was no act to win the judge's favour. George was being fair dinkum about his feelings and regrets about our upbringing. After all these years, it had taken a situation like this to open him up.

I was equally moved and began crying as well. I have never once resented George for making something of his life while I struggled to determine what was right and wrong. True, he was presented with chances that none of his siblings had. But you can only play the cards you are dealt and full credit to George for making the most of his hand in life. How many people can say that? How many people can look back and honestly say they've made the most of their opportunities? There'd be some, but not too many. I certainly wasn't one of them, so I wasn't about to be dirty on George. In fact, I couldn't have been more proud.

The judge awarded me bail. I took a deep breath. Anything but Long Bay, I thought. There were reporters and cameras trailing me for weeks and I had to report to Newtown police station every day, but it didn't matter. Anything but Long Bay. My penalty was still uncertain, but there was already one sanction that had been confirmed that day. My top-grade football career was over. The police had confiscated my passport and prevented me from travelling interstate while I awaited sentencing. That ruled out returning to Leigh or having a final hurrah on the Gold Coast.

There was, however, a silver lining. The notoriety stemming from my very public arrest and charges had a mesmerising effect on the ladies. They approached me from all sides whenever I ventured out that summer. I remember plenty of nights at The Edge nightclub in Coogee, making hay while the sun was shining. I knew that before long I'd be enduring long periods of the day in darkness; when they'd close the door and leave me alone in my cell.

Throughout that time, however, I never stopped thinking about Sam. My temples and sinuses burned when I thought about how he had double-crossed me. About a week after being granted bail, I went for a quiet drive past his house. It was empty. The family had been moved in the dark of night to a secret place, for their own protection. At the time, it was probably a good thing for both of us. I can't guarantee what I would've done had I found Sam at home that day.

I later learned he had been found guilty of drug trafficking and sentenced to 10 years jail. With a wife and two kids, he was compromised. The cops knew that and they also knew he was linked to me, the one they really wanted. In the end, Sam was offered an unconditional release to set me up.

It meant becoming a police informant, the lowest creature on the face of the Earth as far as I was concerned. It meant lying to and cheating his friends, breaking the old code of honour among thieves. That's something virtually gone these days and the cops are so much more effective without it.

Once I realised the streets were squirming with

THE FIX-UP

two-timing, double-dealing scumbags like Sam, there was no option but to scale back. It was by far and away the best weapon police have against crime. Doing anything stupid was out of the question, because the police and NCA were still on my tail.

On Melbourne Cup day a few of the boys, including Nat Wood and Eddie Hayson, went to Randwick. That was the day Nat put the bigger fella on the seat of his pants. Eddie and I had a massive go on the Cup winner Jeune, earning me a six-figure collect from the rails bookies. Late in the day one bagman told me a couple of undercover cops had been questioning blokes in the ring about my activities on course that day. They were obviously looking for extra charges to load me up, because they sensed the current ones wouldn't go very far. 'But don't worry, John, I told them to get lost,' the bookmaker said.

My court date was set for April 1995. Incredibly, I played one final game on the football field the day before I appeared. Lakes United, a team in the Newcastle comp, had wanted me to turn out that season. One of their directors was an old Tigers player and we knew one another from my days at Balmain. He said the coach and officials didn't mind that I was about to be sent to jail. Even one game from an experienced second-rower like me would be a bonus.

I drove up the coast with a couple of Canterbury juniors on the Sunday and we ended up winning. That was the first and last game I played for Lakes United. Less than 24 hours later I was on my way back to the place I dreaded most in the world – Long Bay jail.

CHAPTER 18
FROM OBERON TO LEBANON

Déjà vu – that's the only way I can describe the feeling. More than 15 years had passed, and here I was again. Handcuffed in the back of a prison bus with a dozen other miserable souls on the way to Long Bay. I should have felt more than déjà vu. I had every right to feel sick, given what I had witnessed inside those walls as a teenager. Nothing rivalled the fear I experienced on that trip into the black unknown in October 1979. When I arrived they asked me if I was suicidal. I was 16. Would they ask me again now that I'm 32 – double the age?

I didn't feel as frightened, because I knew what to expect this time. And I wasn't destined for the real Long Bay. My previous visit had been a remand detention, which is the worst kind possible. Not only are you locked away with the most rotten eggs in the basket, you don't know how long you'll be trapped in there with them. It's the uncertainty, more so than the company, that really gets you. I ended up spending 18 months there, but it could have been anything.

This time I knew I'd only be gone for nine months. Already, I had certainty. But better still, it was unlikely that any significant part of my sentence would be served at the state's most notorious prison. When the judge sentenced me earlier that morning, he recommended I be sent to a prison farm. Compared to Long Bay, that's like flying first-class instead of economy. I knew I was in for a much easier ride.

My lawyer John Korn had advised me to plead guilty, but he still made a song and dance about police entrapment. When he delivered his verdict, the judge noted that had the case been heard in America it would have been laughed out of court. In Australia, however, police are given the power to entice people to commit crimes that warrant the same penalty as those enacted under one's own volition.

Even though Alan Jones took the stand as a character witness – recommending that I be made to 'wash buses' as punishment – it would have taken an extraordinarily lenient judge to hand me anything other than a custodial sentence. My judge came close. Because of my record and community service, he had no choice but to put me inside. But he stressed that the sentence be served at what I believe is an excuse for a prison, not the real deal you are faced with in maximum security.

That's why I felt in control as the bus rolled through those gates. The last time I had passed between them, I promised myself never to return. Well, here I was again – but the promise hadn't been truly broken, just a little scuffed. I was only being sent to Long Bay for classification. I knew I'd be somewhere else within a week. I also knew that I'd be looked after. Having resigned myself to prison even well before sentencing, I made some enquiries with a few inmates. They vowed to make my stay as comfortable as possible. There was a TV waiting in my cell when I arrived that night.

The screws classified me as a C2 prisoner – the lowest on the scale. Those serving more than five years are generally classified as As, while three to five years are Bs. The rest are Cs. The lower ranks are placed in what can be described as a safer part of Long Bay while they await transfer. I had a week to pass before being moved on to Oberon, near the Blue Mountains. There, on the freezing highlands, was a prison farm that many of the inmates with a few miles under their belts rated as one of the friendliest in New South Wales.

Although my old mate Neddy Smith had just been sent to the prison hospital after being diagnosed with Parkinson's disease, I was well looked after during those seven days at Long Bay. As well as a TV, I was given civilian clothes and runners. It was much easier going in this part of the jail than my previous digs in Ward 11. We even had a Breville jaffle-maker to prepare our own toasties, which sure beat the new pre-packaged prison food they had introduced.

The week passed without incident, something that rarely happens in my life. On the Monday after my sentencing, nine prisoners and I were herded onto the bus for the climb over the Great Dividing Range. I was the only one headed for Oberon. The rest were being taken to Bathurst – a much tougher jail. Although the 1995 autumn leaves were falling as we set out, I remember it being almost unbearably hot in the back of that bus. The drive from Sydney to Bathurst normally takes about three hours, but it took us five as the heavy-duty bus lugged its illegitimate load up the Great Western Highway.

There was no need for a bus after the others had been

dropped off in Bathurst, so I was loaded into a police bull wagon for the final one-hour leg to Oberon. I had no idea what roads we were taking or which direction we were headed. I later learned from visitors that the prison farm was about 20 km down a dirt track from the main road into town. But I knew about the dirt track from that first trip – and so did the bull wagon's suspension. It was one of the worst roads I'd ever travelled on. One time Ray Dib and his family actually rolled their car and were almost killed as they returned from a weekend visit.

When they say prison farm they mean it. I set eyes on Oberon and thought I'd just arrived at a retreat – not unlike the summer camps you see in those corny American movies. There were 10 quaint-looking cottages scattered around a main hall. And all around were trees and green space. The air was amazingly crisp. This was going to be even better than weekend detention at Silverwater, which represented little more than an annoyance rather than a deterrent.

Each of the cabins accommodated 10 prisoners. Four of the inmates were adults like me. The remaining six were younger kids aged between 18 and 25 who were serving their first sentences. Some of the adults were on low-level charges while others had transferred from maximum security prisons as a means to reintegrate themselves on the eve of their release. It seemed like a surprisingly sensitive and considerate system.

And it worked. The adults in each cabin were expected to mentor the younger ones. 'Yeah?' you might ask cynically. 'Mentor in what? How to steal cars? Deal drugs?' They are fair questions. But that's not how it happened in reality. Freedom and responsibility bred a strange and unexpected hierarchy that all the prisoners adhered to. The younger ones respected their elders and life in the cabins generally progressed harmoniously.

We all had our own bedrooms, which opened onto a communal TV room and kitchen. It was everyone's responsibility to keep the cabin tidy and prepare meals with the rations we were given. This worked remarkably well. If anything, the younger inmates looked up to their elders – they were probably petrified like I was as a teenager and desperate for some sense of assurance.

Most of the older inmates didn't abuse this trust. They instead took the younger ones under their wings. And that's how I became fitter and stronger than I had ever been at any stage of my life. The clean air, the open space, the gym – all the planets aligned at Oberon to inspire me to work out determinedly. As an older prisoner, I appreciated the opportunity to teach the younger ones a thing or two. So I began to conduct daily training sessions on the prison green. Little did I know at the time, but these humble workouts would represent my crude beginnings as a rugby league coach.

The boys all knew I was a former first-grade footballer and jumped at the chance to discover how rugby league players trained. It was a perk they hadn't expected to stumble across when the judge threw away the key. However, I tried to make it as challenging as possible for them. I tried to break them both mentally and physically because that's exactly what the top conditioners do during the pre-season. I wanted to see which prisoners had what it takes, not necessarily to play football but to withstand pain.

The screws at Oberon were so accommodating that they even announced my first training session over the loudspeaker. 'John Elias is about to commence training, if anyone wants to join in,' the message boomed. About 20 kids turned up. By the end of the 90-minute session, only six remained. They were the ones I wanted. The ones who refused to break. They kept training with me until we parted ways.

Those shuttle runs and gym circuits killed two birds with one stone. Not only did they maintain my fitness, they also shook off my selfishness. Up until Oberon, I had only looked out for number one. Whether it be training, pulling fixes at the trots, gambling or collecting – everything I did was designed to satisfy myself. Unlike other men my age, I didn't have a wife or children. I had dated several women seriously, but every relationship was doomed because I only answered to myself. Women need attention and I was too absorbed in the next quick earn to constantly provide that.

The kids in prison, however, looked up to me. For the first time, I felt like the father figure I'd yearned for at their age. I might never have had one, but I could still be one. This possibility stirred an incredible feeling in the pit of my stomach. Whereas other adults prejudged me on what they had read or heard, these kids were more than happy to take me on face value. They could see I had some expertise to pass on and their eagerness to learn became more pronounced the more of an interest I took in them. I still didn't know it at the time, but this was the moment when I decided that I wanted to coach football rather than play it.

The kids were training well and I felt they deserved a reward. I had something unprecedented in mind – a rugby league day featuring the top first-grade players. Inviting millions of dollars worth of talent behind prison doors seemed risky and had never been done before. But the screws were keen, probably because they were big footy fans themselves and wouldn't mind a few autographs. They let me exceed my weekend limit of two phone calls to contact players and organise the event.

In the end Jim Dymock, Nat Wood, Gorden Tallis, Craig Field, Darren Senter and Shane Walker were given permission by their clubs to come. I'd have loved to have kept their appearance a surprise, but secrets don't exist in prisons. Within days of my suggesting the idea to the head screw, the whole place was aware of what I was planning.

It was a Saturday in the middle of 1995 when their bus pulled up. In Oberon at that time of the year, the cold is ridiculous. On the way up the mountains the diesel bus carrying all the footballers had frozen, leaving some of the game's biggest names stranded on the side of a deserted road. Thankfully, they got the bus started again and arrived with armfuls of prawns and other goodies some of the long-timers hadn't set eyes on in several years. The prisoners were like nervous schoolchildren, infatuated but aloof at the same time. But their adoration soon wore off when each of the players was assigned to captain teams of seven players. We had a round-robin touch footy tournament, followed by a big match between the footballers and a prison team. That ended in an honourable draw – the result everyone wanted.

By the end of the day the players were swamped with questions and requests for advice. I had some questions of my own. Just days before I was sentenced, rugby league suffered one of the biggest upheavals in its history. On 1 April 1995, a breakaway competition called Super League secretly signed up some of the code's best teams, players and coaches. The ARL establishment was shocked, but hit back with a war chest funded by Kerry Packer. There was no way Packer, whose Nine network held the rights to cover the ARL, was going to let his old foe Rupert Murdoch rob him in the dead of night. Murdoch's News Ltd was behind Super League, a competition that promised to make the game global but was really looking to cash in on the contemporaneous advent of pay TV in Australia.

The upshot for the players was money. Any footballer in the middle of these warring billionaire tycoons was bound to be showered with rich shrapnel. As I was led away to prison, reserve-graders were signing loyalty agreements with either side for $300,000 a season. Again, I couldn't help but lament my timing. My career had ended just a couple of months before the golden goose dropped her most valuable egg.

All the players who visited Oberon were courted furiously. Although they were all established first-graders, none could believe the sums of money being tossed about. They told me fantastic stories about clandestine negotiations and threats between representatives of the ARL and Super League camps. Most of the players took it all in with a sense of blissful bemusement, like a child being showered with presents for no apparent reason. Their common message was that no-one played the game for money. Until Super League, footballers played it for love while making sure there was enough money to get by. But that all changed when the big bucks arrived. Money is now a major consideration for every player, and the Super League war changed the face of the game.

Naturally, I felt cheated by missing out on this bounty. Good old karma. On the positive side, it would have been much harder to deal with had I been free and unable to find a club. Being trapped in jail robbed me of choices and possibilities and hence I felt less sorry for myself. There was simply nothing I could do but wish my football mates all the best.

FROM OBERON TO LEBANON

Their visit meant a lot to me. But the regular appearances of my then-girlfriend Lisa meant more. Lisa was a very special lady, something I took for granted. She didn't have a driver's licence, but that was no deterrent to making her way from Sydney to Oberon. There were trains and buses and she spent entire weekends enduring slow, cumbersome public transport to visit me. The trip took six-and-half hours each way, but she never complained. In short, I didn't deserve someone so dedicated.

To take a leaf out of actor Jack Nicholson's book, I like to call this the Monkey Syndrome. Women can't grab a new branch without letting go of the old one first. They always need a man. This had undermined my view of women and their approach to relationships. Are they really with me for the person I am, or just the fact that I represent the other half that makes their lives complete? Is this why they tolerated my moods, my preoccupations and my neglect? Was this really better than being single?

If there was ever a woman I would have settled down with, it was Lisa. She was 22 when I went to Oberon, an age when people are more predisposed to having fun on the weekends than sitting beneath the sweltering armpits of train commuters. But Lisa was in love. Eventually, her love sowed a seed of its own in my heart. Years after my release, I decided to marry her. But bad luck and terrible judgement on my part cruelled those plans. When we broke up, Lisa didn't swing straight to the next branch. Her life remained in stasis as she regained composure after suffering from my transgression. Eventually, she met a new man and they are now married. No-one could be more happy for Lisa than me.

Lisa's visits and the regular training kept me satisfied during my time on the farm. In fact, I was more than satisfied. I was happy. As prisoners, our workload was incredibly light. My only duties were to make sure our cottage was clean and tidy while the younger prisoners went out every morning and cut down trees in the surrounding forest. Even their work was easy. They'd be lucky to cut down two trees in an entire day. In fact, Oberon was a bludge. There was no hard work, but there was camaraderie and spirit. Every month, the screws took us on boot camps into the bush. Those weekends were not unlike the pre-season bonding camps footballers are sent on nowadays. We were forced to survive on rations while being made to navigate our way through the bush. To get from A to B, we'd have to master abseiling and rock climbing. Gliding down a pristine rock face, with birds chirping in your ears and the fresh wind rushing through your hair, it was impossible to believe you were still being punished.

Instead, the mindset was positive and trusting. And it's amazing what people will give you in return for a bit of trust. On those trips into the bush, any of us could have elected to make a run for it. We went unsupervised for hours on end. Even the farm itself didn't have any gates. When the players came to visit, they even loaded me onto the bus with them as it drove away. I travelled with them up the dirt road for about 2 km. There was no-one to stop me from going all the way back to Sydney and then who knows where?

But escaping was never on my mind, because there was nothing to escape from. Despite not having my full freedom, I enjoyed responsibility and ownership at Oberon. We weren't treated like mindless automatons, as is the case in maximum security. That's understandable – a lot of prisoners in places like Long Bay are simply too dangerous to be allowed liberties. At Oberon, however, no-one abused their rights. Not to the full extent, anyhow. I did witness younger guys shooting up drugs that were delivered from outside. The kids would stumble into the cottage at the end of a weekend bleary-eyed and mealy-mouthed. It wasn't ideal, but the drug culture didn't extend to dealing and trafficking. It stopped at personal use, something that didn't happen in the really big houses.

A month or so before my release, I decided to put in for a transfer to Windsor jail, located on the north-western outskirts of Sydney. Oberon was getting too far for my family to visit, especially for Mum. Although Windsor would be a tougher proposition, I also viewed it as a reintegration into Sydney. And what's more, I now had a purpose.

It was conceived one midwinter's night in our cottage on the farm. The TV was showing a game featuring one of my old sides, the Rabbitohs. I still had plenty of mates running around for the Bunnies, but it wasn't any of the players that caught my eye. What entranced me were Souths' colours: red, green and white. They were the same colours as the Lebanese flag. In an instant, the thought struck me. Why couldn't Lebanon have its own rugby league team? With the kids from the first generation of immigrants now hitting their teenage years, there was a considerable spike in the number of Lebanese juniors enrolled to play rugby league in Sydney. In the Canterbury district alone, Lebanese kids would have outnumbered those of any other ethnic background. The resources were there, but no-one had thought to set up a system to harness them.

And that's how the Lebanese Rugby League was conceived – on a battered cloth lounge opposite a 34 cm TV that blanked out in snowstorms. During my final month of incarceration at Windsor, I met with my brother George and told him about the idea that had quickly progressed to my sole ambition. Setting up the side consumed me, more so because I'd abandoned all thoughts of returning to a life of crime.

It would be a lie to say the penal system cured me in late 1995. But my stay in Oberon precipitated much soul-searching about my attitude towards crime. Apart from the early days when I brazenly stole cars and robbed businesses, I had come to think of myself as a service provider rather than a criminal. The rest of society would take a different view, but I justified debt collection as a crude means of righting wrongs. Similarly, my tricks on the trotting track were a get-square for the bookies, who had been fleecing punters on the back of rorts since the chariots circled the Colosseum. I didn't think of the innocent people betting, in the conviction they were fair dinkum, on the races we'd fixed. I didn't think of the families of the people I stood over. I neglected to think of the wicked chain of events this type of 'justice' triggered. There were many things I didn't think of because, frankly, if I did, they might have tugged at my conscience and stopped me.

But through all my wrongs and stupidity, what you got was what you saw. For mine, that transcended right and wrong in a world that I'd been convinced was purely dog-eat-dog. You survived as best you could, obliterating all the rules but the one that governed truth. Sam's betrayal shattered this idyll. At Oberon, it dawned on me that the streets were now riddled with police informants and double-dealers. There was no-one I could trust anymore. Crime used to pay, but now suddenly it didn't. The playing field wasn't level anymore. Instead of working together against the police, the crims had now turned on their own kind. It would take both a brave and stupid man to risk such odds.

That's why I meant every word when I appeared on *The Footy Show* in 1996 and sang 'I Fought the Law'. Blocker, who was then a panellist, convinced me to dress up and do a bit of karaoke as a gag. But what looked like a joke carried some serious overtones. The law had won . . . for the time being.

Craig Field was waiting for me outside Windsor jail on 2 January 1996. I was a free man once more. Craig had been doing his best to get me another start at Souths that season, which threatened to be a split competition between the ARL and Super League. He had been in Alan Jones's ear, telling him how fit I had become inside. But it was no good. I'd burned my bridges with the fix controversy, both at Redfern and the other 19 clubs. Jones, however, didn't give me away that easily. Souths had forged an alignment with Newtown, which had been resurrected as a Metropolitan Cup team six seasons earlier. The arrangement was for Rabbitohs-contracted players to turn out for the Jets when they weren't selected for first-grade. Jones offered to use his influence to get me a start at Newtown under their coach Col Murphy, whom I'd played alongside at Henson Park almost 15 years earlier. Not only was it my only chance to keep playing football, it seemed like a fitting one. Here was the chance to finish my career in Sydney where it began – at Newtown.

Between training with the Jets three nights a week and manoeuvring to set up the Lebanese Rugby League, I had little time for anything else. All my old criminal associates were still running around. They got in touch, but I was simply too spooked by Sam's act of treachery to trust anyone again. In time, I would ease back into the bookmaking scene. But only as a commission agent who placed bets for the big fish and scraped the cream off whatever odds I could obtain that were above the agreed rate. But that wouldn't even come until a couple of years down the track. It was all still too raw post-prison.

Nevertheless, I still kept close to my old partner Harry Eden. But now I needed his help to set up the Lebanese side, rather than an SP bookmakers' ring. Harry knew a lawyer, Colin Love. I wasn't sure how they became involved, but I knew Love's support was essential for my dream to be realised. Love – who is now in his 11th straight year as ARL chairman – was also a big-time promoter in those days. He was the man behind the pre-season rugby league sevens tournament, a concept that exploded in the late 1980s. Love's genius, however, was to make the competition global. In 1992 he staged the first World Sevens at the SFS, featuring sides from exotic places like Morocco, Russia and Japan. I knew he was planning another tournament in 1997. It seemed an ideal stage for Lebanon to be introduced to the rugby league world.

Harry arranged a meeting between Colin and me at the NSWRL offices on Phillip Street in September 1996. Like any crusty lawyer, Love was hard-nosed. He was open to the idea of a Lebanon side taking part, but didn't give too much away. There was no doubt he was aware of the pulling power a Cedars side would possess, given Sydney's growing Lebanese community. He could hear the turnstiles clicking over, but remained steely-faced and demanded we reach all sorts of sponsorship targets before Lebanon's inclusion could be rubber-stamped.

Two could play at this game. I agreed to Love's request, but little did he know that my brother George, Ray Dib and I had been working behind the scenes for most of the year to secure support. We had enough sponsors to meet the target before I even laid eyes on Love. A couple of weeks later I revealed the extent of our support and we were in. Come February 1997, Lebanon would have its own side.

Although my focus was on the Cedars, Newtown was also pressing for a nostalgic premiership in the Metro Cup. My old mate from the Tigers, Garry Jack, was coaching Ryde–Eastwood, who would be our eventual grand final opponents. Ryde finished first in the competition but were no match for us on the day. We won 34–12, much to the joy of old Bluebag warriors like Tommy Raudonikis and Brian 'Chicka' Moore, who had come to Parramatta Stadium to witness their old club's first title win in half a century. To cap it off I scored two tries and was named man of the match. People can say what they like about me, but I prided myself on rising for the big occasions even if I lacked consistency at other times of the year. In two grand final appearances (the other for Brisbane Souths), I had been voted best on ground both times.

As the 1997 Sevens grew closer, I became more intense. I'd be on the phone to my old friend Tas Baitieri, who by then was the ARL's International Development Officer, at least twice a day. As Tas and the others involved in setting up the Lebanon team discovered, hyperactivity never disappears. It just picks a different target. The frenetic energy that used to be absorbed by my thrilling stunts and collects was now making the lives of my best mates hell. They needed to get rid of me before the tournament began or else they'd go insane. I would later learn that this was exactly why Tas suggested I play that off-season in France, rather than help put the finishing touches on Lebanon's preparations. In October 1996 he approached me with an offer from a first-division side called Limoux.

Although keen to travel, I was concerned about being absent at the pointy end of Lebanon's build-up after investing so much to establish the team. A few weeks earlier we'd conducted trials at Belmore Oval, which attracted more than 300 kids. From that pool we chose three players to go alongside the Lebanese players at the top clubs. Experienced first-graders Charlie Saab and David Baysari selected themselves, as did a number of exciting up-and-comers like Kandy Tamer, Paul Khoury and a promising little winger from Canterbury named Hazem El Masri.

My brother George and Ray Dib assured me they had the situation in hand, allowing my wanderlust to get its wish. I was off to France again, this time for three months until the Sevens in February. If Limoux were still in contention after the Sevens, I would be contractually obliged to return to France.

Limoux was vastly different from my first side, Avignon. Rather than a built-up town, it was a hamlet of no more than 10,000 people plonked in the middle of southern France's famous wine-growing region. I was given the choice of whether to live in town or on an actual working vineyard with a local family. I chose the latter, thinking it would be a more authentic experience. I wasn't wrong.

The lifestyle was blissfully rural, laid back and easygoing. Strangely enough, my little granny flat reminded me of the cottages in Oberon. Life was good in Limoux. Unlike the tearaway who hit France 12 years earlier in search of nightlife and stolen buses, I was now a retiring 34-year-old who was content to maintain his fitness and sleep levels. Limoux was too far away from the other towns with teams that boasted other Australian players to engender much of a social life. Not that I cared anyway, because Lisa had arrived to spend Christmas and New Year's with me. We lived like a happy couple as 1996 gave way to 1997. I had rarely been happier, my inner beast apparently euthanased by the company of a wonderful woman and endless sparkling wine, a speciality of the region.

Part of my mind, however, was always preoccupied with what was happening in Sydney. This got me in a spot of bother with the Limoux officials after I racked up a $2,000 phone bill checking up on Tas and Ray. Even from the other side of the globe, they were getting no peace. My contract stipulated that I was free to return to Sydney a fortnight before the Sevens. Limoux, however, were having a great season and had made the final of the French Challenge Cup. That meant I would be obliged to step back on a 26-hour flight after the tournament. Although I loved the French lifestyle, I didn't really want to return. It was a measure of how much I was maturing that I honoured that commitment. I was no longer doing what suited me and me alone. I had discovered the value of consideration and commitment.

When I arrived back in Sydney, the Lebanese team had already started training at Guildford under coach Steve Ghosn. Steve immediately announced that I would be captain, an honour that sent me into a bit of a spin. I was, however, concerned about the feelings of my teammates. How would they feel taking orders from a convicted criminal who no longer played first-grade? The answer was they didn't have a problem. At the end of the first training session, I gathered them as a group and said that if one person was uncomfortable about my appointment I'd stand down. The team was more important because we were now representing a nation. For me, the captaincy was a massive bonus. Just seeing the team come together was reward enough.

The boys were great about it. A week before the Sevens kicked off, we booked into a hotel in Camperdown for some bonding. The tournament included the 12 ARL teams, whose players already knew one another. The Lebanese side, however, had been assembled from a disparate collection of players from all over New South Wales and Queensland.

The most intriguing was young El Masri, who had made his first-grade debut with Canterbury the previous season. Canterbury was a Super League club and therefore had no compulsion to permit one of its players to feature in the ARL-run Sevens. But despite our chequered history, Peter 'Bullfrog' Moore gave nothing but his full blessing for Hazem to play in the Sevens. It was the perfect example of the Bullfrog's innate understanding of what makes individual footballers tick. He knew Hazem would deeply appreciate the chance to represent his country of birth. The winger has since gone on to become one of the most revered players to pull on a Bulldogs jersey, breaking the club record for not only the most points but also the most top-grade appearances.

I roomed with Hazem that week, which is a loose description of how we lived. Being a conservative young Muslim, Hazem was the only player granted permission to spend his evenings at home. But the rest of the day, Hazem was himself. I recall one of the first times I came into the room, I saw him kneeling on the floor in deep prayer. Although I'm from a Christian background, I knew all too well how sacred the five daily prayers are to followers of Islam. I left the room quietly and let Hazem be. I also knew it was Ramadan, the holy Islamic month of fasting where believers couldn't eat or drink between dawn and dusk. The extraordinarily long summer days had been especially unkind to

Hazem and the other Muslim players during training. The fact they got through without hydration was extraordinary.

We made a point of demonstrating great tolerance from the start. Our cousins back in the homeland might be divided over religion, but there was no way that was going to be a factor in this side. We were pretty much half Muslim, half Christian and no-one ever mentioned religion. It wasn't a spoken rule either – religion just didn't come into the equation. All of us were either born in Australia or had been raised here. We lived in a secular society where people accepted each other's right to believe whatever they wanted and that's how the team operated. It was for that same reason everyone spoke English instead of Arabic. Some of the team members weren't quite as fluent in Arabic, meaning that if some people decided to speak in the mother tongue it might have made them feel inferior.

There were 24 teams in the tournament, split into eight pools of three. The top team in each pool progressed to the quarter-finals. We were drawn in a pool alongside Melbourne and New South Wales Country. Not having to face an ARL side boosted our expectations. There was no reason why we couldn't progress to the quarter-finals. With the game torn in half because of Super League, crowds were turning away from rugby league in droves. Hard-working fans sensed that their game had been sold out for money above loyalty, the very thing they were asked to show every weekend. The result was a season of appalling crowds across both competitions and the ARL Sevens were no exception.

The turn-out on both days of the tournament would have been embarrassing had it not been for one saving grace – the Lebanese community. When we arrived at the SFS around 1 pm on the Saturday, I recall being bombarded with messages about how massive the support for us was. Apparently, the Lebanese contingent had purchased two entire bays on halfway opposite the tunnel. They had turned up early with drums, flags and bandanas in eager anticipation of being part of sporting history. I felt a shiver of excitement, which I knew had to be tempered if we were to perform without distraction.

As captain, I ordered the team not to enter the stadium before our first game. We instead decided to warm up at the adjacent SCG cricket nets before heading into the sheds to prepare to face Melbourne. I felt overwhelmingly nervous in those final minutes. Steve Ghosn did most of the talking, leaving me to speak louder on the field. He was an incredible motivator, Steve. He spoke about performing for our parents and ancestors, as opposed to the fans and locals who followed club sides. The emphasis was on nationhood. There's a world of difference. Even though I have lived my entire life in Australia, I couldn't divorce myself from Lebanon. My genes were from the old country, and they generated a massive sense of pride as we marched down the tunnel.

At the end was a wall of red, green and white. The tipsters weren't wrong. Lebanese-Australians filled bays 35 and 36 with a din of singing, drumming and general chaos. Our appearance was a celebration for everyone who'd been searching for their identity since arriving on these shores. There's a little bit of that in every migrant – the feeling that they'll never be whole again because part of them stayed at home.

In the middle of the throng was Mum. She's a loud, vivacious and overbearing woman at the best of times, but now was her chance to really come to the fore. She was jumping and singing like a teenager. It took Mum up until her retirement in 1987 to watch me play a game, but she had quickly developed into an expert on the game. There wasn't a match that went by without her giving me some criticism or advice, usually the former.

The fans generated an atmosphere I'd never experienced in rugby league. The 1985 grand final at Lang Park with Brisbane Souths was special, but fell short of what I was now feeling. It could best be described as genuine satisfaction, something I had rarely experienced because I had never worked hard enough. But on this occasion I had seen it through. The idea born in Oberon was now reality and it wouldn't have mattered if there was only one fan at the ground. All that mattered was that we had made it.

The Melbourne side we faced that day had no affiliation to the purple juggernaut that would soon take the NRL by 'Storm'. Instead, the seven players on the opposite side of halfway were a ragged collection of part-timers from the local Victorian comp in what was then a rugby league wasteland. Although we didn't boast any superstars, we looked like a team chock-full of them next to Melbourne. Every time we scored, the fans went berserk. It was a flogging. All that stood between us and a return the following day was New South Wales Country.

We had just two hours to recuperate for the next game. Unfortunately, we had lost one of our most experienced campaigners, Charlie Saab, to a leg injury in the opening minutes. The tournament rules stipulated that squads could only carry 10 players and that no replacements were permitted in the event of injury. We would have to soldier on for the rest of the tournament with only nine men. I spent the intervening period in the members' lounge with players from the top sides. The support Lebanon attracted was a real buzz topic, with Illawarra's Paul McGregor and Manly's Cliff Lyons both coming up to me personally to say how much they were blown away.

Within no time we were back on the paddock, this time to face a much stronger opposition. The New South Wales Country side boasted a number of former first-graders and it turned out to be a nail-biting affair. We led 10–4 with seconds left, but they scored out wide. A successful conversion would send the match into extra time, something we weren't looking forward to given our lack of manpower. From behind the goalposts I can remember the crowd going crazy as soon as the conversion was launched. The kick sprayed well wide, sparking celebrations not unlike those on grand final day. We had lived to fight another day, sending the fans into raptures. I imagine Colin Love would have had a wry smile on his face, too, given that missed conversion had guaranteed his coffers another 6,000 paying customers the following day.

After spending a good 10 minutes embracing the crowd, we returned to the sheds. A local Elvis impersonator, Simon Kanaan, had devised a team song called 'Go, Go Lebanon'. It was a take on an old Roy Orbison tune and we belted it out in the sheds and on the bus back to our team hotel. If anything, we celebrated a little too hard that night. We were drawn to play Parramatta – one of the ARL heavyweights – the following day at 1.30 pm. We should have just had dinner and retired straight to bed. But the hype was overwhelming. Waiting for us at the hotel were hundreds of excited relatives and friends. The party had only just started for them and we had no option but to oblige after the sensational support they had provided. But beneath my smiles and high-fives was a fear that some of the younger players were getting carried away.

FROM OBERON TO LEBANON

The following morning I was also concerned about how they would handle a Parramatta outfit containing internationals like Jim Dymock and Jason Smith. I suspected they would be overawed, and I wasn't wrong. We dropped the ball on our first two sets and were always on the back foot. The crowd on Sunday was probably bigger and more vocal than the previous day, but we were struggling to match their enthusiasm. It was possible we'd played – and celebrated – our grand final 24 hours earlier against New South Wales Country. Nevertheless, we hung in and were somehow level at 6–all just seconds before halftime. Parramatta, however, sneaked in a try as the buzzer went. It was the killer blow mentally. Instead of going into the break on level terms we were trailing one of the tournament favourites – and they had the first possession of the second half. It yielded another try and from then on it was a question of by how much. Not as much as people might have thought. We went down fighting, 24–12, and left the field with not one less admirer. The fact Parramatta went on to win the tournament was also some consolation.

Although I had to return to France a couple of days later, I boarded the plane with a sense of pride. Little did I know then about the biggest challenge of my life that was awaiting me.

CHAPTER 19

DON'T MENTION THE C-WORD

'John, I've got some bad news.'

I'd heard these words many times before, but never before had they scared me so much. Before that visit to the doctor's surgery in mid-1999, all the bad news I'd received was inconsequential. Bad news up until that point was being dropped to the bench or being told a rorted trots race hadn't gone as planned. When a doctor gives you bad news, it's something else entirely. It's no longer just bad news – it's a matter of life and death.

Dr Nabil Rahim is a kind-looking man. I had first met him three days earlier when he did some tests on my stomach, which had been playing up for the previous month. I thought nothing of it. I left Dr Rahim's rooms in Burwood that Friday afternoon and he wished me a nice weekend. The results would be back in a week. There was nothing to worry about until then. Then his secretary phoned on Monday and told me to see him straightaway. I still didn't think anything of it. My stomach still didn't feel quite normal, but it wasn't compromising my life. I just figured that being a very busy and popular gastroenterologist, Dr Rahim needed to juggle a few appointments to fit some other patients in.

I didn't contemplate bad news. Before entering his office, I had been flirting with the secretary – making her lean close to smell my new aftershave before ambushing her with a peck on the cheek. She was close to 60 years old. It made her smile and I felt good.

But now, 10 minutes later, I was faced with bad news. This is the worst part, not knowing how bad it would be. I barely had time to begin contemplating before Dr Rahim spoke again. 'John, I'm sorry, but you've got cancer.'

It all started with a burp in May 1999. First the odd burp here and there, then at regular intervals. I was still training and working, just with a lot more burping. Then the feeling in my guts began. It lived on the left-hand side of my abdomen. It was not so much pain as a presence. Like something lurking. It felt uncomfortable, but by no means unmanageable. I still ate and drank what I pleased without it getting worse. But neither it nor the burping went away. I might have paid it more attention had there been fewer distractions. But, as always, my life was full in the winter of 1999. I had taken steps to further my coaching career, gaining a Certificate One and taking charge of a Canterbury junior side, the St George Dragons. They would go on to win four straight titles under my watch.

My old mate from the Tigers, Wayne Pearce, who was still head coach at Balmain, had also appointed me to his staff. For the past two seasons I had been his defensive coach, overseeing tackling drills at Leichhardt Oval twice a week. And then there was my beloved Lebanon. After a successful debut in the 1997 Sevens, the Cedars played their first full match against Italy at Leichhardt in July 1998. The match was a curtain-raiser to an NRL fixture between Balmain and North Queensland, and attracted 20,000 people. We were continually encouraged by the support for the Cedars and preparations were in full swing for a game against France at the newly-opened Olympic Stadium in Homebush Bay on Bastille Day – 14 July 1999.

Although I had officially hung up the boots a long time ago, I intended to play not only that match and but also for Lebanon in the Rugby League World Cup the following season. I was now 36, but age didn't deter me when it came to playing for the Cedars. There's a huge difference between being able to lift for a game here and there and performing consistently, week in, week out. At my age, I could do the former but definitely not the latter.

Nevertheless, the demands of playing still required a mammoth preparation. I virtually needed an entire pre-season for just one match – our international against the French that would precede the round 14 Tigers–Bulldogs fixture. I was training extra hard for the big night, doing the same conditioning work as the Balmain first-graders as well as solo sessions in the gym and pool.

The only part of my life that had gone into decline at that point was the illegitimate part. I was indelibly scarred by the police set-up five years earlier that led to me being convicted on the firearms trafficking. Of all the emotions, trust is perhaps the strongest yet most easy to break. Mine had been shattered from that experience and I still wasn't prepared to put it back together for the sake of an easy earn.

The temptation, however, didn't go away. In late 1998 I was followed by police and taken to Lakemba station for questioning about a $1 million cigarette heist. I had no involvement and told the cops as much. But what I didn't say was that I'd been approached to help pull the job off. It was an inside job on a cigarette warehouse near Bankstown. Still smarting from the set-up five years earlier, I turned down the offer and missed out on a real windfall. The thieves made away with three semitrailer loads of smokes and didn't get caught. The closest the cops came was arresting me, but I was released after a couple of hours when it was clear they were chasing someone on reputation instead of reality.

With everything that was happening, a bit of stomach discomfort barely rated a mention. But its sheer persistence eventually forced my attention. I've neglected many things and people in my life, but never my health. The discipline I lacked in all the attempts to stay clean manifested itself on the training field. I was compulsively hooked on the endorphins that would fill my body with jubilation after a hard session. Now, without crime or the underworld to provide any thrills, I needed that buzz more than ever. Training hard and eating well not only makes you fit, but also acutely aware of your body.

My family doctor couldn't feel a thing during the first consultation. Dr Jimmy Lahood was not only my regular physician, but also a dear friend. Jimmy was a fanatical Souths fan who would later go on to be on the Rabbitohs board until it was disbanded when Russell Crowe and Peter Holmes à Court bought the club in 2006. Jimmy poked and prodded my stomach but couldn't detect a problem. 'You're as fit as a bull, Johnny,' he said. 'You could even play again.'

DON'T MENTION THE C-WORD

As a precaution he prescribed me some ulcer tablets to take in the next month. I followed his advice to the letter, but the discomfort was stubborn. It didn't budge. I'd experience the same discomfort every few days, for about a day at a time. When I say pain, I use the term very loosely. It still wasn't bad enough to make me lighten my training routine or even change my diet. It was more an annoyance, albeit one that was beginning to mystify me. My bowel movements had also increased and one day I noticed my faeces were blacker than usual. Had I bothered to ask Jimmy, he would have told me this was a sure sign that I was bleeding internally. But I didn't ask and continued my preparations for the France game.

I saw Jimmy once the tablets ran out without fixing the problem. He was now able to rule out an ulcer. But on this occasion he made me sit upright rather than lie flat when he examined me. As he probed, Jimmy said: 'Johnny, I've been thinking about you. Someone with a high pain tolerance wouldn't complain unless there was something significant wrong.'

He was right. Since suffering in silence for a week with a broken arm when I was four years old, I'd prided myself on tolerating pain. Virtually everything I'd done in life had relied on it – whether it be playing through injury on the football field or being beaten to a pulp by a bunch of Greek thugs in the back of a Kombi van. I wasn't like normal people. Perhaps if someone else had experienced the same problem, they might have experienced more pain and sought more urgent medical attention. Then again, Jimmy said that had I not been so fit I wouldn't be as able to detect glitches in my system. He said obese, unfit people regularly had problems that their permanently poor condition hid.

I could see Jimmy's expression change as his fingers dug into my stomach. On the previous occasions there was no pain, but now I felt uneasy when he applied pressure to particular areas. The left side of my stomach was the worst.

'Let's take the next step and do some tests,' Jimmy said. The next step was a visit to the specialist, Dr Rahim. I was booked in for a colonoscopy and endoscopy – two invasive procedures involving cameras being inserted from both ends – that coming Friday. When I woke up I asked him: 'Doc, is everything OK?' He didn't give anything away. 'We'll know within a week when we get the results,' Dr Rahim said.

This is why they called me in earlier. It was really bad news, perhaps the worst imaginable. I had cancer, but I didn't believe it because I couldn't believe it. I actually smiled and laughed at the thought. It was impossible. I ate well. I was fit. Throughout all the visits to Jimmy and during the tests, the possibility had never entered my head. I'd never once mentioned the C-word. No-one had.

'John, you've got stomach cancer and we need to start chemotherapy as soon as possible,' continued Dr Rahim, stirring me from my stupor. 'I want to book you in for two weeks time.'

Two weeks? Hang on . . . there were three weeks left until Lebanon played France. I couldn't miss that game. My life had been geared towards it for six months. Now I was being told I couldn't play. In a twisted way, the news was almost more devastating than being told I had cancer. I still wasn't thinking clearly. It was too much of a shock to take in. Too unexpected. Stomach cancer. Fuck. It sounded serious, but

DON'T MENTION THE C-WORD

surely it had to be a mistake. I knew this feeling – of being in a predicament where you don't belong and that you know you don't deserve it. I'd felt the exact same thing two decades ago when the police charged me with stabbing a bus driver – a crime I never committed. That was a mistake, and so was this. Nevertheless, the consequences remained the same. Whether it be spending 18 months in Long Bay or dealing with cancer (whatever that meant), I was in the shit.

The prognosis made sense of everything else – particularly Jimmy's worried expression as he checked me a week earlier. I had also lost three kilograms, something I'd put down to hard training. But it worried Jimmy and he'd also sent me for blood tests. Those results were still to come back, but Dr Rahim was certain I had cancer on the basis of the colonoscopy and endoscopy.

'Are you serious?' I asked. What a stupid question. Fancy asking a specialist if he was being serious. In reality, though, I still thought it possible for Dr Rahim to crack a smile, pat me on the back and let me in on the joke. 'Ahhhh, Johnny, you're too good – of course I'm not serious. You've just got a stomach bug.'

But he didn't say that. He just said, 'I'm sorry.'

There's no manual for dealing with this, but my own rules dictated that Mum be spared from knowing until it was absolutely necessary. As I left the surgery, I was beginning to feel faint. I breathed deeply and it steadied me. I was rocked but still positive. Dr Rahim had sent me to see a cancer specialist, Dr Joshua Douglas, at Royal Prince Alfred (RPA) Hospital on the Wednesday. By that stage my blood test results would be ready. I decided to ignore Dr Rahim's prognosis and wait for further confirmation until I accepted my fate. It was still too much to believe that I had cancer.

Nevertheless, I couldn't keep it to myself for the next 48 hours. There were two people I decided to tell and I did it straightaway. The first was my beautiful girlfriend Lisa, who was at work when her phone rang. Breaking the news to her was almost harder than being told myself. At least I had control over my emotions. I didn't even think of a plan of attack until Lisa answered. She knew I'd been to see Dr Rahim that morning. 'How'd you go?' she said casually. For some reason I turned to levity. 'I have some bad news for you, young lady,' I said, as if warning her that I had just overcooked the meatballs. 'They reckon I've got cancer.'

Lisa began to cry immediately. The news struck her like an arrow through the heart. I'd been struck as well, but it wasn't a clean blow. I was still stumbling around in a state of misapprehension. It just wasn't real. After I told my brother George, I drove straight to Lisa's apartment in Five Dock to wait for her to return from work. I can recall sitting on her lounge watching *The Bold and the Beautiful*. I'd developed a taste for cheap American soapies while in prison at Oberon. The unreal story lines helped me to escape the equally incredible events of my own life. Now it was happening again. I just sat on the couch and went numb, watching TV. It wasn't unlike the time I heard that my good mate Mark Cronk had been killed, and I just kept on chewing a sandwich. Even before going to prison at 16, I had an innate ability to block things out. To go blank. I could be reptilian. Cold-blooded.

I did think about death on Lisa's couch that afternoon. I knew enough about cancer to begin pondering my own mortality. I'd only contemplated death once before – when Con's goons had held a gun to my head outside Belmore Oval nine years earlier. This was very different. On that occasion I had precious little time to prepare myself. No one could take it in and assess the situation. I was 36. Compared to most people, I'd lived a very eventful life. Even though I'd lived by the sword and was set to die by the scalpel, I could accept it.

If I had cancer, then I'd brought it on myself. Is there anything more unfortunate than a healthy person – who exercises, abstains from drugs, alcohol and cigarettes, and eats well – contracting the most deadly of diseases? Physically, I'd done everything to avoid cancer. But elsewhere I'd provoked the wrath of fate, which had already done its bit to check my football career at regular intervals. There'd been prison terms and injury, but I never learned. It took a deep mistrust of the criminal underworld for me to stop messing around. But I wasn't truly over it. The temptation still existed and if I could ever trust enough people again, I'd probably be back in the same old scene.

That's why I again deferred to karma. I knew I deserved something like this. If I die, I die. I'd made my own grave – the time was near to lie in it. There was just one wish I wanted to fulfil before hopping in and bidding the world goodbye. I was going to play for Lebanon against France no matter what.

I'd told Dr Rahim about the game earlier that day and he looked at me like I was insane. His exact words were: 'You may as well just go and commit suicide.' As far as he was concerned, playing in that match was not an option. I had a growth inside my stomach the size of a tennis ball. There was no telling how big it could get between now and kick-off in three weeks. A basketball? A medicine ball? Who knows?

Dr Rahim was adamant that by playing I was almost certain to be tackled or struck in the stomach. He said a direct blow could cause immense damage, possibly death. Furthermore, I needed to begin chemo as soon as possible. Another week's delay could prove the difference. That's how serious my condition was.

Still, I didn't feel nearly as bad as the diagnosis. And he couldn't stop me from playing. No-one could. I decided to play and told Dr Rahim so with a look that ended our argument. He shook his head, shrugged and left the room. How selfish I must have seemed. Here is an expert in his field, trying to help me and save my life and I'm kicking sand in his face. I can be a stubborn bastard.

Dr Joshua Douglas had a similar response when I met him at RPA hospital. It was cancer. The blood tests Jimmy had taken revealed that my white blood cell count was drastically low. From now on, I'd need injections every week to survive. Dr Douglas explained my condition in a little more detail. It was something called Non-Hodgkin's Lymphoma – a disease that kills white blood cells in a certain area of the body. He said an immediate CT scan was required to ascertain whether it had spread beyond my stomach. If it had, my chances would dip further.

'So what are my chances, doc?' I asked, trying to appear relaxed.

'I'm afraid you are a 50-50 case,' he replied. The doctor said those words with an apologetic look, but I was heartened. Fifty-fifty? That's not bad at all. I liked the odds. When a horse started at even money it was generally heavy favourite to win the race. I had as much chance of living as I did of dying. There was no reason, no excuse, for me not to beat this. At that moment I grew resolve. I liked the odds and was prepared to back myself to beat them.

I was also backing myself to play for Lebanon, much to

DON'T MENTION THE C-WORD

Dr Douglas's disappointment. He said that during a game, my adrenalin levels might be so high that they could mask the pain of a rupture. If that happened and I wasn't treated immediately, it would be curtains. I didn't care. I was playing. Perhaps it was the promise of more adrenalin that made me ignore the experts. After all, I'd always traded my safety for a buzz. And this would be the ultimate high. They always remind us that rugby league is just a game, not a matter of life and death. But for me, it now was.

I left RPA emotional but buoyed. I remembered how I'd survived Long Bay as a teenager – the stabbings, the bashings, the violent screws. I shouldn't have spent a second in that prison, but instead it defined my life. Now it was paying me back a dividend. The fight I'd learned inside those walls, the ability to block out what was really happening and just survive, was what I needed to do once more.

My brother George was aghast when he heard I was committed to playing for Lebanon. My chemo had duly been delayed another month. No-one knew how much suffering I'd inflicted on myself by not starting it straightaway. I had no idea about what to expect from the treatment. I'd only known one person who'd died from cancer – the old Balmain strength coach Bruce Walsh. I remember he was at training one day. Then six months later he was dead.

Dr Douglas told me more about the chemo. He clearly didn't want to get my hopes up. He basically said the doctors needed to inject my body with poison to kill the red blood cells that were carrying the cancer. The problem, however, was that the chemo would also kill my white blood cells. He said some patients actually died as a result. The best others could expect was a life of misery and pain. Nausea. Vomiting. Cramps. Dehydration. Sleeplessness.

When I finally told Mum, she was surprisingly stoic. There were no tears. She simply said: 'Don't worry, I know you can beat it. You'll be OK.' It was what I needed to hear, especially with the game against France just a fortnight away. I didn't change a thing. I was like a chicken that kept running, despite losing its head. I'd been rocked by cancer, but outwardly I maintained the same training routine, to keep my condition as quiet as possible. I didn't want anyone to know.

There were, however, exceptions. One was Steve Ghosn, who was still the Lebanon coach in 1999. One night at training at Guildford Oval I pulled him aside. I told him about the cancer, but also about my desire to play. I spoke quickly to ensure he didn't try to talk me into standing down. I was still the captain and nothing would stop me from leading the boys.

I should never have doubted Steve, because he never questioned my decision. We instead spoke about a game plan to enable me to get through the match. No matter how tough I thought I was, I didn't want to find out whether I could survive a ruptured stomach. Not in front of 25,000 spectators. I had to play the game smart. Essentially, I would be out there to lead the team – not carry it. Steve said he wanted me to talk a big game, not play one. On the field I was to play in a dinner suit. This was common for halfbacks, who, if injured or tender, can get through matches without being tackled. But for a second-rower? The only forward I knew in the history of the game who had played with a dinner suit was Phil Gould. He gave plenty of orders, but didn't make a lot of tackles or runs. As much as he sickened me, that's the man I decided to model my game on.

As game day approached, I started to feel more at ease

with my decision. If this was to be my last game, then what better way to bow out? Playing a match with cancer – and against France, no less. The French invaded Lebanon for a large period of history – an occupation the older generations haven't been able to forgive. Although ancient history wasn't a concern for the players, we were committed to beating France for our parents and ancestors. So it meant something indirectly. Kick-off was 5.30 on a freezing evening – 14 July 1999. Like the Sevens, we deliberately avoided seeing the crowd until we took to the field. The facilities at the newly built Olympic Stadium were incredible.

I had used all my experience, all my street smarts, to switch off. Somewhere in my mind I knew I had cancer and I knew this was no normal game. But when I said my regular three Hail Marys and three Our Fathers, I didn't ask the Man Upstairs for any special favours. I kept everything painstakingly regular.

Just when I was immersed in the personal reverie that descends before kick-off, Steve took the floor. I was expecting the usual pre-game speech, but again, I should have known Steve better. He was a master motivator, right back to that Saturday afternoon when he put the *Rocky* video on to fire up Wests for their first game at Orana Park in 1987.

'You boys might think this means a lot to the mums and dads out there in the crowd, but there's one person it means a lot more to,' he began. My face started burning. I knew what was about to come, but remained silent. 'There's a bloke here who's about to take that field with cancer,' Steve continued. 'That bloke is Johnny Elias. Johnny has cancer but that was never going to stop him from playing. If you can all show that type of commitment, we'll walk off that field a proud team.'

From directly next to me I could hear sobbing. The sound was coming from Darren Maroon, my back-row partner and a former Souths teammate. As soon as I saw my mate Darren crying, the tears welled up for me as well. It wasn't how I'd wanted the preparation to end. As usual, I wanted everything to be cold and silent. I didn't thrive on outward emotion. But here I was crying before a match for the first time since the 1985 grand final with Brisbane Souths.

Looking back, I could have been dirty on Steve for telling the rest of the team without my permission. Worse still, I could have been dirty on him for trying to exploit my ordeal for motivation. But I knew Steve wasn't that type of guy. Everyone was going to discover my cancer eventually, so why not just before we took the field? These guys were my teammates, my family. They deserved to know. I might have felt a bit embarrassed with all the attention when they approached me individually before kick-off, but I didn't feel angry or resentful. For my own safety, this was the right course of action.

The other players all vowed to lift and make it easier on me. They tried to shield me from tackles and runs, but I was always a bull at a gate. I lasted 70 minutes that night before Steve replaced me. With more than 150 first-grade games to my name, I knew how to play to avoid injury. Whether it be trying to protect a dodgy ankle or a cancer-infested stomach, there's ways and means to stay healthy. I ran the ball in a certain manner, using my elbows to prevent players from striking me in the abdomen. I had so much adrenalin pumping that the game simply flew and within no time the scoreboard read: Lebanon 26, France 10.

I desperately wanted to score a try to cap the perfect night, but had to be content with addressing the crowd on the field afterwards. I thanked everyone and implored them to stay around to cheer Hazem El Masri, who was playing for the Bulldogs against Balmain.

As soon as I arrived back in the rooms, the players and officials bombarded me with questions. Everyone was talking about my cancer, but somehow none of the media picked up the story that night. It would take another few weeks for it to emerge that I had played with cancer.

Although the taste of victory was sweet, I hadn't come through unscathed. As I left the ground, people were commenting on how pale I looked. My energy levels matched my complexion. I felt utterly exhausted and wanted nothing more than to head straight home and go to bed. However, a supporters' function awaited. As captain, I simply couldn't do a no-show. So I turned up haggard and overwhelmed for a few soft drinks.

The next morning, however, was a different story. I could barely lift my head from the pillow when the sun rose. Sure, part of me still felt great from what I had achieved the night before. Instead of undergoing chemotherapy, I'd played a game of rugby league at age 36 – with cancer – before 25,000 people. It was unlikely that anyone else in the history of the game could say the same.

But the triumphant part of me was diminishing with every passing minute. I felt completely lethargic, like my body had been switched to a failing back-up power supply. I was about to black out. I was almost completely lifeless, so an urgent phone call was made to Dr Rahim. He demanded that I check into Ashfield private hospital as soon as possible.

He knew I'd played the game the night before and his voice carried that tell-tale 'I told you so' tone. At the hospital, the doctors immediately discovered that my white blood cell count had dipped to extraordinarily low levels. Had I left it much longer, I'd have collapsed. I was put straight on a drip and made to stay the night, with Lisa by my side.

I was allowed to leave on the Tuesday, but my chemo was due to begin three days later. I fronted RPA that Friday not knowing what to expect. I'd been warned many times over that it would be testing. But the doctors said different people react differently to the treatment, so I was hoping I'd get through without too much discomfort. I was hoping very hard, because they'd booked me in for six courses – with a month's break between each treatment.

Whatever hopes I had about that evaporated when I saw the nurse deliver the bag of chemicals that would be fed intravenously into my system. He looked like someone prepared to enter a nuclear wasteland. He was dressed from head to toe in protective clothing, with his face covered by a shield. It was like I was about to be treated by a cross between an astronaut and a character from the movie *Outbreak*.

The panic started then. 'Why are you dressed like that?' I asked nervously. Eyeing me with a sorry look, the nurse replied: 'Mate, this stuff is toxic. If it spills it can cause enormous damage.' Toxic – not quite the word you want to hear applied to a substance that's about to be pumped directly into your system. I was now almost overcome with panic, eyeing the one-litre bag with the letters C-H-O-P written across the front. The liquid inside certainly looked toxic. It was bright red, almost the same colour as blood.

I didn't want to know any more about chemotherapy. What would be, would be. I no longer had any control over my fate. It might make me sick, it might kill me – I couldn't afford to worry. All I had to do was keep my mind clear enough to deal with whatever came next.

The needle went in and all I felt was cold. Like a deadly

frost, it crept from my left hand, up my arm and across my chest. It was a sensation like no other I'd felt, like the blood in my veins had been replaced by a frozen thickshake. I didn't feel anything at first. I felt quite normal. This lasted for five minutes, and then 10. The bag took an hour to empty but I dared not look in its direction. I instead buried my head in a copy of *New Idea*, devouring each inane article with feigned interest.

The nurse kept returning to check on me every five minutes, but I was OK. When he came the final time, nothing had changed. I felt no different than I had earlier that morning when I arrived at the hospital. None of the side effects they had warned about were evident. That wasn't so bad, I thought. Despite being OK, I was made to stay overnight. This was a precaution imposed on all first-time chemo patients. By the next morning, there was still no adverse reaction. It was unbelievable, given that goo was supposedly so toxic. How could something like that have no impact on me? What was I? A robot?

The four weeks before my next treatment went by without incident. I felt well enough to continue the same diet and even light training. I drove myself around town and enjoyed the odd meal with a few of the boys. I was still knocking about with Craig Field, Darrell Trindall and Steve Roach.

I was decidedly more relaxed when the time came for my second bout of chemo in late August 1999. I wouldn't even have to stay overnight on this occasion. Instead, a female nurse led me into a large room where I witnessed one of the most bizarre scenes I've ever encountered. Seated around the room in recliners were about 30 people, all of whom were chatting and laughing. None was under 60 and they all looked worse for wear. But these golden oldies were having a grand old time in each other's company. It was like I'd stumbled across the shuffleboard deck on a cruise ship. Instead of cocktails, they were being fed intravenous drips. Inside their bags was a red liquid I now knew as CHOP. I turned to the nurse and said: 'This can't be that bad – look at them.' She looked at me with an expression of remorse. 'John, the truth is the chemo is not working on them,' she said. 'If it was, they wouldn't be feeling so good.'

Her words destroyed me in so many ways. The first was that my hopes of beating cancer without a fight had been dashed. After the first bout of chemo passed without incident, I'd almost come to think it would be a breeze. I'd taken nothing for granted, mind you, but I had let my guard down. The second was that I began to fret about whether the chemo was doing me any good. If the first dose hadn't caused any reaction, how could I be sure it had worked? Was it a waste of time?

My doubts were answered within five minutes of the second treatment starting. Out of nowhere a horrid cramp struck my stomach. It curdled and rushed upwards, forcing me to choke and gasp. Although I hadn't eaten a thing that morning under doctor's orders, I felt an overwhelming sickness. I cried out for the nurse, shattering the social climate of the room. She came running with a bowl, shoving it under my chin just in time to catch the first load of saliva and bile. I turned to her and said, 'Is it working now?'

It was working all right. For the next hour my body shuddered as it tried to purge the poison. After an hour of dry-retching I was in a sweat and fever. It would last for the next three weeks. During that time I went to a place where no-one, not even the most determined, pain-resistant soldier, should be sent.

DON'T MENTION THE C-WORD

I barely set foot out of my bedroom. My days were spent vomiting and moaning. Anything I ate came straight up. Ditto for water. All I could taste was metal. I was dehydrated 24 hours a day, all of which I suffered in consciousness because sleep just wasn't possible. Mum did her best to take care of me but I could see that even she was disturbed. I must have looked like the possessed girl, Linda Blair, from *The Exorcist*.

It took me three days to gather the strength to walk to the mirror, which was on the far side of my room. When I stood in front of it, I simply didn't recognise the person staring back at me. He was a ghoul. A bony, pale ghost with black lips and eyes. I must have dropped at least 10 kg since the game against France.

The farthest I made it in those three weeks was the bathroom. The rest of the time I was condemned to my bed out of a mix of helplessness and embarrassment. I refused all visitors, including Lisa. They simply couldn't be subjected to such a sight and I couldn't bear inflicting it upon them. I now understood why the doctor had told me that it's sometimes the chemo – not the cancer – that ends up killing people. The poison that was destroying my troublesome red blood cells was killing everything else as well. My body was being thrown out with the bath water and I could feel life slipping away. There was simply no escape. Nothing alleviated the discomfort, not even the painkillers I'd been prescribed. Only death could provide the respite I craved.

Then, without notice, I kept down a piece of toast. It performed wonders, like a freak shower in the desert. It was towards the end of the third week and I'd forgotten what it was to feel anything else but like death warmed up. Now, it seemed I'd turned a corner. In the coming days I kept meals down and managed to get out of the house. By midway through the fourth week I felt close to normal, so close that I even managed to drive myself to Jimmy's surgery to have a white blood cell injection.

Sitting in the waiting room that afternoon was my brother George's wife and my niece. It was a total coincidence that I bumped into them, and I'm not sure they completely appreciated it. Although they were delighted to see me up and about, my appearance left them deeply shocked. Even Jimmy was taken aback, although he hid it well. After finishing the injection, he sent me straight to Dr Rahim for more tablets. Jimmy's surgery is in Belfield, a five-minute drive from the specialist's rooms in Burwood. I had driven 20 minutes from Punchbowl, so I thought nothing of ducking up the road under my own steam. I was feeling as good as could be expected, even thinking that I'd made it a third of the way through the chemo. I was upbeat and hopeful and . . .

WHAT THE FUCK WAS THAT?

It felt as if my left side had just exploded. I'd never been shot, but it couldn't have felt much different to this. The pain quickly seized my entire left side, rendering half my body numb and bathed in sweat. Not for the first time, I thought I was going to die. But this time, more so than at the tip of Con's gun, more so than the cancer diagnosis, more so than the chemo . . . I was really convinced. This was it. The feeling that had exploded inside me was so alien to anything that I had experienced. It had to be death.

I kept driving. All animals live to survive and I was no different. My thoughts were racing but they paused momentarily at an article I recall reading that advised against panicking in urgent situations. Panic can only weaken. I needed every ounce of strength to make it to Dr Rahim and any chance of survival.

On the field, the difference between good and great players is their ability to perform under pressure. All the great ones – such as Andrew Johns, Darren Lockyer and Wally Lewis – didn't just handle pressure, they thrived on it. But instead of the difference between good and great, performing under pressure was now the difference between life and death. In any other situation I imagined myself collapsed on the floor, writhing in pain. That was completely natural. But that wasn't an option as I continued to drive along Georges River Road.

I made out red traffic lights ahead at the intersection where I needed to turn left into Dr Rahim's street. At the opposite side of the intersection was my old mate 'Tricky' Trindall. What were the chances? Tricky spotted me straightaway and began frantically waving. He could see I was looking directly at him, yet not responding. I simply couldn't. Nothing else mattered but getting to Dr Rahim's rooms. As the lights changed and our cars passed, Tricky leaned out the window and yelled: 'You think you're too good to say hello, John?' He looked furious.

I turned left and drove the remaining 500 metres to Dr Rahim's surgery. It was a surreal journey. For once, karma dealt me a break. Right out the front was a parking spot.

The waiting room was brimming with patients and every one of them looked horrified when I walked in. I was hunched over and creased with pain. Dr Rahim's secretary let out a short gasp before rushing to get help. The other patients recognised death when they saw it and gladly allowed me to jump the queue.

Dr Rahim didn't waste any time. Without even asking

me a question, he jabbed me with a strong painkiller. Within minutes I felt myself emerging from the pain. It was almost as if I was stepping out of my body. I smiled as I told Dr Rahim about the explosion in my guts. If I was going to die, then I'd do so with a smile. That's the one consolation of junkies who overdose. Opposed to drugs all my life, I suddenly shared their ill-gotten bliss. Nothing else mattered.

The fight in me had taken flight and I was ready to be taken away as the ambulance sped towards RPA hospital. For no particular reason, I remained alive. The doctors and nurses were scurrying like ants before a thunderstorm when I was wheeled through Emergency. I still didn't know what had happened.

My brother George, Ray Dib, Mum and Lisa had all arrived by the time the painkiller had worn off. I could now feel my insides crawling. I was overcome by cramping and breathlessness. It was dangerous to give too much pethidine, but my screams of agony sent the textbook flying out the window. The second jab didn't work as well, but it was sufficient to bring me close enough to reality to understand what was happening.

The emergency surgeon, Dr Kevin Storey, was furious. He cursed and screamed all sorts of insults at the hospital administration for making me wait so long to be treated. Apparently another patient was being operated on and it was impossible to stop the procedure for my sake. I remember the clock – 3.03 pm. The nurses were now shoving tubes into me. I looked at George and said: 'If I die, make sure to bury me in the Lebanon jersey.'

DON'T MENTION THE C-WORD

Lisa's face was all I could see when I woke up. She was wearing her work clothes – a blue suit. Lisa had no car and little money, so I thought it wonderful that she was with me. 'Lisa, do you have enough money to get home?' I asked. There was no time for her to answer because I had fallen straight back to sleep. The clock read 1 am.

It wasn't until after breakfast the following day that I discovered my stomach had burst while I was driving. The surgeons had removed three-quarters of it during a seven-hour operation the night before. Dr Storey told me on my arrival that my chances of living were 30 per cent. That made the 50:50 I'd been quoted about beating cancer seem even better. There was no way I was going to die now. Not after beating this.

It was the second bout of chemo that had done what a game of rugby league couldn't. The poison had eaten my insides to such an extent that it had made my stomach explode. But although I was only left with a fraction of my guts, the doctors said I wouldn't need a colostomy bag. The trade-off, however, was that for the rest of my life I could only eat tiny meals. Anything too big would simply make me throw up.

To this day, I still get it wrong. Midway through 2008 – almost 10 years after the surgery – I ate too much at my favourite Italian restaurant in Rozelle. It ended with me spewing 15 minutes later in the toilets at a nearby hotel. As a result of having such a small stomach, I now have to eat six small meals a day at regular intervals.

The road back was more difficult than my recovery from chemo. It was like climbing to the top of a mountain from a ravine, only to descend into an even deeper chasm on the opposite side. Everything seemed futile, but I now owed it to God to keep going.

In the seconds before the anaesthetic sent me to sleep I made the Man Upstairs a promise. In return for helping me survive the knife, I promised never to engage in crime again. It was all I had to offer and God had held his part of the bargain. Time would tell whether I'd be capable of living up to mine.

I'd lost 15 kg in one hit because of the operation. It was simply unfathomable how different I looked. To make matters worse, I couldn't eat for another two weeks. Instead, a drip did all my feeding. It was a depressing time during which I didn't even have the dignity of hiding my horrendous appearance from the rest of the world. Visitors flooded in from all the walks of life I had run with . . . footballers, conmen, family and even the odd priest.

The first thing I tasted was chicken broth. As far as I was concerned, it was liquid gold. And better still, I didn't bring it up. My spirits had been gradually lifting until this point, with the removal of each tube representing a huge milestone in my recovery.

It was a relief to finally get home, but only a mild one. I still had four bouts of chemo to come plus a possible stint of radiation. One bonus of the stomach operation was that the surgeons were pretty convinced they'd removed all the cancerous growth. The specialists, however, were unwilling to take any chances. They demanded I finish the chemo, even if they were open to cancelling the radiation if the results were favourable.

The surgery had delayed my third batch of chemo for a month, which was not ideal because it was supposed to be applied in strictly spaced increments. But from my point of view, the timing didn't seem to make a difference. Once again, there was a nurse catching my bile within five minutes of the deathly cold sensation that entered my body. Once again, I shuddered and vomited at home for three weeks.

Mum did her best to humour me, but I became aggressive and intolerant. Whenever she told me that everything would by OK, I'd snap back. 'What would you know?' I'd shout. 'How can you possibly know what I'm feeling?' It was an immature and rude reaction to someone who would sacrifice her own life to see me take another breath. But I wasn't myself in those horrible days of October 1999.

The horizon was dark most days, but a light appeared later that month when the Lebanese side booked its trip to Europe for the 2000 World Cup qualifiers. We had to win two matches to qualify – the first against Italy and the second against the winner of USA and South Africa. Although I was no hope of playing any official role in the campaign, I desperately wanted to be there to support the boys.

The tour was only 10 days long – enough time to get me thinking. It also fell perfectly in the window just before my fourth bout of chemo, when I knew I'd feel better. If the doctors would grant a few days grace, it was possible.

As soon as I started thinking like that, there was no stopping me. Naturally, all the experts advised against it and said I was insane. But they were powerless to stop me. If it was possible, then I'd be there. I also needed a solid incentive, something concrete to live for. Steve Ghosn and the boys were over the moon to hear of my plans. We flew out and I must have still looked like a ghost, because they upgraded me to first class on the basis of my condition.

It was extremely cold at that time of the year in Toulouse, France. But I don't mind the cold. I'd tag along with the team to lunch and training. Some days I'd just hang around the hotel. I recall one afternoon the whole team went to a café and we were sitting outside having coffee. I got so tired that I fell asleep as everyone chatted around me. It was cold, but I was comfortable. It felt good to be among a team again – I'd missed that so much in the solitary confines of my bedroom.

On the eve of our qualifier against Italy, replacement skipper Darren Maroon gathered the team together for a final bonding session. He challenged each member of the squad to say a few words about what making the World Cup meant to them. When it came to me I simply stood up and said: 'I need you to go give me the inspiration to beat cancer. If you qualify for the World Cup, I'll come back and play alongside you.' The boys took the first step the next afternoon by thrashing Italy. It was straight on to New Orleans for our death-or-glory game against the USA.

Yours truly, however, would never see that game. When we arrived in New Orleans there was a squad of official-looking people waiting in customs. I leaned over to Darren and said, 'Look, mate, there's the whole US media here to interview the Lebanese captain.'

They wanted an interview all right, just not with Darren. It was me they wanted to speak to – and these hombres weren't reporters. They were US customs officials.

I was taken into a room and told there'd be no way I could be granted entry because of my criminal record. I was being sent back to France on the next flight. I told them about my cancer and the game, but it fell on deaf ears. Arguing would only place me at risk of a worse fate, although I couldn't imagine one that would outweigh missing the game.

I flew back to Paris to be met by my old mate Pierre van Dome, who had helped me co-ordinate the game against France in July. Pierre kept me at his house in Perpignan, where I received that fateful call from across the Atlantic. On the other end was Steve – and with good news. We'd easily accounted for the USA. We'd won a place in the World Cup. Forget pethidine, there was no greater painkiller than this. All our toil was worth the effort.

And what's more I now had something that made the next three months of hell worthwhile. I vowed then and there to finish the chemo, beat cancer and play for Lebanon in the 2000 World Cup. If death wanted to take me after that, then it was entitled to. I'd have nothing more to give.

Thankfully, the last half of chemo was better than the first. The period in which I was incapacitated started to shrink with each treatment and after the sixth and final bout I only suffered for 10 days. It was time for another CT scan to check whether the cancer was still lurking. I went to see Dr Douglas in March 2000 with great confidence. I knew inside that I had the bastard beaten. He confirmed my thoughts with four simple words: 'The tests are negative.' I'd faced the toughest opponent imaginable and won. No game of rugby league, no big collect, no massive plunge had ever instilled me with what I felt now.

The movie was still eight years away from hitting cinemas, but I already felt like Mr Incredible.

CHAPTER 20

COACHJELIAS@HOTMAIL.COM

The delusion of being bulletproof wasn't foreign to me. Throughout my life, there'd been phases where I felt above reproach or beyond the law. When I was younger I'd brazenly steal dozens of cars in a single night and dump them wherever I pleased. As I got older, I'd barge my way into football matches and concerts. I satisfied my urges without any consideration of the consequences. When you feel bulletproof, there suddenly aren't any consequences. You feel like you can do anything without having to pay a price.

That's how I felt after my final chemo treatment in early 2000. If I could beat cancer, then I could beat anything. The specialist at RPA, Dr Joshua Douglas, had told me there was no need for radiation therapy. I thought I was in the clear. I thought I'd been given the green light to take on the world. And that's exactly what I aimed to do. The 2000 Rugby League World Cup was scheduled to be staged in Great Britain in October. Lebanon was one of the 16 sides that had qualified, thanks to our victory over the USA the previous November. Although I would be nearly 38 by the time the tournament began, I was hell-bent on playing.

It wasn't all just in my head, either. I had evidence that this incredible comeback was possible. Before I was diagnosed in 1999, my old Newtown teammate Tommy Raudonikis had called me out of the blue to see if I wanted to have a run with Wests. Tommy was coaching the Magpies that year and the battling club was struggling more than ever. Tommy was light on props and felt I might fit the bill, despite the fact I had played my last first-grade game in 1994. I took up his offer to trial at training and felt adequate among the other players. I could still keep up with them. But just as Tommy was about to draw up an incentive-based contract after a week's training, my mates on the Wests board caught wind of his idea. And that was the end of that.

My mind clicked into gear and the weight started to return. So did the muscle. I was like the bionic man – building myself up from scratch. Three months after finishing chemo, I was back into full training at the gym and pool. People who had been shocked by my sickly appearance now expressed equal amazement at how quickly I'd regained full health. I was also making up for lost time away from training. Apart from the trip overseas with the Lebanese team, I'd virtually spent the past nine months marinating in my own sickness at home.

I needed to get out and exercise some of my invincibility. I never crossed the line into criminal activities, but the candle was burned at both ends most days. I happily traded regular status at the cancer treatment room for some of the new clubs and bars that were sprouting up all over Sydney. On most weekends I'd party hard and recklessly, never

COACHJELIAS@HOTMAIL.COM

drinking big or taking drugs, but it's probably fair to say I threw my weight around. After all she'd done for me when I was sick, Lisa deserved better.

It took a routine visit to Dr Douglas to rein me in. I fronted him full of chutzpah and confidence. 'Well, I've got it beat, eh doc?' I chuckled. Not for the first time, Dr Douglas looked at me as if I was a simpleton. 'John, I think there's something you should know,' he said. 'The fact is you could very well still have cancer as we speak. For all patients, the highest risk period is the five years after onset. It generally recurs then. You will now have a much lower life expectancy, but if you can get through the next five years you can then start thinking about being in the clear. You still have a long way to go. You are only in remission.'

Remission? The way Dr Douglas spoke, it felt like my body was still riddled with cancer. But instead of attacking me, it had been put to sleep. Should it stir at any time over the next five years, I'd be back where I started. Back in my bedroom vomiting bile and tearing my eyes out at 3 am while the rest of the city slept soundly. Five years?

I visited Dr Douglas in June, meaning the World Cup was now just five months away. In a matter of minutes he had turned my dream of captaining Lebanon at the tournament into a nightmare. I'd ignored him a year ago and played against France, but something felt different this time. The spell of my invincibility suddenly wore off. I felt small and vulnerable – a man at the mercy of damnation. When I took the field against France, I'd taken a risk that had landed me in hospital on a drip two days later. I had a full stomach back then as well. Now I only had a quarter left.

But there was something else eating away at my conviction to pull on the jersey. I was being selfish. I was putting myself ahead of the team – a terrible thing for any captain to do. At nearly 38 and coming off a nine-month battle with cancer, there was no way I could replicate the player I was. Instead, I'd be a shadow of my former self trying to nurse his way through the tournament with secret fears that my stomach could collapse altogether at any moment. That was no way to represent one's country. It was an insult to the team, and what's more, to the young player who would have to make way for me after helping the side qualify.

Yes, I was being foolish. For once, I took some advice and let my stubbornness take a back seat. Playing for Lebanon in the World Cup had been my inspiration for the past six months, but it was now revealed for what it was: a pipe dream. I decided then and there to let it go.

When I left RPA that afternoon, there were a lot of things going through my head. On one hand I was glad that I'd stopped myself from making a terrible mistake and cheating the team. But on the other I now felt impotent. More than anything, I wanted to be part of the campaign – to make a difference. How could I possibly do that if I wasn't going to play?

There were also problems in the background that made me doubt myself. Around that time one of the directors – whom I won't name – started making moves to rid me from the team in any official capacity. Although I had founded the side, he believed my presence on the board was a deterrent to potential sponsors. I found his attitude reprehensible, given this particular person was a long-time friend. Worse still, he had relied on my services in the past. That's not a friend, that's a turncoat.

Before his feelings became widely known, this director had confided his thoughts with our coach Steve Ghosn.

COACHJELIAS@HOTMAIL.COM

Being a persuasive and clever salesman, the director managed to talk Steve around to his way of thinking. When I found out that Steve was part of the campaign to have me removed, I was livid. United and passionate just six months ago, our front office was now unravelling along a fault line. We soon had a split camp, with both sides muscling the other for control. I still blame the director for brainwashing Steve.

It might have ended differently had my brother George and I not enjoyed the support of Tas Baitieri and Colin Love. Both were influential figures within the International Federation of Rugby League (IFRL), the body that stages the World Cup. They made George and me a promise to deal only with us, and that settled the argument. The director and his supporters were forced to resign from the board and walk away. It was a sad start to what should have been one of the most special times in our lives.

Steve was still coach, but I felt he had to go as well. It had nothing to do with his ability and profile. Steve had not only been a great friend of mine, but also a wonderful coach who could motivate his players to run through brick walls. With a passionate country like Lebanon, that's exactly the kind of man you need in charge. No, the reason why Steve had to go was because he crossed the line and showed disloyalty. You can't have that in a team sport and once it sets in it can be harder to cure than cancer.

Around the time Dr Douglas dashed my hopes of playing, I rang Steve and told him we had decided to advertise for a new coach. Silence. Steve was devastated. He'd coached the side for nothing since 1997 and was now being shafted when his reward was due. We shouted and argued, but I didn't budge. I said he was free to apply for the position, but that was even more insulting to his integrity. That phone call destroyed a 14-year friendship. He would one day speak to me again, but not until many years later in a place that was as far away from the football field as one could imagine – Silverwater jail.

With time running out and the team without a coach, I made a series of phone calls to all the top candidates. My good friend Wayne Bennett was the first, but he wanted to spend that off-season with his family. Tim Sheens said he was too busy, as did Wayne Pearce. Junior had coached both Wests Tigers (Balmain and Wests had merged that season) and New South Wales in 2000. He was spent. Queensland coach Mark Murray was also unavailable, leaving me with just one man to turn to.

Big Artie Beetson hadn't picked up a clipboard since being dumped by Easts in 1988. Despite his time away from coaching, I knew he had the smarts and charisma to get our players up for the challenge. Artie remains one of the most respected figures in the game and shaped as an inspiration for the Lebanese kids, many of whom were either park footballers or Metro Cup players.

'I don't have the capacity to do it fulltime,' Artie said. 'But I'm happy to come along and help out. Who else are you thinking of?' I told him my options were bare. We'd placed an ad in the paper, but no-one had applied. 'Then why don't you do it, John?' Artie asked.

His words were like a shot of clarity. I'd played under many coaches and been tutored by the likes of Warren Ryan and Wayne Bennett. I'd also spent the past four years coaching the St George Dragons, a junior side in the Canterbury comp, and was Wayne Pearce's defensive coach at Balmain until I got cancer. I knew I wanted to be a coach, but that

COACHJELIAS@HOTMAIL.COM

desire had never translated to leading Lebanon until the phone call to Artie. I always saw myself as a player, not as a coach, when it came to the Cedars. Suddenly, I thought differently. After moping for a couple of weeks because of the cancer warning and my run-in with Steve Ghosn, I was the old bull at the gate again. Then and there I decided to team up with Artie to lead the side at the World Cup.

Although the Lebanon position was not in my sights, I'd been preparing myself for a tilt at coaching that season. Every time the Broncos came to Sydney, I'd accompany Wayne Bennett in the coach's box. Wayne was kind enough to grant me the chance to simply observe him in action and ask the odd question afterwards.

Given the Broncos won that season's premiership in a canter, it was a fascinating experience to watch a man at the top of his game relate to his players. At all the matches I attended, Wayne never lost his cool with the side. He kept careful track of the stats and relayed all his instructions through his assistants. At halftime, he didn't say a lot except for one game when the Broncos were trailing by a fair margin. Wayne was angry that afternoon, and he didn't attempt to hide it. But instead of humiliating the players with criticism, he bluntly reminded them of what they were capable of. The manner was harsh, but the message was still positive. I know you can do better – now get out there and do it!

After matches Wayne always shared his emotions with the players, just as he trained with them during the week. If Brisbane won, he was just about the happiest bloke in the room. If they lost, he'd find a corner and barely say a word. Wayne knew how to be on their level. He never used words like 'I' or 'you' when addressing the players. It was always 'we'.

Coaches have to be many things – statisticians,

motivators, technical gurus, psychologists and father figures. But if there was one thing Wayne taught me, it was that the coach is above all a team builder. Every decision, every idea, had to be considered with the dynamics of the team in mind. And a team is a complex organism, full of different personalities and backgrounds. Before teaching them how to play football, the coach has to teach them to play together.

Putting the team first always leads to hard decisions because certain individuals will inevitably be forced to take a back seat. I immediately learned this when I was forced to omit several players from our 22-man World Cup squad who'd been great servants of the team. One was my cousin, Anthony Mansour. Although the players who missed out were great friends, the reality was there were better youngsters coming through. It was difficult to break the news, but I'm relieved to say that every player who missed out was mature enough to accept the decision and not complain.

We only had three players with first-grade experience – Hazem El Masri, Michael Khoury and Sami Chamoun. And had I put my personality above the team's best interests, Sami might not have been there either. He and I didn't get along from the start.

Our differences stemmed from the fact that we were so alike. A prop forward with the Illawarra Steelers, Sami thought he could throw his weight around in camp. During the build-up for our game against France in 1999, I remember him being a smartarse at training. He tried to influence the other players and was quietly subverting the control from the coach and older guys.

I recognised what was going on because he reminded me a lot of myself at his age. Sami was a young guy with plenty of ability and an even bigger opinion of himself. Perhaps if I had been his age, we might have been best buddies. In my mid-30s, however, I was looking for respect and it wasn't coming from Sami.

Our simmering feud came to a head later that year at Paris airport, when the team was waiting to board a flight to Toulouse for our World Cup qualifier against Italy. Although I was weak and gaunt because of the cancer treatment, I challenged 103 kg Sami to a fight there and then. He had encouraged some of players to go out drinking the night before and I could still smell the alcohol on his breath. Officials had imposed an alcohol ban before the game and Sami had insulted the team by not only ignoring it, but also persuading other players to do so.

The irony was that I'd done exactly the same thing as a player 12 months earlier. We toured Japan at the end of the 1998 season and Steve had put an alcohol ban and curfew in place before the game. One night, however, I was having such a good time in Tokyo that I didn't return to the team hotel until 5 am. Steve was livid the next morning and wanted to sack me.

Although I barely had the strength to throw a punch let alone sustain one, I confronted Sami before dozens of stunned Parisian passengers at the departure gate. 'Righto, you and me outside now,' I said. My jacket came off and I began to shape up. I had no hope of beating him in a fight. He was at the peak of his physical condition, while I was at the depth of mine. He looked shocked. He couldn't believe someone so ill was prepared to take him on over a principle. Sami didn't react and the other players quickly restrained me. But I gained his respect that day, something crucial now that I was coach and he was one of our best players.

The lesson I hope Sami learned was there's nothing better than discipline, something I've always had a love–hate relationship with. While I was motivated on the training field, I lapsed away from football. In some parts of my life, I had absolutely no discipline. My gambling habit and relationships with women are two examples. A lack of discipline in those departments dashed any chance I had of a happy personal life, even before crime came into the equation.

Above all, I wanted to make sure the team was disciplined. It starts with little things like being at training on time and not cutting corners on a witch's hat. If anyone did either they'd be condemned to extra sessions with our head conditioner Tony Green.

I was also conscious of using my experience as a player to understand how to best communicate with them. One of the things I appreciated most was having input. It made me feel like I was a respected part of the team, rather than just a tool at the coach's disposal. I made sure to constantly seek input from the senior players about what they thought of the coaching drills and training methods. You have to be above them, but not too far above them, otherwise you lose relevance. Like Wayne Bennett, I did the conditioning work with them. If they can't relate to you, they won't play for you.

Pride didn't stop me from admitting that I was inexperienced and in need of much help. Artie was great in this regard. He lived in Sydney at the time and we trained at Leichhardt. Every session was meticulously planned together. I also got fresh faces to training, like Alan Jones and Wayne Pearce. I remember Jones gave one of his stirring speeches, which ended with the line: 'If any one of you 22 blokes is happy just being here, then you should go home now.' The boys were mesmerised.

COACHJELIAS@HOTMAIL.COM

We were drawn to play New Zealand, Wales, and the Cook Islands in the pool phase. The top two teams would progress to the quarter-finals. On paper we had no chance of beating the Kiwis – the second-best team in the world. But an upset over Wales and victory against the Cook Islanders would be enough to see us through. It was a long shot with only three first-graders, but not impossible. By the time we arrived at our base in Swansea, Wales, we were rock-hard fit after three months training.

I did nothing fancy in the lead-up to our first game against New Zealand. There were no hypnotists or *Rocky* tapes. Just a boring old alcohol ban and nightly curfews. The only tweak I made was to ensure the Christian and Muslim players were mixed in their rooms. I speculated that the non-drinking Muslims would be a good influence on the Christians, whose religion didn't forbid them from straying into the many bars that Swansea had to offer. It worked. Not one player put a foot out of line. The only vice I allowed them was gambling at a mini casino down the road. In Australia, the blackjack tables use eight decks of cards. In Wales, however, there were only four. Being old pros, Artie and I fancied our chances of being able to count the cards. Predictably, we lost big-time while the amateur players cleaned up.

Unfortunately, there was another thing out of our control – the weather. Conditions for our game against New Zealand were the worst I've ever encountered. It was a freezing, miserable day. During the match, six of our players suffered from hypothermia. We had gone into the game with a plan to try and move the big Kiwi forwards around. But the sticky mudheap and slippery ball made us stationary targets for their brutal pack. After a solid resistance in the first 20 minutes, we were obliterated by more than 60 points.

I couldn't wait for the game to end, but I didn't feel embarrassed. I had every right to, with the team being belted by a cricket score in its first outing under my watch. New Zealand, however, were an extremely strong side. It was a mismatch from the start and the conditions accentuated that. The truth was that playing New Zealand first-up was a terrible draw. Had we met them with a few runs under our belt, I'm sure the scoreline would have finished up more respectable. I also had no doubt that the players had given their all. That's the least you can ask. Their execution, on the other hand, was appalling at times. Artie and I had much work to do to lift their spirits before the game against Wales at the newly-built Millennium Stadium the following week.

Artie and I spoke at length about how to rebuild the players' confidence after such a drubbing. Artie advised me to forget about the game and pretend it didn't happen. But I had other ideas. Although Artie was a football great, he lacked insight into the Lebanese psyche. We are a very proud race and don't take humiliation lightly. The greater the humiliation, the greater the urge to settle the score. It was in my control to further embarrass these players to the point that they'd be ready to kill in seven days time.

Every night before the Wales game I showed them the video. I didn't need to provide an in-depth analysis because the pictures said it all. On each viewing, new and even more cringe-worthy incidents would be brought to light. I let them take it in. There were no reminders of how bad they'd been, just how much better they could be. I owe that one to Wayne Bennett.

The next motivational trick was all me. I'd noticed the

bookies had given us a 22-and-a-half points start against the Welsh. The hosts had some handy players in Iestyn Harris and Kieron Cunningham, but I still felt our fitness would be far superior. If we could control the ball and defend well, we'd have a shot in the final 15 minutes. The handicap was ridiculous, so I implored all the players to back themselves.

The final motivational twist came on the bus to the game. When we departed Sydney, I had one of the team officials videotape messages of support from all the players' families and children at the airport. The tape had since been edited and was waiting for a moment like this. I didn't see the point of using it before the New Zealand game, because I knew it would make no difference. For maximum effect, the tape could only be used once. When it began playing, the bus went silent. There was an air of determination on board.

Hazem had also put together a video of his own. It was a montage of clips of the bombings in Lebanon, particularly those that had forced his family and many others to move to Australia. There's not a Lebanese-Australian who can't relate to these war-torn images of their mother country. Both videos generated a potent emotional cocktail that had the team ready to explode against the Welsh.

But we started terribly. It was almost as if we were too hyped-up. Wales skipped out to an 18–0 lead in no time, before we steadied and came into the sheds at 22–6.

One thing struck me about the players. They were hardly puffing. There was only 40 minutes left, but the team had enough fitness reserves to start all over again. I gathered them together and pointed this out. I spoke to each player and convinced them they had what it took to come back. They did extremely well, cutting the margin to 24–16 with five minutes to play. Wales were now standing still and I was sure that if there were another 10 minutes left we'd win. Michael Khoury confirmed as much when he crossed with 90 seconds left to cut the margin to two points. But it was a fraction too late. Our World Cup was over.

The first person I wanted to seek out afterwards was Wales coach Clive Woodward. I wanted to know whether he thought the turnaround was due to complacency on his team's behalf, or purely our efforts. 'John, your boys had me very worried there,' he said. 'We were doing our best, but you were too good for us in the second half. It was a good thing you started so poorly.' To come so close and lose was frustrating, but I couldn't show any negative emotions. The players had done exactly what I'd asked in the second half. They'd come within a whisker of beating the side that would go on to lead Australia 20–8 at halftime in the second semi-final. Anger was not the answer.

Although the form guide suggested we should account for the Cook Islands, a 24–all draw eventuated. I was happy with that result, too, and more so because the game was the first rugby league match staged at Millennium Stadium in Cardiff. It was a dead rubber and I was satisfied the players had done everything possible to lift themselves. The Cook Islands also played well and we matched them. We didn't have a win to show for our efforts, but we hadn't been disgraced either. Plenty of the so-called 'minnow' sides were belted by Australia and New Zealand, so no-one judged us on that first drubbing against the Kiwis.

The experience of coaching Lebanon had left me wanting more. Yes, this is what I wanted to do with the rest of my life. I felt I had not only the football know-how, but also the life skills to take charge and mould young men. I was no longer all about looking out for myself. If anything could be salvaged from my life of misdemeanour it was ensuring that kids didn't stray down the same path.

My criminal record and reputation were testament to what eventually awaited everyone who thought they were bulletproof. But it was precisely those two things that prevented me from getting a real coaching job in Australia. My reputation was shot. No club in its right mind was about to hand control over impressionable youngsters to a bloke who sold machine-gun parts and allegedly fixed games. Not enough time had passed to convince them otherwise, and nor had I provided enough evidence as a coach to make any club CEO believe the risk was worthwhile.

Upon returning to Australia in late 2000, this was made abundantly clear by Canterbury's recruitment man Mark Hughes. Mark was in charge of coaching appointments for the Bulldogs junior rep teams and I enquired about the Harold Matthews (U15s) coaching job for 2001. Mark looked at me like the doctors used to when I asked dumb questions and insisted on playing football with cancer. He looked at me like I was crazy.

There was no way Canterbury – or any other top club – was going to take the risk. They were scared stiff about what sponsors and the community would think. But I also believe they were scared stiff about giving control to someone they couldn't control. That's one of the saddest things in rugby league and sport in general. The administrators might like to believe they are professional, but it's still a big boys' club where who you know is handier than what you know.

If that was the game, then I had no choice but to play it. I contacted my old mate in France, Pierre van Dome. He had enough influence to get me a start over there and soon came back with an offer from a club called the Pia Donkeys. Pia were the perennial cellar-dwellers of the French first division, having not won a thing for 27 seasons. The money was also poor, but beggars can never be choosers. I didn't have to think to accept.

It was a chance to start a very long journey that I hoped deep down would end in the NRL in Sydney. I prepared for the assignment by accompanying Wayne Bennett as often as I could. I also needed to sign four imports and invested plenty of time and effort choosing the right guys – Laloa Milford, a winger from Balmain; Adam Nable, a hooker from Manly; and Cowboys pair Bruce Mamando (forward); and Danny Lambert (halfback). I also hired a head trainer, Tim Rogers, who came highly recommended by Tas Baitieri. Tim prepared the team for two months before I arrived in Pia just a fortnight before our first game, in October 2001.

My first training session was a mix of tragedy and comedy. I was unable to communicate with the players in French and had to rely on a bilingual prop, Carl Javaux, to translate instructions. Not that it mattered. Even a coach of my limited experience spoke a language far too complex for these part-timers. They were very ill-disciplined compared to teams in the NRL. A park football side probably had more idea about the finer details of the game, like the kick-chase and marker play. It was these simple things I tried to stress in the lead-up to our round one clash against Toulouse, a side coached by former Gold Coast mentor Phil Economidis. We were flogged 46–0.

I phoned Wayne Bennett that night and poured out my soul. What had I got myself into? I didn't think I had any answers, and even if I did I wasn't sure whether the players could understand what I was saying. As ever, Wayne refused to buy into any panic. He stayed calm and pressed me for positives. 'There must have been something,' he said. And there was – none of my imports had played in that match.

The following week at training, I reminded the local players about the impending threat to their positions. I also didn't neglect to point out my willingness to promote players from the under-18s side if performances didn't improve. But I didn't drop anyone straightaway. I remembered Steve Ghosn's faith in me after my first game for Wests – the shocker in Canberra. His loyalty lifted me to perform and I hoped that extending the same chance to these players would embolden their respect and desire to play for me. It worked. With the addition of our imports, we won the next six games to be eyeballing top-of-the-table side Villeneuve.

Discipline was the key. Anyone late for training was immediately dropped. I tried to shock them, to wake them from their complacency. The time-honoured steaks and sugar cubes were replaced with bowls of pasta before matches. The players noticed the difference and respected me for it. I had also bought videos of top-grade games from Australia, which I showed them repeatedly. It was all about taking them out of their comfort zone and showing them a different way to do things. The entire club had been stuck in a rut for so long it had accepted the battler's tag without question.

Part of the problem was geography. Pia was next to Perpignan, which boasted one of the competition's real hot-shot teams, UTC. Over time, Pia had earned the nickname Little Brother. Over time, the players and officials believed it. They never questioned the beltings and bullying from

UTC, because, like any little brother, they expected no different.

Apart from the football side of things, I was also enjoying the role of father figure. This is what attracted me to coaching in the first place – way back to those impromptu training sessions in the yard at Oberon farm. I liked the idea of being the male role model I never had. It made me feel partly complete, compensating in some way for the absence I'd endured as a child without anyone to look up to.

Wayne Bennett was particularly invaluable in teaching me the finer points of this role. I'd try and phone him every Monday night – if we lost, the conversation would be lengthy, if we won, it would be brief. On one occasion he gave me a piece of advice I'll never forget as a coach.

'John, there's one player in your team you are going to rely on all season,' Wayne said from his farm on the other side of the globe. 'That bloke will most likely be your best player. Injuries permitting, he's going to play every game. You have to work on your relationship with him. You need to build a team within a team with that player.'

For Wayne, that player was Darren Lockyer at the Broncos. For me, it was a kid called Saba at Pia. Saba was only 19 but one of the most naturally gifted fullbacks I'd seen. He was a class above the other plodders. He could do it all – tackle, evade tackles, score tries and kick goals. But he didn't want to do it all every week. He was high-maintenance and problematic.

Taking Wayne's advice, I had to make an extra effort to reach Saba off the field. He was simply a tearaway who thought he knew best. He was unmotivated off the field – the classic bored teenager in a small country town. You find them outside cities all over the world. Saba needed a job, so

COACHJELIAS@HOTMAIL.COM

I arranged one with the local fire department. He appreciated my interest and began to reciprocate with consistent performances. I also gave him input, despite his age. It paid huge dividends and he was one of our best as we charged towards the 2002 French Challenge Cup final against the all-conquering Villeneuve.

The big game had many parallels with the Brisbane Souths versus Wynnum grand final in 1985. It was another David and Goliath battle, with Villeneuve the Wynnum of the French comp in those days. They boasted virtually the entire national side and were odds-on favourites to brush us aside. But for some untimely injuries, we would have won that afternoon. I remember being buoyed by the fact my old friends from Leigh, Tim Street and Samantha Martin (Scotty Mahon's girlfriend) flew across the English Channel just to be there.

We were leading 19–12 with 20 minutes remaining when both Laloa Milford and Danny Lambert had to come off with shoulder injuries. The lethal Villeneuve side sensed blood and pounced, eventually winning by six points.

Nevertheless, our performance earned me coach of the year for that season. Having come to France on minimum wages, I was suddenly in demand. UTC made a huge offer for my services for 2002–03, but I decided to stay loyal. I was very happy at Pia, despite the fact we bowed out of contention in the finals after finishing second. Once again, Villeneuve were responsible for our demise.

Although we pulled up short, the turn-around was remarkable. Sponsors and fans were back on board to celebrate Pia's resurrection. Nothing less than a title would suffice the following season. I returned to Australia in 2002 looking for a new batch of imports who could take us one step further.

SIN BIN

This time, I had no girlfriend to greet me. I had broken up with Lisa the previous year – something that began with my recklessness after beating cancer. Just when I should have been treasuring her for nursing me through the disease, I neglected her. It is one of the biggest regrets of my life.

The first player I approached was my old mate from South Sydney, Craig Field. Craig had endured some tough times during my spell in France. In 2001 he was sacked by Wests Tigers after testing positive to cocaine and then getting involved in a punch-up at Balmain Leagues Club. His first-grade career was over, although he did have a lot of offers to play in the bush. I sensed, however, that Craig was a broken man when it came to football. When I came back he had taken the unexpected step of managing an Italian restaurant on Norton Street in Leichhardt.

It was there that I implored him to come and play for me at Pia. We were great friends and it didn't take long to convince him. If I've got any other regrets, one would definitely be the fact I never became a salesman. From the day I flogged all those raffle tickets and walkathon sponsorships at St John's, I was born to sell. The gift of the gab is an integral part of coaching. At the end of the day it's all just a big sell. You are selling your ideas of how to approach a game. How much they believe you depends on how well you sell, particularly when you don't have a reputation.

Jimmy Serdaris came out of retirement to join me and I also convinced prop Tim Madison and pivot Tom O'Reilly to have a season at Pia. Laloa was also backing up after being crowned top try scorer in 2001–02.

I felt we had the mix right, but there's always something lurking in the background to take you by surprise. On this

COACHJELIAS@HOTMAIL.COM

occasion it was a cancer in the form of our new football manager, Guy Delaunay. Guy had begged to come across from neighbouring UTC, the team that was still chasing my services for 2003–04. Until he arrived at Pia, we got on well, sharing meals and nights out. I wouldn't have allowed him anywhere near our club if I'd had any inkling of just what a grub he was.

Because of his links to UTC, Guy knew that their president Bernard Guasch had offered me a two-year contract. But that wasn't the most lucrative part of the offer. It had just been revealed that Perpignan had been accepted to join the UK Super League in 2005 in the guise of a new franchise named Les Catalans. Bernard had told me that if all went smoothly over my two seasons, I'd have a fair crack at being the inaugural coach of Les Catalans. This represented a massive opportunity to develop my career, an opportunity that wasn't going to come from anywhere else in the world, because of my reputation.

Still, I didn't agree to leave Pia straightaway. In 2002–03 we improved again, thanks largely to Craig Field's captaincy. He demonstrated his commitment to the team on the day we arrived in France from Australia. We had a trial match just four hours after making it to Pia from Paris, but Craig wouldn't hear of jet lag. He played with a heart and commitment that continued in the same vein for the entire season.

I was also improving as a coach. Part of that came with understanding the players better, but there was also a bit of trial and error. I liked to experiment with different forms of motivation – one being music. In late 2002 I returned to my duties with Lebanon for our one-off Test against France in Tripoli. It was an historic occasion – the first rugby league match on Lebanese soil. Over 10,000 people turned up to watch us thrash the French 36–6. But I'd like to think that a little trick I devised before the game played a small role in our performance. That night, I decided to say nothing in the dressing room. Instead, I set a CD player on the floor and played 'Time to Say Goodbye', the classic by Andrea Bocelli and Sarah Brightman that never fails to inspire me. The boys went silent and did their country proud. That taught me how good a motivator music could be and I pulled the same trick for Pia's local derby against UTC later that season. I also played 'Amazing Grace' before another game.

It was during my sabbatical with the Lebanese side that Guy got down to his dirty business. Although he had promised me he wouldn't utter a word about the UTC offer, he let the cat out of the bag to Craig Field. Guy wanted to create a contingency in case I left. He couldn't see the point of paying Craig Field big bucks and then shelling out more money for a coach. So Guy asked Craig if he wanted to be captain–coach in 2003–04.

I'd taken the club from rags to riches in 12 months, and here was this bloke, knifing me in the back before I'd even decided what the future might hold. There was still every chance that I could stay at Pia, despite the lure of Les Catalans three years down the track. I loved Pia. Not anymore. When I discovered the board were in on Guy's plan to white-ant me, it all began to unravel. I just can't tolerate duplicity and backstabbing in a team environment. I can understand Guy's concern that I might leave, but he should have spoken to me about the contingency before going behind my back.

I immediately took up the UTC offer and quit Pia. Other coaches might have tried to survive in such a poisonous environment, but I felt it would be bad for everyone. The team relies on integrity and honesty. Without that it has

COACHJELIAS@HOTMAIL.COM

to be dismantled and rebuilt from scratch. Craig took over both roles and managed to steer Pia to a second straight Challenge Cup final against Villeneuve. But he couldn't do a Wayne Bennett and avenge the previous year's defeat.

Meanwhile, I was back in Australia. I had reason to be positive with the move to UTC the following season, but something inside me had turned dark over my departure from Pia. It was all that was needed to make me do the unthinkable.

CHAPTER 21
RAY

Now I'm the one holding the gun.

It's pointed at Ray's chest. I don't look at his eyes, just his enormous chest. It moves up and down fast, gathering breaths like each one might be his last. I'm on the verge of shooting Ray in the chest. I'm on the verge of killing a man. I've never thought about this before, but here I am just after 10 am on a Saturday, ready to murder Ray. We're standing face-to-face outside a McDonald's restaurant. The staff don't notice a thing. They are too busy replacing the breakfast muffins with the burger buns.

My finger is on the trigger. The gun is loaded. I know this because the guy who gave it to me the night before said so. I've never fired a gun before, so this bullet looks as though it will be both my first and last. I might never see the outside again if I do this.

Still, I can't afford to let Ray live. Last night, he knocked on my mother's door and threatened her life. For her sake,

I can't give Ray the chance to make good his threat. One press of the trigger will do it. Ray will be gone and Mum will be safe. She should never have been dragged into this. Somewhere in the background my voice is screaming for him to stay away from my family, to never come near me again . . .

I look in his eyes. I want to see the look of a man who is facing death. I'd been in the position several times myself, once with a gun to my head in 1990, but I'd never seen the eyes. They twitch back and forth, between hope and despair. They want to live, but death is easier if you accept it beforehand. Ray's eyes can't decide which way to go.

They used to be such kind eyes. Ones that carried promise, generosity and friendship. Then they were blinded by an addiction. Gambling. It changed Ray's life, turned him from a nice guy to someone I'm about to kill. I couldn't help but think about his wife and kids . . . *his kids*. I'd met them plenty of times – a boy and girl, beautiful, well-raised children who were a credit to their mother. Sadly, they were forced to put up with a father consumed by greed. They deserved their old dad back, the man who bought them gifts instead of losing their house on the punt.

No kid deserves to grow up without a father. I should know. That's what happened to me and look where I am now. A twice-jailed felon about to shoot a man in broad daylight. If those kids ended up following in my footsteps, it would be on my conscience because I was the one who killed their dad.

Let it be on Ray's conscience, I thought. I can't kill this man. For the sake of his kids, I can't kill this man.

I lower the gun and pull the trigger.

RAY

Ray entered my life in late 1993, when I was training with the Balmain Tigers for the following season. I noticed him straightaway when he lobbed at training. The guy was huge – at least 120 kg. He came down to Leichhardt Oval to watch us train. Ray was a regular at training that off-season – a really big Balmain fan. Literally. But he wasn't like some of the other diehards who'd come to training because they had nothing better to do. Ray had something to offer in return.

He worked for a phone company called MLC Communications, Balmain's new major sponsor. Ray managed MLC's nearest shop at Rozelle and lined all the players up with $1,000 mobile phones. Being a big Balmain fan, Ray was starry-eyed about getting to know the players. He badly wanted their acceptance, to be part of the group. Because he was friendly and approachable, no-one had a problem with him hanging around. There was a feeling that Ray was trying to buy membership into the players' inner sanctum, but most of the boys weren't willing to knock back a free dinner. And there were plenty when Ray was around. He'd always insist on buying the boys drinks and food. In fact, he got them anything they wanted.

Personally, I liked the guy for who he was, not what he could get me. I was quite capable in that regard. I never needed favours from anyone, no matter how desperate they were for my attention. Being Lebanese, Ray got on well with me. I was happy to have him around because he seemed genuine and honest. He reminded me a lot of a young Eddie Hayson. When Eddie joined our crew at the trots a couple of years earlier, he was also looking to buy acceptance. But I liked Eddie for who he was and still remain friends with him today.

Ray, however, is a different story. The rot set in without notice. A couple of months after latching on to us, Ray began spending more and more of his spare time at the local TAB or racecourse. He had somehow befriended the infamous Gary Clarke, the professional punter involved with bookmaker Robbie Waterhouse in the 1981 Fine Cotton scandal. Although he had been banned, Gary was still doing the form across the state. He regularly gave Ray tips, tips Ray believed were the gospel. Gary had an opinion on every race and Ray thought it was possible to clean up every time.

Ray made a bright start, which is the worst thing anyone with a tendency to get hooked on gambling can hope for. He tasted the buzz first up and would quickly come to spend his life chasing the next one. It wasn't much different to a junkie, really.

Ray loved the adrenalin, something I could relate to. But he had no means of staying above water. I'm no angel when it comes to gambling, but it was a habit that came *after* my other work on the streets. A big collect would lead to a big wager – not the other way around. Ray, however, would bet first and think later.

Within months he was calling in loans – sometimes up to $10,000. The casino was also featuring and he'd mortgaged the family home in South Strathfield. By 1996 it was gone. Ray owed money to bookmakers all over town, but his quick tongue and double-dealing kept him ahead of payback time. He'd rob Peter to pay Paul. He had turned into a liar who'd name-drop to get himself out of strife.

It soon came to my attention that Ray had been using my name around town. It was 1998 and I'd long since stopped seeing him regularly. He was no longer the mate I'd come

RAY

to like at Balmain. He was conniving and cunning, a desperate who was hopelessly brainwashed by the punt. It had possessed his body like some demon, forcing his family into a rented property when their house was repossessed. I wasn't impressed to learn that Ray was trading on my name. I decided to pay him a visit at home.

'Listen Ray, I want you to stop mentioning my name,' I said. 'In fact, I want you to stay away from me altogether. You stay away from me and I'll stay away from you. OK?'

Ray looked more desperate than ever. Nearly five years had passed since I last saw him, but he still looked like a man on the run despite piling on what looked like another 20 kg. It was a hot day in March 2003 when we met again and he was sweating. The stresses of gambling and debt that ruined his life all those years ago had not gone away. I could see it in his body language, something I learned to interpret well during my collecting days. Ray was in deeper than ever and needed my help. I was reluctant to meet him. The last time we'd spoken I stressed that we should never talk again. But a lot of time had passed and I'd secretly hoped it had been enough for Ray to recover.

He was such a wonderful guy in those early days, even going as far as donating $20,000 at an auction to raise money for the 1997 Lebanese Sevens side. I never stopped liking that guy and felt he was good enough to beat gambling.

The fact was that he'd failed. Ray reeked of desperation as he sat down opposite me at my favourite café in Balmain. He hardly had time for pleasantries. It was straight down to the business of money. That was his life now – money, money, money. He bet it, he owed it and he craved it.

343

Ray told me about a horse trainer he knew with a good reputation for preparing two-year-olds. He said the trainer was confident of a strong autumn campaign in 2003 and wanted to bet big. But, being a trainer, he couldn't put his head on show. So he'd called Ray to organise the wagers. Ray, however, had a slight problem. There was no longer an SP bookie in town that he hadn't burned. He needed someone else to lay his trainer's bets. Someone with a better reputation for settling their debts and excellent connections.

Ray figured that someone was me. And he was not totally wrong. I got on well with a lot of the bookies and would have no problem betting big because they knew I'd always paid up. But did I really want to get mixed up with Ray? Hadn't I told him never to come near me again? I was torn, because he looked so pathetic grovelling for my help. In a strange way I felt pity for him. He was simply not the same guy. The guy I knew had been hollowed out and filled with the poisonous addiction for the punt.

I reasoned that we could make a good earn out of this trainer. If we did, maybe I could convince Ray to pay his debts with the winnings and quit with a clean sheet. Most of all I wanted to help him out – he looked like he needed fast relief. There was virtually no risk. If we thought the trainer's bet was astute, we'd act as commission agents and get him set with another bookie. But if we thought it a poor judgement, we'd take him on ourselves and collect on his loss. I agreed that afternoon.

I'd be lying if I said I was completely comfortable. Although I'd done a fair amount of commission work with Harry Eden since my last prison stint, I was wary of running with Ray. Still, I felt I had enough experience to control the situation. Although my criminal activities had been put

RAY

to bed, I still felt I was the bigger fish. There would be no problem so long as I was running this show.

The trainer started with a $5,000 collect on Grand Armee, a Group One race on a bog track at Randwick. We were down, but not out. It was a manageable amount. Over the next three weekends, his judgement didn't prove so astute. The trainer lost in bigger and bigger increments. First it was $17,000, then $24,000 and finally $34,000. The trainer was a reliable man. We'd made an arrangement to settle the bets at Balmain on the following Friday night after the races. If we won, Ray and I would then split the cash 50-50. But the final $34,000 proved problematic.

As always, Ray wanted the cash straight away. There was little doubt what he wanted it for – more punting. I'd now concluded that the guy was a lost cause. I figured that we were better off letting the cash sit for the next day. I was worried that the trainer was due for a big win. He couldn't keep losing in such massive amounts.

I waited for the trainer at our usual place that night, but he didn't show. Ray had got to him first via an intermediary and convinced him not to hand over the $34,000. It would be an understatement to say this upset me. But my agitation was nothing compared to the fury that gripped me when Ray called later that night and taunted: 'You are a c——. You wanted to take all the money for yourself. You're going to rob me.' I could tell he had a car load of goons – the same ones who got to the trainer – egging him on. It was incredible how much the bloke had degenerated. Never in my life had I witnessed a scarier example of how the punt can infect one person.

Principles were at stake. We agreed to meet at Belmore Oval at 10 o'clock that night to settle the dispute. I figured

Ray would bring his posse for company, so I arranged for my good friend and partner Georgie Boy to be in the area. I'd learned from my previous mistake with Con 13 years earlier that flying solo could be a huge health hazard. I waited an hour for Ray, but he didn't show. I called his phone but he didn't answer.

Words can't do justice to how angry I felt. It was not just Ray that I was livid at – it was also myself. After being so good for so long, why had I let myself back into a situation like this? The cool option would simply have been to walk away and forget it. But principle was at stake. I simply can't stand by and watch someone so degenerate profit from the destruction of basic principles that separate humans from animals.

I arrived home with my head spinning. And that's when I really lost the plot. My eldest brother Joe, who had moved back with Mum after the breakdown of his marriage, had some distressing news. 'We got a visit from your friend Ray tonight,' Joe said, turning my blood to ice. 'He told me to tell you that if you don't leave him alone there will be problems for us.' Us? That meant Joe, Mum and God knows who else I loved dearly. I was ready to explode. I could handle people threatening me, but my mother was not negotiable. Ray had gone too far. He would have to pay.

But the thing that really spooked me was that Ray had a gun on him when he visited the house. He later denied this in court. On that night I was too distressed and too unhinged to think properly. The simplest solution seemed the most appropriate. If Ray had a gun, then I needed one too.

I visited a friend to get myself a gun. I remember talking to people on the way to collect the weapon, people who tried to get me to change my mind. They knew what the consequences would be if that gun, Ray and I ever met. Deep down, I knew as well. But the difference was I didn't care.

I was Danny Karam. I discovered the simple difference between him and every other wannabe gangster. Fear. At some level, everyone fears the consequences – be it a jail stint or the ultimate price of death. But like Danny, I no longer cared. All I cared about was Mum. After all I'd put her through, there was no way I was going to let her be threatened. Over my dead body.

As I returned home with the piece, I received another phone call. It was from another friend, Greg. Evidently, he had also been in contact with Ray that evening. Greg had a message from the man newspapers would later call my 'business associate'. 'Ray wants to meet you at the McDonald's in South Strathfield at 10 am tomorrow to sort things out,' Greg said.

Three words summed up my response: Bring. It. On.

The gun recoiled in my hand. Then it went off again. All I saw was Ray jumping about like a cowboy in a bad Western flick. He was about eight metres away. I was pretty sure I'd missed, but Ray insisted otherwise. 'Call the ambulance! Call the police!' he wailed. 'John Elias has just shot me in the leg.'

I heard his cries but paid no attention. Instead, I calmly stepped into my car and drove off in the direction of Randwick racecourse. To me, it was now just another ordinary Saturday. I felt nothing.

I had decided to get the gun after seeing a carload of goons that I figured were accompanying Ray. Before spotting them, I didn't have a clear plan of how to handle him. Ray found me inside the McDonald's just after 10 am. I was having a coffee. I looked relaxed, but was very much on edge. And it wasn't the gun that made me nervous. Ten minutes earlier Greg had called with another message. 'Be very careful when you meet Ray – the word is that he's planning an ambush,' Greg said.

It was broad daylight and there were half a dozen people enjoying their McMuffins and hash browns when Ray arrived. I didn't think it was possible that he'd do something brazen in such a public place. This particular McDonald's was next to the Hume Highway, after all.

'John, I want to speak to you outside,' he said. I followed Ray out towards a side street. By coincidence, he led me straight to where my car was parked. I still wasn't quite sure what game he was playing, but Greg's warning was ringing loud in my ears. Ray seemed completely alien to the person I knew, even the desperate gambler. He walked with a bulletproof air. He clearly thought he was in control.

Then I saw the car – a white Toyota. It was packed with at least four goons. I held the line until the car stopped at the top of the side street and began reversing. That's when Greg's warning turned into reality. I didn't have any more time to hang around and have a gun put to my head. I'd been there, done that. This time, I'd get in first.

If Ray hadn't led me to my car, I might not be here to tell this story. I opened the boot and whipped out my gun. It was so quick, because I didn't think. I acted on instinct, something honed from the last time I was ambushed. I still didn't know how it would end. But when I pointed the gun at Ray's chest, killing him seemed reasonable enough until I remembered his kids and aimed at his leg instead.

●

There was no shortage of curiosity at Randwick when news of the shooting emerged that afternoon. Ray had hardly endeared himself to the punting fraternity, and I certainly didn't feel remorse. Not at that stage, anyway. I must have been a madman. My demeanour after shooting Ray was just so detached. Had I aimed for his chest, the term cold-blooded killer would have been more than apt.

I was later asked in court why I didn't go to the police instead of taking the law into my own hands. For a person with my history and values, going to the police isn't an option. For starters, I didn't have the cleanest reputation. It was unlikely they would have believed me. More importantly, I was dead against snitching. I despised police informants and was loath to become one, even if it meant putting Ray away.

To this day, people still ask me what I would do if someone threatened my family. Would I retaliate in the same brutal manner; shooting a man in the leg and leaving his family to live with the consequences? Would I organise someone else to do it? Would I go to the police?

Thanks to how I mishandled the situation, I've had plenty of time alone to come up with an answer. I just can't put myself in the same position again. But many people thought I'd earned a lifetime of repercussions for shooting Ray, who had his own network of undesirables. For a while, a very ugly and bloody street war loomed.

Incredibly, it was avoided because of Danny Karam. Although Danny had died more than five years earlier, his nephew Alex Taouil – better known as Little Al – had since grown up to earn plenty of respect on the streets himself. It was Alex who cooled the tensions between Ray, myself and our various associates and that's why he's earned another moniker: 'The Peacemaker'.

Nevertheless, it was scary how I switched off emotionally in the hours after the most dramatic incident of my life. In a strange way, I was still performing under pressure. This wasn't over. Deep down, I knew there was another twist to come. I didn't think that Ray would go to the police. But that's exactly what he did as I spent the afternoon at Randwick. The following morning I awoke to headlines in the Sunday papers: ELIAS WANTED OVER McDONALD'S SHOOTING.

As a precaution, I'd spent the night in a hotel at The Rocks. I didn't want to go near Mum's house just yet. My decision to sleep elsewhere was by no means an attempt to dodge the police, even though I did check in under a false name. It was to keep Mum safe. I felt sure Ray's goons would come for me and I didn't want it to happen with her around. If they found me elsewhere, then fair enough. I'd fired a couple of bullets, so it was only fair that I be prepared to cop one as well. That's the way I was thinking at the time.

Late on the Saturday night I received a mysterious phone call from my good mate Nat Wood. Nat said he'd been phoned by John Singleton earlier that evening. Singo had caught wind of the shooting – probably from his many mates at Randwick – and wanted to know if I was involved. I was reluctant to say anything, but Nat and I have a special bond. Whenever we need to know the truth from one another, one of us will say *Hyet Allah*, an Arabic phrase that means 'I swear to God it's the truth'. Nat said: '*Hyet Allah*,

John, did you shoot Ray?' I told Nat the truth – he is a wonderful friend – and then rang Singo. The clock read 1 am, but Singo answered straightaway.

It was absurd – here I was just hours after shooting a man talking to one of Australia's most powerful media moguls in the middle of the night. I had maintained loose contact with Singo since our days at Newtown in the early 1980s. He was a great larrikin and didn't judge me on anything else but what we'd done together.

Singo wanted to know what had happened, but I was short. 'No-one threatens my family,' I replied. He sensed I wasn't in the mood to elaborate and ended the conversation with a brief offer of help. 'John, if there's anything I can do, just let me know, OK?'

Reading the paper the following day, I gathered the rules had changed. Ray had gone to the police, meaning that he didn't intend to take the law into his own hands. This surprised, and yes, disappointed me somewhat. The rules that govern the world we both lived in indicate our differences should have been settled 'in-house'. I even sent Ray a message expressing such a desire late the previous night. He obviously didn't listen; which meant mixed news for me. On a positive note, it meant that Mum or family would not be harmed. On a negative note, it meant I'd soon be arrested.

I also received a helping hand from another well-known source. John Ibrahim is Sydney's premier nightclub owner and portrayed in the media as the city's answer to an overlord. I met John at DCM nightclub on Oxford Street that night and told him about what had happened with Ray. A week later he offered to pay my legal costs. People might be wary of John, but that's the same mistake they make with me. If they got to know him, they'd discover a man who is extremely loyal to his friends. Because I don't expect to be judged, I would never do the same to someone else.

There was no point delaying the inevitable. I contacted my solicitor John Korn and organised a meeting in the city. John rang the police from his office to tell them we were prepared to come in and answer questions. Incredibly, the police said there was no need. They weren't looking for me just yet. A wise man would later say they wanted to get me alone without my lawyer and that's exactly what they did.

At 7 pm on the Sunday I was walking down Darlinghurst Road, Kings Cross, when a cop car cruised past. The officers took a good look at me as they drove by. I didn't take my eyes off the car. It did a U-turn and headed back in my direction. There were no skid marks, no sirens. I didn't try to escape. When the four police officers approached me, I raised my hands and emptied my pockets. I knew the routine, although I would have preferred it not to have been carried out in one of the busiest strips in Sydney. At the end of the day, though, it didn't make a difference.

I wouldn't be around to experience the shame my family endures until this day.

CHAPTER 22

THE FINAL STRETCH

When I first laid eyes on Bilal Skaf, I couldn't believe how small and vulnerable he looked. He was a monster. But standing before me was a naive, scared little dark kid who couldn't handle prison. The other inmates told me that he'd cry every day. That's not a good start when you're staring at 50 years behind bars. Along with his brother Mohammed, Bilal had been convicted for gang-raping a teenage girl in 2000. The Skafs were sentenced to record terms.

Bilal was no longer a stranger to Long Bay. He'd been in the protection wing for well over a year before I arrived. But I could see that he would never adjust, despite the fact that the rest of his life was destined to be spent behind bars. He was broken before his term had even started.

Watching young Bilal drift through the corridors during those long afternoons took me back to my first stint here. I was even younger than him – just 16 – but felt the same sense of helplessness and fear. Somehow, I'd been able to survive. I learned to block out what was happening on the outside and deal with negotiating the next hour of the day – whether it be rotting in my cell alone or watching for a knife-wielding maniac in the yard. Prison was a fulltime drain on your attention and senses.

Now I had to face it all over again. For the next four-and-half years I had to somehow deal with the failure of being back at the bottom of the pile. I'd let down so many people by lapsing again – Mum, the friends who'd defended me, the Lebanese team. Worst of all, I'd failed myself. Again. I'd promised more than once not to re-offend – making a vow to the Man Upstairs as I was wheeled into surgery with a burst stomach in 1999.

He'd delivered and got me through. This is how I responded – by not being able to control myself. I forgot the promises I'd made, forgot the consequences and lived in the moment. It was a huge mistake to shoot Ray, even in response to what he'd done. I'd tried to protect Mum, but I'd probably hurt her even more by being sent back to prison for another stretch.

She was beside herself in court when the jury declared me guilty of intent to commit grievous bodily harm. My solicitor, John Korn, advised me to plead to self-defence in the hope of securing a not guilty verdict. He thought we had a decent case given Ray's threats to my family and the carload of goons that had appeared at the McDonald's. I was also asked in court whether I owed Ray money. I told the jury I didn't. It was the truth. Think about it: if I owed Ray money, why would I try to meet him? Wouldn't the natural course of action be to avoid him? You be the judge.

But none of that mattered now. All that counted for me was the next moment. Everything that was happening

THE FINAL STRETCH

outside these walls – the war in Iraq, the 2004 federal election, the Athens Olympics, the Asian tsunami – didn't affect me. When I first landed in prison on remand in June 2003, a lifer approached and gave me some valuable advice. 'John, I've been here for over two decades and there's only one way to survive,' he said. 'You've got to block it all out. You've got to convince yourself there's no other world but the one you live in now. It's your only chance to adapt and to survive.'

So many prisoners failed. The solitary nights locked alone in their cells from 3 pm to 8 am drove them insane. The answer was drugs. All the prisons that I served my term in – Silverwater, Long Bay, Windsor and Parklea – were swimming in drugs. I'd seen the most hardened, mentally staunch criminals descend into junkies within months. They couldn't handle the confinement. They couldn't block out the possibilities of what lay beyond the walls. They couldn't let go of their freedom.

The other option was suicide. I never contemplated drugs, but the thought of taking my own life gate-crashed my consciousness during the first few months of my incarceration. I'd reached the point where life wasn't worth living. I was back on remand, a period of excruciating uncertainty for any criminal.

John Korn had told me to expect between eight to 12 years. Good references from the likes of Alan Jones and Arthur Beetson later convinced the sentencing judge to give me six years with four-and-a-half non-parole. A letter from Dr Nabil Rahim was also crucial to the judge agreeing to a lesser term. Dr Rahim testified that I had a lower life expectancy given my cancer scare, thus exacerbating the impact of any sentence.

At age 40, however, four-and-a-half years was simply too

long. I'd been in trouble before, but felt I'd just turned onto the road to redemption before I shot Ray. The possibility of coaching in the UK Super League had convinced me there was hope I could make it back in people's estimation. I don't even know how UTC found out that I wouldn't be able to make it to France that season.

Now redemption seemed a road blocked forever. Those who'd resisted the urge to judge me on my former acts and reputation had no reason to defend me anymore. I'd let them down and made them look stupid in front of those who maintained all along that John Elias was a good-for-nothing criminal. I still didn't see myself that way, because I'd acted out of an instinct to protect my family. But everyone else did, and it might as well have been the case. Perception was reality and I'd lost the right to be judged on my merits.

I was never going to commit suicide, but the symptoms were there. From where I sat, there was nothing to lose. But I recalled what Neddy Smith used to tell me about suicide during my first stretch. 'I don't respect people who take their own lives,' he declared. 'It's a selfish act. They get to absolve themselves of all responsibility, and leave behind everyone else to clean up the mess.' If I owed Mum and my family anything, it was at least to spare them that.

So I lived, if you can call it that. The first six months of my term were served at Silverwater jail, a fairly modern facility. I was in maximum security, but it was nowhere near as bad as Long Bay 25 years earlier. The food, however, was inedible. Where they used to prepare our meals on the spot in the 1970s, everything was now cooked and served four days later. Unless you had no money, there was no way anyone would ever eat the food in the mess hall.

Money was a major tool of survival in prison. Without

THE FINAL STRETCH

it, life was infinitely harder. The food was just one example. Money could buy you a rice cooker, stovetop and Breville sandwich maker. With a few basic ingredients, it was possible to get by on a fair diet of relatively fresh food. Although everyone's groceries were kept in a common fridge in the kitchen, the consequences of stealing another's supplies could be dire. Severe bashings and stabbings were not out of the question.

Cash also purchased small comforts like toothpaste, soap and toilet paper. All these were issued by the prison for free; but, again, you'd be a brave man to use the complimentary stuff. The soap was so harsh that it would turn bed sheets into cardboard. And these days, cigarettes were also purchased – not handed out for free as was the case during my last stint.

Prisoners received a weekly allowance of $14 into their account to buy supplies and make phone calls. It didn't go very far. If you had a job in the prison, you'd earn at least $20 a week. That made a bit of a difference. All the money was credited and debited from personal prison accounts so that the screws could track and control exactly what we were spending it on. There wasn't meant to be any cash inside, but of course there was. The main currency among inmates, however, was cigarettes.

Although it had only been built recently, Silverwater had wasted no time catching up to the other prisons in New South Wales in the vermin stakes. Our cells were infested with cockroaches. Each night before bed, I'd lay out a silver tray smeared with margarine and a dollop of strawberry jam in the middle. This had to be done religiously, without fail, or else you could be assured of waking up with roaches all over you. Every morning I'd find at least 20 filthy roaches stuck to the tray, scrambling mindlessly for the jam in the middle. No matter how many I trapped and killed, their numbers would never diminish. Thank goodness I had enough money to afford the 'luxury' items needed for the trap. Cash really does make a huge difference on the inside – even to the point of keeping cockroaches from crawling on your skin.

Of all the inmates who relied on cash, Rodney Adler was the one who lived and died by it. Adler was the disgraced businessman convicted of fleecing investors for millions following the collapse of HIH insurance group in 2001. He joined us at Long Bay towards the end of 2004 (I'd been transferred from Silverwater earlier that year).

Although I did my best to avoid hearing about the outside world, even I knew who Adler was. Everyone did – he was a bloody celebrity. In prison, however, notoriety is not a good thing. The key is to avoid attention at all costs. Adler was famous because his face had led nightly news bulletins and front-page stories for three years. Worse still, he was famous for having made a buck or two.

This was not lost on the boys at Long Bay. Once they discovered Adler had been placed in maximum security rather than protection (he would have been safe from harm there), all bets were off. He was a walking target.

Inmates knew the bloke was cashed-up and a bidding war began for his protection money. It was a service Adler could not afford to live without, because without it he wouldn't have lived. Eventually, a group of Middle Eastern prisoners won the coveted 'contract'. The word was that Adler paid them $1,000 a week for protection. They did a good job, too, because I never once saw the slimy little criminal get stood over.

THE FINAL STRETCH

I detested white-collar criminals like Adler. His ilk – conniving lawyers, accountants and financial planners – probably ruined more lives than any drug dealer could. How many families lost it all because of Adler? Plenty. Yet he and his mates always seemed to think they were above the common crims like us. They'd argue that they hadn't been violent and therefore didn't deserve to be in the same yard.

But Adler was worse. Despite being publicly humiliated and loathed, his arrogance was astounding. I recall one time in the yard a mate of mine approached him to ask how things were.

'Not so good, mate,' a glum-looking Adler replied. 'My wife's doing it a bit tough. She's had to sell the home at Rose Bay and move into one at North Bondi.' My mate almost clocked him then and there. 'Rodney, let me give you a tip,' he warned. 'I wouldn't go telling that story to too many blokes in here. Most of them can't even afford to feed their families.' He threw in a few more choice words for effect and I reckon Adler got the message. I never could understand how that bloke only got two-and-a-half years. Money talks – on the inside and outside.

Fittingly, I also served part of my sentence with Adler's partner in crime Ray Williams. Ray was not found as culpable for HIH's collapse as Adler and served his sentence at Windsor, a far less intimidating place than the Bay. As my term came to a close I was moved to Windsor in late 2005.

It was there I encountered Williams in curious circumstances. He was sitting with us at a table when a young prisoner approached whom only a few of the group knew. We introduced him to Williams and the kid said, 'Hey, old man, you look familiar. Are you that Ray Williams?'

Ray nodded and the kid's face suddenly changed. 'I hate you, you fucking prick... you cost my grandmother her house.' Before anyone could react, the kid launched a savage right into Williams's temple. Given the old man was in his 70s, he was lucky to survive the blow and being knocked to the ground.

Attacks like that on older prisoners were not common. Strangely, there was a healthy respect for elders on the inside. The kids called us OCs – old crims. Having served as both, I can categorically say it's easier to get by as an OC. My transfer to Long Bay was made smoother because of Shami, my old mate from the trots. Shami had arrived a couple of weeks before I did and made sure I was looked after. Firstly, he got me transferred from Ward 7 to 10 to be with him. Safety in numbers was an important thing in that place.

Shami had a good rapport with the screws, something I'd never managed during my first stretch. I can't emphasise what a difference this makes. The biggest advantage is that it can lead to work, which means less time alone in your cell. And Shami had a plum job that he was keen to get me on. He had scored a gig as a cook for the Violent Offenders Therapeutic Program (VOTP). The VOTP was a 12-month course designed to cure the 25 most crazy, psychopathic and dangerous felons at Long Bay.

Now, being lumped in with so many unpredictable murderers and mutilators might not seem desirable, but it had its attractions. For starters, the VOTP was sealed off from the rest of the prison, meaning we weren't tied down to the draconian schedule the rest had to follow. We got more time out of our cells and more time to ourselves. In short, it was as close as you could get to freedom.

THE FINAL STRETCH

The trade-off was the inmates. They were heavily guarded because of their reputations, but not even the screws could watch them 24/7. The funniest thing was that they behaved calmly and reasonably most of the time. In early 2005 we met a kid from Kempsey named Phil Jared. Whenever we saw Phil, he'd always tell us about his cousin. 'He's a great footy player – he's just been signed by the Melbourne Storm,' Phil would boast. Shami and I would roll our eyes. It seemed everyone in prison knew someone on the outside who was destined for greatness. But Phil ended up being on the money. His cousin's name was Greg Inglis.

Then there was the 200 kg triple murderer Berwin, who was also doing the VOTP course while we manned the kitchen. If you didn't know better, you'd think the guy was a member of Mensa. He had obtained a masters degree in psychology inside and scoffed at the doe-eyed university graduates who came to give the VOTPs advice.

But the difference between Reeves and other academics was his temper. The slightest thing could trigger him. I know a thing or two about that myself, but these guys were operating on an even shorter fuse. On one occasion, Shami neglected to give a big, mean Islander some leftovers from lunch. The Islander came into the kitchen asking for his seconds, but Shami told him he was too late. There were none left. This wasn't acceptable. With incredible speed for a man his size, the Islander grabbed a steak knife and put it to Shami's throat. 'You'll be kissing this ground if you don't give me more food,' the Islander growled. Then he stopped. Inexplicably, he dropped the knife and just walked away.

He snapped out of the trance as if nothing had happened and returned to his cell. He even followed us up later that night for a friendly chat. There was no mention of the near-death experience that we had all shared just hours earlier in the kitchen. The big bloke had forgotten all about it. He was a dead-set schizophrenic – as most of them were. As much as I admired the prison system for trying to rehabilitate them, I don't think role-playing exercises and fact sheets were the answer. These guys needed medical attention. They were head cases.

But for all the wackos in VOTP, it was much preferable to maximum security. That place was a zoo – especially the yard. Every morning for three hours, they'd pack about 70 inmates into a patch of dirt the size of a Tokyo studio apartment. Mortal enemies stood shoulder to shoulder and on most days the air was so thick you could cut it with a knife. There were punch-ups and stabbings all the time, especially on Thursdays when the drug money was due. Dozens of inmates would be unable to pay, or had arrangements on the outside fall through. The retribution was savage and usually ended with a stretcher being hauled into the yard.

One afternoon in 2005, however, was unrivalled. In prisons across New South Wales, a race war between the Lebanese and Islanders erupted. It stemmed from a vicious attack on an Islander kingpin named Moses at Junee prison a couple of weeks earlier. The attack was carried out by a group of Middle Eastern maniacs and their ethnic rivals were now bloodthirsty. The Islanders had been planning retribution for weeks and had secretly planned a co-ordinated ambush on all Middle Eastern inmates across the state. The ambush was to take place in every prison simultaneously at 10 am on a Tuesday.

The first I heard of the ambush came 15 minutes before it was due to take place when an Islander kid called John

THE FINAL STRETCH

approached me with a tip-off. The son of an ex-footballer, John had followed my career with interest and must have had a soft spot for me because I could relate to his old man. 'Johnny, there's going to be a big attack on all the Lebos at any moment. We don't want anything to do with you, so I'm just warning you to stay away,' he said.

I appreciated John's advice. The rest of the Lebos tended to hang together, making them an easier target than a flock of bloated gazelles. He must have sensed that I would tip the others off, so John waited until the last possible moment to tell me. Even if I had wanted to, I didn't have time to warn them. Moments later, a huge roar erupted. The Lebanese clique was suddenly under siege from all sides. They were being hammered with knives, sticks, boots and fists. They were caught completely off guard and had copped several blows before they could even think of reacting.

It shaped up like a bloodbath. Even though I was standing away from the trouble, the yard was so small that it eventually collected me. Thanks to Johnny, I was ready. I had just began throwing a few punches of my own when a horrible stinging sensation hit my eyes. Tear gas. The coppers had responded in brutal style, lobbing canister after canister of the stuff into that sardine tin of a yard. It was harsh, but effective. The fighting stopped straightaway.

When the haze cleared, I can only remember seeing blood, hair and bits of skin everywhere. The yard resembled a genocide site and that's effectively what the Islanders had wanted. One particular Lebo, Joseph George, was stabbed 10 times. No-one was told whether he lived. Similar attacks all over the state forced the authorities to react swiftly. They could no longer afford to mix ethnicity. The Lebanese and Islanders were placed in separate parts of the prison.

Being Lebanese, that spelt the end of my sabbatical in VOTP. My time came just as I was due to be transferred to the medical wing, where I was booked in for a colonoscopy and endoscopy to check for any cancerous regrowth.

In prison, just the fact that you are due for medical treatment is no guarantee that you will get it at any stage in the present decade. I had to wait eight months for these simple procedures. People who have never been to prison might chastise me for complaining. What right does a convicted criminal have to timely medical treatment? Why not let him rot like he deserves? I can understand that view, but I'd only wish that those who peddle it spend a week in Long Bay. There seems to be a perception that prison is a bit of a soft touch, that the inmates are pampered hotel guests. That might be accurate when it comes to weekend detention and prison farms, but not maximum security. The hardest lock-ups in New South Wales are a nightmare.

Sometimes, the standard of medical treatment verges on laughable. Because the screws are so wary of the prisoners getting their grubby mitts on strong painkillers, the only form of pain relief is Panadol. It's the solution to every ailment. Just had your left eyeball gouged out with a fork prong? Here, take a Panadol. Just been stabbed? Here, take a Panadol. Just been fucked up the arse? Here, take a Panadol. So there's no prizes for guessing what they offered me when I contracted an embarrassing rash from the washing powder. Yep, it was Panadol. Anyone who thinks life in prison is a holiday can sit on it.

When I arrived in the medical wing, I was reunited with my old fellow inmate Neddy Smith. I use the term reunited loosely, because Neddy was no longer the hardened warrior whom I'd left in 1981. He was now the furthest thing from

THE FINAL STRETCH

it – a frail, wheezy old man who shook like leafless branches in a hurricane. Parkinson's disease had completely overwhelmed him.

Because of his condition, Neddy no longer commanded such a luxurious cell. The big TV and magazines were now replaced by a computer, which he used to write his memoirs. Despite his frailty, the old bloke still had it upstairs and remembered me immediately. 'John, you are the last person I expected to see back in here,' he lamented. It just reinforced my self-loathing. Even one of the more notorious murderers in Australia had put his faith in me to stay clean. I was no better than him.

The move to Windsor came soon after my colonoscopy and endoscopy results returned. They were clear, marking a rare celebration in those dark days. I had survived five years without the cancer reappearing. According to the experts, there was now a good chance I could fulfil something of a normal life (notwithstanding the fact I was completing my third prison sentence). Nothing could detract from the occasion. I had officially beaten cancer.

At Windsor, I reunited with my mate Shami. Compared to Long Bay, Windsor was like a five-star resort. It had a decent-sized yard where I could once again recommence my field sessions with the younger inmates. It even came to my mind to enter a team in the local A Grade comp in 2006, but that was swiftly knocked back.

There was also a telephone in our wing where prisoners were allowed to make as many calls as their bank balance allowed. You'd just dial in your PIN and phone away. I was able to speak to Mum every day, but there was one person the authorities prevented me from contacting. Alan Jones was on the no-talkies list because the screws were terrified that I'd dish out some dirt on the prison that the broadcaster could then use to embarrass them on his talk-back show. All my phone calls were monitored anyway, so I couldn't see what the problem was. Besides, I was now nearing the end of my stint and had no interest in jeopardising my parole.

In the absence of phone calls, Jones and I traded letters. His letters arrived at Windsor on 2GB letterhead, astounding the screws, who combed every word of correspondence that went between us and the outside world. Like Wayne Bennett (who also wrote regularly), Jones was a great inspiration in those years.

The other visitor who brightened my world was an up-and-coming hooker from Wests Tigers, Robbie Farah. I had first got to know Robbie when he made the squad for Lebanon's game on home soil against France at the end of 2002. He was an unknown teenager then, but demonstrated extraordinary confidence for a kid who was yet to play any higher level than Jersey Flegg (U19s). It's probably fair to say Robbie's confidence verged on arrogance, but I think that's a good thing in people who have the ability to back it up. Although he was a nobody, Robbie went to the effort of sending me a highlights video to press for selection. I watched the tape and liked what I saw. Others in the camp favoured a slightly older hooker, George Ndaira, but I got a good vibe from Robbie. He has since gone on to win a premiership with the Tigers and is now their captain.

Along with other members of the Lebanese side, Robbie made plenty of trips to Windsor. But the visitor who warmed my heart more than anyone was an American lady named Tracey. We had met at the end of 2002 as I awaited a flight from Frankfurt to Beirut for our game against the French. Terrible weather had grounded all the flights,

THE FINAL STRETCH

leaving everyone stranded inside the terminal for seven hours. I settled in for the long wait by pulling up a chair at a café.

Sitting next to me was Tracey. She was my perfect opposite – hailing from a wealthy background, she was elegant, smart and classy. This girl from Baltimore ran a multi-million-dollar business and had no right to be interested in a knockabout like me. But we chatted like old friends for the entire time and vowed to stay in touch. Shortly before I landed back in prison, she came to Australia to visit me. We had an amazing connection, something I assumed had been destroyed along with everything else that was worthwhile in my life when they threw away the key.

Then, one random weekend, she lobbed at Long Bay without warning. I simply couldn't believe anyone would fly 30 hours to see a pathetic sod in prison. I'm not even sure how she found out about my sentence. Tracey also visited me at Windsor. On both occasions, she saw neither the Opera House nor Harbour Bridge. Her fleeting journeys Down Under were purely for my benefit. It seemed crazy, but her presence could not be disputed.

I gained immense confidence and reassurance from her support and commitment. By going to such lengths to see me in jail, Tracey made me feel like I still had something to live for. That was crucial as my time inside drew to a close. Four-and-a-half years is a long time to spend away from society, particularly when you're taking extreme efforts to avoid updates about the outside world. All my visitors knew I had this mindset and tried their best to avoid talking about what was happening out there. We instead passed the time by talking on a more personal level.

The mental component was just one of three vital things

I felt I had to get right to survive. The others were physical – and I trained the house down to stay in shape – and spiritual. There's no way I'm going to try and convince anyone that I'm an overly religious person. I was, however, raised in a Catholic household and taught by nuns at primary school. Religion was therefore a part of my programming, albeit one whose tenets were regularly ignored at the expense of easy money and a short fuse. In prison, however, I tried to get in touch with religion. I'd never say I found God. But what I did want to find was the fulfilment that comes with living your life in accordance with the accepted mores of right and wrong. If you were so inclined, jail was the perfect place to achieve this.

At Windsor there were Christian services every Sunday. They were held by an ex-bikie overlord named Steve. Now he's someone who really did find God behind bars. Steve went from dealing drugs and firearms to being the in-house pastor at John Maroney II. His services attracted quite a crowd, though it must be pointed out that many in the congregation only showed up for the free biscuits and soft drinks that were served afterwards.

I was one of the flock that didn't need any edible inducements. They say religion is food for the soul and I discovered that at Windsor. I haven't really gone to church since getting out, but the spirituality I discovered has definitely helped me tolerate this mixed-up world a whole lot better.

Windsor also offered a service for Muslim inmates. The prisoner who started that on Fridays was an Afghani imam, Rahim. Again, Rahim was an unlikely man of the cloth. He was arrested after attempting to import large quantities of heroin from his homeland. The international climate and September 11 bombings didn't aid his cause either. Rahim's

THE FINAL STRETCH

sermons were constantly monitored, with authorities suspecting that he was preaching jihad against Australia to his fellow inmates. The fact they had fingered him as a possible terrorist meant Rahim was never going to get parole.

The job Shami got me at Long Bay was good, but he went one better at Windsor. There, he managed to wrangle us a gig serving food at the rifle range, where workers from high-risk government agencies like DOCS would train. For a couple of hangdog prison hounds, the grub was amazing – quartered sandwiches, roast chicken and gourmet salads. The screw who monitored us was also not such a bad bloke and would allow leftovers to be taken back to the quarters. Those old sandwiches and drumsticks earned us plenty of bargaining power in the yard.

The best perk, however, was the pool. Windsor can get insanely hot during summer – sometimes 10° degrees warmer than the coast 60 km away. There was nothing in our job description about cleaning the pool, so we decided to be proactive. Our inspiration would soar on scorching days, when we'd actually have to get into the pool to clean it as the other prisoners went into meltdown outside. We'd stay there until the screws noticed, yelling out 'Elias . . . get out of that pool immediately!' They'd never punish us, though.

Given that lifestyle, I was more than happy to serve the rest of my time at Windsor with Shami. But it wasn't to be. With six months left before my parole, we were transferred to Parklea after the New South Wales government decided to close John Maroney II in early 2007. The shutdown came as a result of an industrial dispute between the screws and the pollies. The screws at Windsor were filthy at the staffing levels and pay.

Even if I'd had expectations of Parklea, that jail would

have underwhelmed them. It was a complete cesspit. We were transferred to a wing that was meant to be accommodating 70 prisoners on weekend detention. But by the time all the refugees from Windsor arrived, there were 140 lodgers. The solution was simple – just throw an extra mattress in every cell. For the first time in my seven-and-a-half years behind bars, I shared a cell for an extended period.

My 'room-mate' was a young Lebanese kid who'd been picked up for importing cocaine. We got on well, which was a godsend given the bloody consequences that usually arose when two cellmates didn't get along. My buddy liked the odd game of chess, something I wasn't too bad at. But neither of us was a match for the Kiwi drug trafficker – Jimmy Shepherd. Jimmy was part of the notorious Mr Asia syndicate, run by none other than Terrence Clark. Jimmy was a demon on the chessboard – no-one in the prison system could match him.

Although I detested it at the time, the Parklea squalor was a bonus. I'd become too comfortable at Windsor, something that would work against me upon release. It's no secret that a large majority of prisoners re-offend and land back in the slot. I've got no doubt they do so because of a subconscious urging to get back inside. After so long behind bars, they simply can't handle the outside world and its challenges of independence and responsibility. There might not be any freedom in prison, but there's routine and reliability. Some find it easier inside than out.

But I'm certainly not one of them.

POSTSCRIPT
YOU BE THE JUDGE

The phone is ringing again. It rings a lot these days, and I'm generally happy about that. It tells me there are still people out there who've got faith in my redemption, that I haven't been completely deserted after stuffing up so many times. This call, however, is one I'd prefer not to take. On the other end of the line is a big-time Sydney nightclub owner. He probably owns about a dozen venues between the CBD and Kings Cross. I haven't spoken to this person since my release from Parklea in December 2007. Eight months later, he's suddenly tracked me down. I'm guessing it's not to catch up for dinner.

The nightclub owner has an offer to make. They always do, don't they? As I drive to Balmain to meet a friend, he tells me I'm the only man for the job. It's a gig worth up to $10,000 a week, depending on business. All I've got to do in return is look after his clubs. Looking after his clubs doesn't mean collecting the mail and ensuring the rates are paid on time. This bloke wants my head on show every weekend, just to remind the patrons who his friends are. Apparently, I've still got a bit of pull in this town. That's what he reckons. He's now being very flattering. 'John, there's no-one else with the respect out there that you have,' he implores. 'You are the only person I can trust to do this for me.'

He is a smart man. He knows how to push my buttons. Along with loyalty, integrity and honesty are the two most important qualities I look for. I'm flattered that he thinks I enshrine them. I continue to listen. He keeps talking, pushing the sell harder. I like what he's got to say and the money is good. It's been a long time since I've had that type of cash. For someone accustomed to the thrill of illegitimacy and easy dough, life in the regular world can be like going from an autobahn to a cobbled street. I've been stuck in the slow lane since my release, vowing never to switch over again. And it's been a pleasant change after so many near-death experiences. Cancer, gunfights, prison stabbings . . . haven't I had enough adrenalin rushes to last a lifetime?

The answer was obvious: Yes. And so I told the nightclub owner: No.

He was taken aback. 'Nobody rejects an offer from me,' he replied. Well, my friend, there's a first time for everything. Finally, I'd learned to say that all-important word: No.

If only I'd said it on all those other occasions. Stealing cars with Kenny? No. Robbing Eddie's businesses in Punchbowl? No. Pinching Peter Moore's credit card and taking my teammates to a brothel? No. Rejecting Wayne Bennett's offer to become a foundation player for the Brisbane Broncos? No. Entertaining Dave's offer to fix a game? No.

Dealing drugs to Tony? No. Neglecting my beloved Lisa? No. And finally, letting Ray back into my life? No.

It was Ray who finally sent the message home. When he convinced me to take those bets in 2003, it seemed like such a harmless idea. There were no guns, no stand-overs, no violence. But I made one important oversight. I didn't see where the offer could possibly lead. What else is involved? Had I stopped and thought, I might have figured out that Ray, in his frayed and emotional state, could invite trouble. I knew myself well enough by then to realise that I wouldn't back down from a dispute. It was foreseeable that it could end exactly the way it did. For the sake of Ray's children, I hope they know the true story of why their father has a bullet wound in his leg. And I hope they found out before I wrote this book – from Ray himself. Ray is not and will never again be my enemy. At the same time, he is not and will never again be my friend. But there is good in everyone, and Ray demonstrated that during the early part of our relationship.

Foresight is the difference between then and now. Right now I'm thinking about where this offer might end. On the surface it seems harmless. Go out on the weekends and put my head on show. Collect a cool $10,000 and relax for the next five days. Sadly, it's not that simple. I stopped and I thought. I thought about the type of people I'd be mixing with, the scene that I'd be returning to. It would be akin to a reformed alcoholic taking an all-access tour of a brewery. Once I mastered that, there was no turning back. No offers like these were worth entertaining because they all led to the same sad conclusion. Every time I said yes, it eventually got me in trouble. Sure, there were good times and big collects. But every street on my life's road map ended on a cliff's edge. In time, I'd always finish up hurtling into an abyss.

The nightclub owner had a few of his mates try to change my mind in the coming weeks, but they were wasting their phone credits. The answer was and always will be: No. Learning to say no is a start, but I still don't have any idea how to earn society's respect. It's something I lost when I stole my first car in 1975 and have never earned back.

Three jail stints later, I'm now a caricature. In cafés, I see couples whispering and pointing. Potential girlfriends have Googled me on the internet and run a mile. Drunken blokes approach me at the footy for a photograph. They see it as their big chance to say they got close and personal with a gangster – and lived to tell the tale.

No-one likes being a cliché. And although I might have got a kick out of it as a young punk, it's no fun being feared either. Being feared means you can never be understood. And not being understood means you can never be trusted.

That's exactly why I still can't find work almost two years out of jail. No matter how many nights I spend feeding the homeless, no matter how many African children I might sponsor, the stench won't go away. It's like Lady Macbeth's 'damned spot'. The original sin can never be erased. People talk about giving others a second chance, but I've asked for many more than that. In short, I've used up all my get-out-of-jail cards.

The saddest thing is that society is right. It doesn't owe me a thing. I'm a big believer in karma, and everything bad that has happened to me seems like reasonable payback for the harm I've inflicted. The untimely injuries and suspensions that checked my footy career are examples. Even cancer. To this day, I believe it was karma's way of somehow levelling the scales. The people I feel genuine pity for are those who get cancer and lead wholesome lives, both morally and physically. I'm not among them. In fact, society has probably given me more than I deserve. The fact that people like Wayne Bennett, Arthur Beetson, Alan Jones, John Singleton, and boxing trainer Johnny Lewis have stood by and supported me is unbelievable. Three-time Olympic boxer Rick Timperi and my old friend Georgie Boy, Mick Manning, Norm Nicholas, Tas Baitieri, Sam Ayoub, Darren Maroon, the lawyer Mark Gates and Les Kalache (who always looked after me in prison) are others who've stood by me when others rightfully decided enough was enough. In return for their unconditional friendship and support, I consider them family. As for my blood family, I can't thank them enough – particularly Mum and my brother George. There's other relatives I'd like to mention on Mum's side – nieces, nephews and cousins – but I feel it's wiser to keep their names under wraps because of the life I've led.

All these people could have walked away at any point – I've done more than enough to abuse their trust. Their continued friendship and support is what keeps me going against all odds. Now I must do the same to work my way back, to prove them wise instead of stupid.

I can now understand where Phil Gould was coming from when he tried to stop Nat Wood from fraternising with me. My problem was he didn't talk to me directly. I can handle that better than people going behind my back, whispering and judging without the facts. I also find hypocrisy hard to handle. There's dozens of current rugby league administrators and directors who've done things to warrant a jail sentence themselves. There's some who've even asked for my help with illegitimate business, but now don't want a bar of me. I find their hypocrisy impossible to swallow, because they are meant to be representing the good of the game – not themselves.

But their character is for others with cleaner hands to judge properly. If Gould or any others I've clashed with – Jason Taylor and Paul Langmack included – see fit to respond, I've got no problem. After all, people are entitled to wonder what right a sinner like me has to cast stones. One word sums up my answer: honesty. I've vowed to be truthful and when you go down that path you're going to mix the good with the bad.

So far, there's been little encouragement. I've applied for a handful of coaching jobs, as well as the head spot at Les Catalans. They all knocked me back. No-one says why – the standard excuse is that they don't have the space. But I know why. I'd prefer they tell me straight, rather than chatter in the background like the jittery couples in cafés.

I've learned to deal with disappointment – being sent to Long Bay jail at 16 will do that for you. Being told you've got cancer is another sure-fire way. Although I'd prefer if someone gave me a start, getting knocked back isn't going to make me despair. As well as the ability to say no, I've also obtained perspective. If I ever get depressed, it's because I don't have a means to pass any of this on to kids who are in danger of following my lead.

All I see when I look at the lot of young footballers these days is the potential for trouble. They've got loads of money and just as much spare time. There are plenty of times when I found myself in that situation and it generally resulted in trouble. Sure, most kids won't make the same litany of bad choices that I did. But when they put themselves in certain situations, the choice is no longer theirs.

I fear their attraction to alcohol, gambling and drugs. I've got no doubt that the majority of young NRL players are dabbling in two of the three. For some of them, that can't end well. Who better to tell them about the consequences? To the youth that I hope will read this book: I'd tell them I got it all wrong. I thought I was a big-shot gangster leading a sexy lifestyle. But now I've got a criminal record that includes three jail stints. Because of that, I probably will never get another chance at coaching first grade, either here or in Europe. It's basically over and I've got to deal with it in the full knowledge that every mistake I made was through my own choices. And that's why I deserve to be where I am now with the sole hope that others can at least succeed where I failed in learning from my mistakes.

In my opinion, most first-grade coaches are out of touch with reality. They might all have wonderful football brains and communication skills, but those things are a given in this professional age. The key to getting the best out of people is understanding them as individuals and working on their level. In my experience, no-one comes close to Wayne Bennett. He is without doubt the coach of our generation, perhaps even our lifetimes.

So where do I go from here? Now that you know my life's story, I'm hoping you can be the judge.

AUTHOR'S NOTE

All proceeds from the sale of this book have been donated to the Chris O'Brien Lifehouse Cancer Centre at Sydney's Royal Prince Alfred (RPA) Hospital. Without the sacrifices and dedication of the nurses and doctors who work tirelessly to save lives every day, John might not have been one of their success stories.

INDEX

Abbott, Hubbie 89, 92
Ackery, Paul 83
Adler, Rodney 358–9
Alexander, Ben 202
Alexander, Greg 202
Andary, Ben 102
Anderson, Bill 217
Archer, Paul 168–9
arrest
   demanding money with menace 200–1
   first 40
   shooting Ray 352
attempted murder charges 49, 58
Avignon 78–80, 83
Ayoub, Sam 375

Baitieri, Tas 78–9, 81, 89, 92, 277, 279, 319, 330, 375
Baker, Neil 83
Balmain Greg 159–66, 169
Balmain Tigers 3, 15, 175–203, 214–8, 223–4
   Alan Jones as coach 192–203, 214

defensive coach 288–9
first-grade 177–8, 182, 195–6
grand final 1989 178–81
groin injury 187–8
hawks Nest boot camp 182
joining 175–6
man of the match 183
mid-season transfer 223
1990 season opening match 182–3
off season 1993-94 215
old boys' reunion 214
reserve grade 177, 188, 194
set plays 195, 202
training 182, 192, 215
training camp 198
two year deal 192
Wayne Pearce as coach 214, 217–8
Banaghan, Jim 94, 97
Barnes, Keith 6, 175, 182, 188, 192, 203, 211
Baysari, David 278
Beattie, Michael 217, 246, 252–9
Beetson, Arthur 'Artie' 71, 144, 148–52, 155–6, 173, 320, 324–6, 355, 375
Belcher, Gary 95, 104, 121, 132, 134

379

Bennett, Justin 99, 105
Bennett, Trish 99
Bennett, Wayne 43, 91, 94–100, 103–15, 118–22, 125, 140–6, 184, 186, 195–7, 245, 320–2, 324, 326, 330–2, 337, 366, 375, 377
Big House Hotel 148, 155, 173
Bilbiga, John 131, 134
Billy Joel concert 215
Blake, Phil 83
The Bold and the Beautiful 294
bomb threat, school 46
boredom 34, 68, 95, 137, 150, 155, 188
Bourbon And Beefsteak 181, 189, 216
Boutros, Louie 144
Bowden, Bruce 64
Boyle, David 83
Brasher, Tim 3, 178, 219
Brisbane Broncos offer 143–6
Brisbane Souths 91–121
   Best Import 119
   centenary dinner 119
   first-grade 96, 99–100, 108
   grand final 1985 101–5, 107, 283
   man of the match 1985 105–6, 135
   pre-season bonding camp 98
   QRL gala dinner 105–6
   Redcliffe game 103, 109–10
   reserve grade 96, 108
   silent treatment 100, 110–1
   team dinner 98
   training 93–100, 107, 110, 112
   trials 95
brothels, visiting 126–8
Brothers (football team) 36, 62–5, 91
Bugden, Mark 118
Burwood Police Boys Club 136

Canberra, agreement to join 141
cancer 287–317
Canterbury-Bankstown 1, 117–26
   attempting to leave 120–1
   banning from leagues club 125
   first-grade 122, 124
   initiation 122
   man of the match 123
   run-on debut 122–3
   sacking from 126–8
   training 124
Canterbury-Bankstown Under-10s rep side 28
car theft 33–5, 39–40, 44–5, 48, 62, 69
Carr, Norm 104
Carrion, Ray 52
Carrion, Roy 52
Cartwright, John 202
cash 'bonuses' 145–6
Cedars rugby league team 273, 275–85, 335–6, 366
   France, game against 289, 291–2, 295–301
   World Cup 2000 311–25
Chamoun, Sami 322–4
charities helping family 20, 48, 192
chemotherapy 296–7, 301–15
Chequers 222–3, 230, 240
City Firsts 135–7
Clark, Terrance 370
Clarke, Gary 342
Cleal, Noel 124
clothes 191–2
coaching
   Canterbury junior St George Dragons 288, 320
   Certificate One 288
   coach of the year 333
   defensive coach, Balmain 288–9
   knock backs 115, 376
   Lebanon Cedars 320–9, 335–6
   Oberon prison farm 267–8, 332
   Pia Donkeys 330–7
   UK Super League 356
   UTC 333–7, 356
Coleman, Craig 'Tugger' 83–4, 88, 97, 209–10, 218, 245
Combined Brisbane side 118
community service 213, 243, 257
Conescu, Greg 103
Confirmation 25
Conway, John 45
Coorey, George 82
Courier, Andy 180, 193
Courier Mail stories 101
Cox, Mr 46
Coyne, Gary 91

INDEX

criminal conviction, first 39
Cronk, Mark 31, 62, 294
Crowe, Russell 290
Cunningham, Kieron 327
Cunningham, Les 134

Davidson, Les 83, 88
Davis, Joe 19
Davis, Paul 189
debt collecting 1–15, 85–7, 124, 135, 150–1, 157–8, 161, 212, 274
Delaunay, Guy 335
Dib, Ray 119, 266, 276, 278–9, 308
D'Jura, Bronco 83–4, 88
Douglas, Dr Joshua 293, 296–7, 313–5, 317, 319–20
Dowling, Greg 91, 184
drinking 87–8, 105
drugs 35–6, 68, 87
    drug and alcohol culture 87–8, 176, 206–7, 214
    selling 248–54
Dymock, Jim 244, 269, 285

Easts 145–56, 173–4
    Artie's sacking 156
    cash 'bonus' 145–6
    first-grade 151, 174
    fractured cheekbone 150
    knee injury 152
    leaving 174–5
    regret 145–8
    reserve grade 174
    signing for 144–5
    training 149, 156, 173
    trial game 150
Economidis, Phil 330
Eden, Harry 158, 200, 212, 214, 246, 276, 344
El Masri, Hazem 278, 280, 322, 327
Elias, Benny 3, 64, 66, 154–5, 175, 179, 182, 184–5, 194, 219
Elias, George 17, 23, 25, 27, 30–2, 36–7, 66, 93, 117–8, 120, 138, 143–5, 255–9, 273, 276, 278, 294, 297, 306, 308, 319, 375
Elias, George (uncle) 19
Elias, Jennifer 17, 23, 27

Elias, Jennifer (grandmother) 20–1
Elias, Joe 17–9, 23, 25, 27, 33, 40, 93, 101, 346
Elias, John (father) 17, 26, 98
Elias, Lou 19
Elias, Susan 17–32, 40, 48, 65, 93, 98–9, 114, 141, 146, 184, 188, 192, 199, 255, 258, 273, 282–3, 298, 308, 311, 346–7, 354, 356, 365, 375
    mum's house 61, 68, 85, 120, 135, 252, 350
Elias, Tony 19, 20–1
Ellis, Grant 65
England, playing in 203–10
expulsion from school 31, 45–6
eye-gouging 184–7

Fairfax, Russell 149, 154, 156, 174
Fallah, Allan 131
Farah, Robbie 366
Farrer, Andrew 2, 204
father figures 21, 26, 29, 99, 120, 136, 175, 268, 332
Fenech, Jeff 164, 188
Fenech, Mario 83, 89
Ferguson, John 'Chicka' 72, 180
Field, Craig 224, 226, 269, 275, 303, 334–7
fighting 41, 49, 215–6
Finlayson, Wayne 52
Fittler, Brad 'Freddy' 22, 202
Flood, Lee 44, 48
Folkes, Steve 118, 123–4
The Footy Show 275
France
    Avignon 78–80, 83
    French Challenge Cup 279, 333, 337
    Koalas team 81
    Limoux 277–9
    Pia Donkeys 81, 330–7
    playing in 77–83, 89, 92–3, 185, 277–9, 285
    training 79–80
    UTC 331–7
Freeman, Gary 'Whiz' 195
Freeman, Ian 131, 133
Frilingos, Peter 183–4

381

Fullerton-Smith, Wally 103
Furner, Don 140, 245

Gaddafi nickname 95, 110
Gale, Brett 131
Galileo 18
gambling 82, 88, 119, 135, 151, 155, 157, 173, 176, 182, 191, 209, 218–9, 246, 275–6, 324–5, 342
    backing his team to win 102–3, 119, 139, 218
    card nights 92, 97, 100, 109, 148–9, 155, 182
    grand final 1985 102–3
    grand final 1988 153–5
    match fixing 221–40
    trots 45, 48, 72, 102, 109, 157–68, 199, 274
gangs 40–3, 49
Gates, Mark 375
George, Joseph 363
Georgie Boy 4–7, 9–11, 200, 230–3, 235–7, 241, 346, 375
Geyer, Mark 140
Ghosn, Steve 129, 131–6, 139, 141–2, 144, 147–8, 212, 279, 282, 298–300, 311, 313, 318–9, 321, 331
Gibbs, Ron 124
Gibson, Jack 129, 211–2
Gillespie, David 2, 118, 204
Gillmeister, Trevor 'The Axe' 148
girlfriends
    Flood, Lee 44, 48
    Lisa 271, 278–9, 294, 302, 305, 308–9, 317, 334
    Prescott, Barbara 207–10
Gorman, Tony 159, 162, 169–72
Gould, Phil 'Gus' 64, 128, 150, 152, 169–71, 202, 298, 375–6
grand final
    Brisbane Souths 1985 101–5, 107, 283
    Metropolitan Cup Newtown 1996 277
Grant, James 178
Green, Tony 324
Guasch, Bernard 335
Guildford, playing for 212–4, 225
    suspension 214

Gunn, Matthew 209–10
Guttenbeil, John 188

Hadley, Ray 162
Hagan, Michael 118
Halpin, Dr Neil 67, 150, 187
Hardine 17–8
Harding, Bruce 168
Harding, Jeff 164
Harold Park trots 7, 45, 48, 72, 157–9, 165, 214
    selling suits at 72, 158
Harrigan, Bill 179
Harris, Iestyn 327
Hayson, Eddie 164–5, 261, 341
Hill, Terry 164, 244
Hockey, Brad 24
Hohn, Mark 185–6
Holmes à Court, Peter 290
Hughes brothers 120
Hughes, Garry 123
Hughes, Mark 329
Hurley, Mick 84
hypnotist 133–4, 141

Ibrahim, John 13–4, 351
impersonating a police officer 200–1, 213
Inglis, Greg 361
injuries
    broken ankle 67–8, 71–2
    broken arm 22–3
    broken collarbone 67
    fractured cheekbone 150
    groin 187
    knee 152
International Federation of Rugby League 319
Isaac, Kenny 119
Izzard, Brad 202

Jack, Garry 180–2, 194, 196, 205, 277
Jackson, Peter 'Jacko' 94, 97, 101, 104
Jackson, Steve 180–1
jail
    attempted escape 53–4
    drugs in 273, 355, 362
    football at 52–3

INDEX

Long Bay jail 2–4, 49–58, 65, 66, 69, 93, 200, 221, 247, 256, 259, 261–5, 297, 353, 358, 360, 364, 367, 369, 376
  money in 356–8
  Oberon prison farm 264–74
  Parklea 369–71
  rugby league day 268–9
  Silverwater 356–7
  suicide, contemplating 356–6
  weekend detention 202, 213, 266
  Windsor 273–5, 359, 365–70
Jared, Phil 361
Jarvis, Pat 74
Javaux, Carl 330
Johns, Andrew 307
Johnson, Brian 253
Johnston, Malcolm 72
Jones, Alan 192–203, 214, 223, 236, 239, 241–3, 264, 275, 324, 355, 365–6, 375
Jones, Ronnie 144–5, 153, 174

Kalache, Les 375
Kanaan, Simon 284
Karam, Danny 69–72, 77, 85–8, 92, 100, 106, 123–4, 136, 149–51, 347, 349, 349
'Kenny' 32–5
Khoury, Michael 322, 328
Khoury, Paul 278
Khoury, Ray 42
kidnapping 'Con' 12, 191
King, Sister Anne 19, 28–9, 58–9
Kings Cross 3, 12–4, 35, 42, 63, 70, 149
Korn, John 213, 256–8, 264, 352, 354–5
Koutonos, Jim 52
labouring work 43, 62, 95

Lahood, Dr Jimmy 290–2, 306
Lakes United 261
Laloa, Milford 334
Lamb, Terry 2, 118, 123–4
Lambert, Danny 330, 333
Langmack, Paul 122, 376
Lebanon 17–8, 20, 24

Lebanon Cedars rugby league team 273, 275–85, 335–6, 366
  France, game against 289, 291–2, 295–301
  World Cup 2000 311–25
Lee, Johnny 88
Leeds, Andrew 202–3
left-foot step 97, 104
Leigh 205–10
  drinking 206–7
  first match with 206
  return to Sydney 210
  training 208
Leo (Newtown Jets selector) 63–4
Lewis, Johnny 243, 375
Lewis, Wally 91, 101, 104–5, 184–7, 307
Limoux 277–9
Lockyer, Darren 307, 332
Long Bay jail 2–4, 49–58, 65, 66, 69, 93, 200, 221, 247, 256, 259, 297, 364, 376
  attempted escape 53–4
  football at 52–3
  second time 261–5
  third time 353, 358, 360, 367, 369
Love, Colin 276–7, 284, 319
Lucky Bills 32–3, 39–40, 42–3, 50, 61–3, 68–9
Lumby, Ash 94
Lyons, Cliff 284

McCarthy, Bob 117
McClelland, Jim 97
McCullah, Brian 36
McDonalds shooting 339–52, 354
McGahan, Hugh 148
McGregor, Paul 284
McGuire, Bruce 175, 177, 179, 205
McKinnon, Don 73, 104
Madison, Tim 334
Mahon, Scott 206–10, 333
Mamando, Bruce 330
man of the match
  Balmain 1990 183
  Canterbury-Bankstown 123
  grand final 1985 105–6, 135
  Metropolitan Cup grand final 1996 277

Manning, Mick 375
Mansour, Anthony 322
Mara, Les 84
Mares, Paul 78
Maroon, Darren 300, 312, 375
Martin, Ray 243, 245
Martin, Samantha 333
Masella, Martin 219
match fixing 221–40
Meninga, Mal 94–5, 97, 100, 121, 132, 134
Merriman, Jim 52
Metropolitan Cup 212, 218, 275, 277
migration 5, 18, 94
Miles, Gene 184
Milford, Laloa 330, 333
Miller, Andrew 24
Miller, Carol 24–6, 28
Miller, Jamie 24
Miller, Ron 24–6, 28, 36, 99
Minda Boys' Home 40, 43
Montgomery, Rick 84, 88, 218
Moore, Brian 'Chicka' 72–4, 277
Moore, Peter 'Bullfrog' 117, 119–21, 123, 125–8, 280
Mortimer, Steve 2, 118–9, 123
Mundine, Anthony 180
Murdoch, Rupert 269–70
Murphy, Col 275
Murray, Graham 177
Murray, Mark 320

Nable, Adam 330
national competition, NRL 143
National Crime Authority 7, 243–7, 253, 255, 261
Ndaira, George 366
Nebauer, Roger 168–9
Neil, Mick 179, 219
Nelson, Barry 125
news stories 183–4, 350
    A Current Affair 243
    Courier Mail 101
    Rugby League Week interviews 101, 209
Newtown Jets 63–4, 137
    bankruptcy 74–5
    bar job 71

broken ankle 67–8, 71–2
broken collarbone 67
first-grade debut 73
man of the match 277
Metropolitan Cup 275, 277
reserve grade 73–4
return to 71–2
signing with 66
third grade 65, 67, 71, 73
training 63–4, 66, 68, 71, 73
tryout for 63–4
Newtown Police Boys Club 243
Nicholas, Norm 375
Nichols, Laurie 188–9
nickname 95, 110
Niebling, Bryan 103
Non-Hodgkin's Lymphoma 296
Noyce, Steve 204, 211

Oberon prison farm 264–74
O'Brien, Steve 189
O'Reilly, Tom 334
O'Toole, Adrian 138

Packer, Kerry 198, 269
Palmer, Ronnie 149
Panasonic Cup 118, 138
Parker, Terry 85, 88–9
Pearce, Wayne 'Junior' 175–7, 189–90, 193, 214–5, 217–8, 288, 320, 324
Pethybridge, Rod 141–2
Phelan, Chris 100–1, 109
police badge 200
Politis, Nick 149, 155, 170
practical jokes 44–5, 82, 182, 200, 209–10
Prescott, Barbara 207–10
pre-season ARL Sevens tournament 276–85, 289
Puckridge, David 65
Punchbowl 18, 19, 24–5, 32, 34, 40, 42–4, 47, 61, 66, 68, 78, 83, 85, 92–3
Punchbowl Bulldogs gang 40–1
Punchbowl High 45–6
Punchbowl Hotel 135
Punchbowl Pipe and Bricks 43

INDEX

QRL gala dinner 105
QRL rules 121, 140

race-fixing 96, 161–7, 268, 274
Rahim, Dr Nabil 287–8, 292–3, 295, 301, 306–8, 355
Rampling, Tony 83
Ransdale, Dennis 206, 208
Raudonikis, Tommy 63–4, 277, 316, 316
Rea, Johnny 65
Reeves, Berwin 361–2
Rhind, Steve 52
Ribot, John 142–3
Ricketts, Steve 101
Ridge, Matt 196
Riley, Murray 56
Rix, Lyn 42
Rix, Margaret 28, 33
Rix, Peter 23–4, 27, 28, 31–3, 41–2, 62–5, 125, 153–4
Rix, Ray 28, 33, 45, 63, 157
Roach, Steve 'Blocker' 3, 70, 175–6, 179, 181–2, 194, 214, 275, 303
robberies 42–4, 47–8, 69, 135, 157
   jewellery stores 123–4
Roberts, Ian 83, 88, 196
Rocky video 133, 299
Rogers, Tim 330
Roselands swimming pool 6, 20
rugby league
   introduction to 23–4, 36–7
   prison day 268–9
   watching 63
Rugby League Week interviews 101, 209
Rugby League World Cup 289, 311–3
Ryan, Warren 'Wok' 63–4, 79, 97–8, 118–20, 122–3, 128, 133–4, 150, 152, 154, 156, 175, 177–82, 188, 191–3, 195, 197, 203–4, 208, 320

Saab, Charlie 278, 283
Saba 332
Sailor, Wendell 109
St Jerome's primary school 19, 23, 27, 29, 31, 59

St John's High School 23, 29–31, 36, 45, 62
Sait, Paul 84
Sattler, John 183
school
   bomb threat 46
   expulsion from 31, 45–6
   rugby league, introduction to 23–4, 36–7
   St Jerome's primary school 19, 23, 27, 29, 31, 59
   St John's High School 23, 29–31, 36, 45, 62
   suspension from 27
Scott, Colin 91
Scullion, Detective Neville 50
selling
   bullet proof vests and gun parts 246–54
   drugs 248–54
   suits 72, 88, 112, 122, 158, 175–6, 201, 213–4
Senter, Darren 269
Serdaris, Jimmy 334
Sevens tournament 276–85, 289
Shalala, Alex 70–1
Shami 159–62, 167, 170, 216, 360–1, 365, 369
Sheens, Tim 140, 320
Shepherd, Jimmy 370
Shine, Ken 234, 239–40
Sigsworth, Phil 64
Silverwater jail 356–7
Simms, Steve 208
Sinclair, Jacin 197, 226
Singleton, John 74, 350–1, 375
Sironen, Paul 'Sirro' 175–7, 179, 189, 194, 215
Skaf, Bilal 353
Skaf, Mohammed 353
Slattery, Brian 175
Smith, Arthur Stanley 'Neddy' 51, 56–7, 216, 231, 237, 265, 356, 364–5
Smith, Brian 193–5
Smith, Jason 285
Smith, Justice Cameron 58–9
Smith, Tyrone 226

South Sydney 83–9, 93, 223–40, 245
   Alan Jones as coach 223, 236, 239, 241–3
   drug and alcohol culture 87–8
   first-grade 84, 89
   match fix 221–40
   mid-season transfer to 223
   reserve grade 84
   signing with 83
   third grade 84
   training 84, 87–8
SP bookmaking 135, 157–8, 199, 214, 218
stand-over work 3, 87, 96, 147
State of Origin 92, 105, 113, 135, 177, 185
   New South Wales 218
   Queensland team 121, 132, 140
Storey, Dr Kevin 308–9
stomach cancer 287–317
stomach rupture 309–10
Street, Tim 208–9, 333
Super League 226, 269–70, 275, 280–1
suspension from school 27

Tallis, Gorden 269
Tamer, Kandy 278
Taouil, Alex 350
Taylor, Jason 216–7, 376
Timperi, Rick 375
Trewella, David 148
Trimbole, Robert 158
Trindall, Darrell 'Tricky' 170, 224, 226, 303, 307
Tronc, Scott 95
trots 45, 48, 72, 109, 157–67, 173, 199
   Albion Park 102
   corruption 158–64
   Harold Park trots 7, 45, 48, 72, 157–9, 214
   ICAC inquiry 160–1, 168
   Miracle Mile 1992 161–2
   Newcastle 166–7
   Penrith 162–3
   race fixing 158–67
   stealing swabs 163–4
   Western Derby 165–6
Tunks, Peter 118, 122

van Dome, Pierre 312–3, 329
Vautin, Paul 124

Wade, Rick 129, 142
Walker, Shane 269
Wallabies 192–3, 195
Walsh, Bruce 297
Waterhouse, Robbie 342
Watsford, Wally 84, 137
weekend detention 202, 213, 266
West End 93, 97–8, 101
   card nights 97, 109
Wests 128–44, 203–4, 210–1
   beer theft 141–2
   bonding camp 136
   first game with 131–3
   first-grade 131–4, 139
   hypnotist 133–4, 141
   leaving 211
   1987 season 137–8
   off-season 135–6
   Parramatta, beating 133
   return to 203–4
   suspension 138–9
   training 131, 142
   wooden spoon 133, 144, 147
   working at leagues club 141–2
Willey, Ron 83–4, 89, 97, 152, 154
Williams, Danny 52
Williams, Jason 149, 174
Williams, Ray 359–60
Wilson, Ken 64
Wood, Nat 170, 215–6, 261, 269, 350–1, 375
Woodward, Clive 328
World Cup 2000 289, 311–25
World Sevens 276

Young, Andrew 49, 57–8
Young, Craig 74